THE PURITAN HOPE

David Livingstone, 1813–1873, travelled twenty-nine thousand miles in Africa for the cause of the gospel: 'O Jesus, fill me with Thy love now, and I beseech Thee, accept me, and use me a little for Thy Glory.'

THE PURITAN HOPE

A STUDY IN REVIVAL
AND THE INTERPRETATION
OF PROPHECY

Iain H. Murray

THE BANNER OF TRUTH TRUST

THE BANNER OF TRUTH TRUST

78b Chiltern Street, London WIM IPS

*

© Copyright 1971 Iain H. Murray
First published 1971

*

Set in 11 on 13 point Monotype Baskerville
and printed in Great Britain by
Billing & Sons Ltd, Guildford and London

CONTENTS

ILLUSTRATIONS

INTRODUCTION

*Elstow, where John Bunyan was born in 1628 – a
time when the gospel was in the ascendancy
throughout England*

The word *hope* I take for faith; and indeed hope is nothing else but the constancy of faith.

JOHN CALVIN
Commentaries on the Epistle of Paul to the Hebrews
chapter 3, verse 6

But our chief consolation is that this is the cause of God and that he will take it in hand to bring it to a happy issue. Even though all the princes of the earth were to unite for the maintenance of our Gospel, still we must not make that the foundation of our hope. So, likewise, whatever resistance we see today offered by almost all the world to the progress of the truth, we must not doubt that our Lord will come at last to break through all the undertakings of men and make a passage for his word. Let us hope boldly, then, more than we can understand; he will still surpass our opinion and our hope.

JOHN CALVIN
Quoted by J. H. Merle D'Aubigné, *History of the Reformation in Europe in the time of Calvin*,
1876, vol 7, 49

Strong and certain was the conviction of the Christians that the church would come forth triumphant out of its conflicts, and, as it was its destination to be a world-transforming principle, would attain to dominion of the world.

J. A. W. NEANDER
History of the Christian Religion and Church
translated by Joseph Torrey, vol 2, 1851, 395–6

Though our *persons* fall, our *cause* shall be as truly, certainly, and infallibly victorious, as that Christ sits at the right hand of God. The gospel shall be victorious. This greatly comforts and refreshes me.

JOHN OWEN
The Use of Faith, if Popery Should Return Upon Us, 1680
[*The Works of John Owen*, 1851, vol 9, 507–508]

There will come a time when the generality of mankind, both Jew and Gentile, shall come to Jesus Christ. He hath had but little takings of the world yet, but he will have before he hath done.

THOMAS GOODWIN, 1600–1679
Sermon XXXIV in *An Exposition of the First Chapter of the Epistle to the Ephesians* [*Complete Works*, 1861, vol 1, 520]

There will come a time when in this world holiness shall be more general, and more eminent, than ever it hath been since Adam fell in paradise.

THOMAS BROOKS
The Crown and Glory of Christianity, 1662
[*Complete Works*, vol 4, 434]

There have been great and glorious days of the gospel in this land; but they have been small in comparison of what shall be.

JAMES RENWICK, martyred 17 February 1688
*A Choice Collection of Prefaces, Lectures, and Sermons
by James Renwick*, 1777, 279

Plain it is, there is not a more stupifying, benumbing thing in all the world than mere despair. To look upon such a sad face and aspect of things through the world as we have before our eyes; to look upon it despairingly and with the apprehension that it never will, never can be better. . . . But hope is a kind of anticipated enjoyment and gives a present participation in the expected pleasantness of those days, how long soever they may yet be off from us. . . . Religion shall not be an inglorious thing in the world always.

JOHN HOWE
Sermons on *The Prosperous State of the Christian Interest Before the
End of Time*, 1678 [*Works*, 1837, 578–579]

I had a strong hope, that God would 'bow the heavens and come down' and do some marvellous work among the Heathen.

DAVID BRAINERD
Life and Diary for 22 July 1744, *Works of Jonathan Edwards*,
vol 2, 1840, 349

Hope is one of the principal springs that keep mankind in motion. It is vigorous, bold, and enterprising. It causes men to encounter dangers, endure hardships, and surmount difficulties innumerable, in order to accomplish the desired end. In religion it is of no less consequence. It makes a considerable part of the religion of those that truly fear God . . .

ANDREW FULLER, first Secretary of the Baptist Missionary Society,
in a circular letter to the Churches of the Northamptonshire
Association on *The Excellency and Utility of the Grace of Hope*, 1782
[*Complete Works*, 1841, 714]

I long to be engaged in the blessed work of saying to the heathen, 'Behold your God' Do not think that the future scenes cast me down. No! behold I go full of hope.

ROBERT MOFFAT, Pioneer missionary to South Africa, to his parents before departing, 1816. *The Lives of Robert and Mary Moffat*, J. S. Moffat, 1896, 23

'We also rejoice in *hope*. We have many and express assurances in the Scriptures, which cannot be broken, of the general, the universal spread and reign of Christianity, which are not yet accomplished. Nothing has yet taken place in the history of Divine grace, wide enough in extent, durable enough in continuance, powerful enough in energy, blessed enough in enjoyment, magnificent enough in glory, to do anything like justice to these predictions and promises. Better days, therefore, are before us, notwithstanding the forebodings of many.

WILLIAM JAY, 1769–1853, Nonconformist leader *The Autobiography and Reminiscences of the Rev. William Jay*, 1855, 162

David was not a believer in the theory that the world will grow worse and worse, and that the dispensation will wind up with general darkness, and idolatry. Earth's sun is to go down amid tenfold night if some of our prophetic brethren are to be believed. Not so do we expect, but we look for a day when the dwellers in all lands shall learn righteousness, shall trust in the Saviour, shall worship thee alone, O God, 'and shall glorify thy name.' The modern notion has greatly damped the zeal of the church for missions, and the sooner it is shown to be unscriptural the better for the cause of God. It neither consorts with prophecy, honours God, nor inspires the church with ardour. Far hence be it driven.

C. H. SPURGEON
From an exposition of Psalm 86.9, 'All nations whom thou hast made shall come and worship before thee, O Lord; and shall glorify thy name'. *The Treasury of David*, 1874.

MY father was a Christian who believed in prayer but I knew and understood little of his praying until after my own conversion at the age of seventeen. From that time as I listened to my father's petitions I concurred with them all – all, that is, except one, and this one had to do with a subject which was so much a part of his praying that I could not miss the divergence in our thought. Our difference concerned the extent to which the success of the kingdom of Christ is to be expected in the earth. My father would pray for its universal spread and global triumph, for the day when 'nation shall not lift up sword against nation, neither shall they learn war any more', and when great multitudes in all lands will be found numbered among the travail of Christ's soul. According to the teaching with which I was then in contact these petitions were misguided, the product of a theological liberalism which believed in the upward progress of man and in the coming of a better world. Evangelical belief, so I thought, bound one to a contrary persuasion, namely, that growing evil must dominate the world-scene until Jesus Christ comes again in power and glory. Until then the gospel must be preached as a testimony unto all nations, though not with anticipation that large numbers of the human race will receive it.

I was therefore ill at ease over this one aspect of our family prayers, especially so as I supposed that belief in the imminent second advent of Christ is a necessity in evangelical experience, whereas the petitions from which I dissented could hardly be offered unless one supposed that 'the end is not yet'. Was not that a supposition which would destroy the readiness for his appearing which Christ commanded?

In the urging of his petitions I realized that my father was often employing scriptural language. I conceived his mistake to be that he was applying to this age and to the present course of history what is descriptive of a period which is to follow the return of Christ. Only after his personal appearing will multitudes – including the Jews as a nation – enter his kingdom; only then will ensue an age of peace when 'the earth shall be full of the knowledge of the Lord, as the waters cover the sea'.

With this view of the future one can both believe in the present progress of evil and in a period yet to dawn when the predicted prosperity of the kingdom of God in the world will at last become a reality. In consequence one must also believe that the conclusion of this present age is not to witness the end of the world but the return of Christ and the ushering in of a new era – often called 'the millennium'. When that has run its course, the last judgment shall take place and time shall be no more.

In accepting this outlook upon the future – an outlook which has been known as millenarianism – I was unaware of an objection which has long been urged against it. It is an objection which can be simply stated: the return of Jesus Christ is represented in the New Testament in terms which exclude the possibility of a new era intervening between his coming and the end of the world. His second advent and 'the end' will occur together (1 Cor. 15. 23,24). He is to remain in heaven, not until the commencement of a millennium, but until 'the time of the restoration of all things' (Acts 3. 21), elsewhere spoken of as 'the regeneration', which Jesus identifies with the last judgment (Matt. 19. 28). When he comes all the dead will be raised, Christians glorified, the kingdom complete and the day of God's longsuffering towards sinners will be over. The witness of many texts which speak of these truths renders impossible the idea that Christ's appearing can be connected with, or followed by, a new era of spiritual blessing for those hitherto unsaved. For this reason all the Confessional statements of the Reformed Churches four hundred years ago refused to identify millenarianism with historic Christianity and spoke rather of the return of Jesus Christ as coincident with the day of judgment. The Thirty-Nine Articles declare, in connection with the resurrection of Christ that he ascended into heaven 'and there sitteth, until he return to judge all men at the last day'. The Scottish Confession of Faith (1560), The Belgic Confession (1561) and the Heidelberg Catechism (1563) all repeat the same truth. 'We believe, according to the Word of God, when the time appointed by the Lord (which is unknown to all creatures) is come, and the number of the elect complete, that our Lord Jesus Christ will come from heaven, corporally and visibly, as he ascended with great glory and majesty, to declare himself Judge of the quick and the dead, burning this old world with fire and flame to cleanse it. And then all men will personally appear before this great Judge, both men and women and children, that have been from the beginning of the world to the end thereof.'*

Thus I came to see that there is an insuperable objection to the view of prophecy which I had accepted in my early Christian life. I retain my respect and affection for those who have held and still hold that view; I know also that they urge Scripture to support it, but, when Scripture is alleged against Scripture, it is of cardinal importance that the dependence we place upon texts which are obscure in meaning or capable of more than one sense should be less than that which we place upon doctrinal texts where the sense is clear and confirmed by parallel scriptures. As the *Westminster Confession* says, 'All things in scripture are not alike plain in themselves, nor alike clear unto all'. Therefore, in view of the total absence of supporting evidence from the New Testament, it is exceedingly hazardous to claim that a thousand years intervene between Christ's coming and the end of the world on the grounds that Revelation 20 teaches

---

* The Belgic Confession, Article 37, *The Creeds of the Evangelical Protestant Churches*, edited by H. B. Smith and P. Schaff, 1877, 433.

a millennium. The truth is that Revelation 20 contains what has been called 'the darkest passage in all the Bible'; widely differing meanings have been given to it by those who share a common faith in the inerrancy of Scripture, and it is better to admit that our view of that difficult chapter is uncertain rather than to commit ourselves to an interpretation which can only be harmonized with the remainder of Scripture by introducing confusion into the meaning of many passages otherwise clear.*

In reply to this plea that one should begin with the plain, not the obscure, and build upon what is written large in the Word of God, it may be asked who is to decide what is 'plain'? Ultimately every Christian must form his own judgment, but in this area it is wise to consider what has been the consensus of Christian opinion in the past. When, for example, we read the same testimony in the Nicene Creed of the fourth century – 'He shall come again, with glory, to judge the living and the dead' – as in the Confessions of the Reformation – all professing that Christ's advent is the final judgment – there ought to be strong evidence before we conclude that this belief does not represent the clear witness of the New Testament.

For some while after I gave up the millenarian view of future history the only truth respecting unfulfilled prophecy which I could regard as clear was this great one that Christ's coming will be at the consummation of his kingdom. Therefore all conversion-work yet to be seen in history must occur before the Second Advent. Of the certainty or extent of any future work of

---

* It would be unfair to imply that only millenarians have erred by putting too much weight upon the uncertain. Some of the Puritans were also over-influenced by their view of the closing chapters of the book of the Revelation – applying too much to earth which belongs to heaven – and some of the postmillennialists of the eighteenth and nineteenth centuries carried this further when they spoke of the world being conquered by holiness for a thousand years before the Second Advent in language inconsistent with what Scripture elsewhere declares of the mixed spiritual conditions which will remain until the end. Whatever wider blessing attends the Church's witness in the future it will still remain a fact that wheat and tares are to grow together while the world shall last (Matt. 13. 30). It is a mistake to treat as synonymous the Puritan and postmillennial view of unfulfilled prophecy.

grace I was entirely in doubt. I still retained the conviction that the testimony of Scripture on human depravity requires the expectation of an ever-darkening world and the signs of the twentieth century seemed to point me to the same conclusion.

Only very slowly did I come to believe that the Christian Church has indeed a great future in the world and this conviction came as the result of several lines of thought. For one thing all the scripture texts claimed as proof that the coming of Jesus Christ must now be close at hand have also been confidently so used in former generations. Not a few Christians in the past have been erroneously convinced that their age must witness the end. When the Teutonic barbarians overturned Rome and reduced a stable world to chaos in the fifth century A.D., many in the Church despairingly drew the wrong conclusion that the world could have no future. Even larger numbers did so at the approach of the year 1000, believing that the closing millennium would end the world. In the gloom of the fourteenth century such tracts appeared as *The Last Age of the Church*, and in terms very similar to that old title a great number have written since.

All this does not make scripture predictions a subject for legitimate scepticism but it does prove that the signs of the end are not nearly so clear as some men would make them. To believe that 'the end is not yet' is not therefore so patently unscriptural as it is often represented. In the absence of any certain evidence to the contrary, the possibility that history is not about to close cannot be other than a real one. The acceptance of this may not change one's thoughts profoundly but it can open the way to other considerations. Supposing the church, after all, is to have a future in history, and that our individual end will not coincide with the end of the world, what then may that future be? To be disinterested in such a question simply because it does not affect our own individual salvation would not be an attitude worthy of a Christian.

Another subject which increased my doubts about the rightness of my pessimism was the significance of revivals. One common reason for believing that the world must grow worse and worse has always been the evidence of abounding moral decay. Confronted by this evidence it has too often been supposed that the only work left for God is judgment. Yet the history of revivals should teach us that even in the midst of prevailing evil it is possible to form precisely the opposite conviction. For example, when John Wesley arrived in Newcastle-upon-Tyne in May, 1742, he wrote these memorable words: 'I was surprised; so much drunkenness, cursing and swearing (even from the mouths of little children) do I never remember to have seen and heard before in so small a compass of time. Surely this place is ripe for Him who 'came not to call the righteous, but sinners to repentance'.* And the great evangelical revival which was then dawning proved this conviction to be right. The gospel of grace does not need promising conditions to make its reception a certainty. Such a result depends upon the will of him who declares his love to the ungodly. Thus in various centuries revivals of apostolic Christianity have broken out in the most improbable circumstances and have powerfully, rapidly and extensively affected whole communities. 'When the enemy shall come in like a flood, the Spirit of the Lord shall lift up a standard against him' (Isa. 59. 19). The wonder of God's saving works ought therefore to make Christians slow to believe that only doom and catastrophe must await the vast population of this evil earth. If, as men predict, the world population is to double in the next thirty years, why should it not be that God is going to show on a yet greater scale that truth is more powerful than error, grace more powerful than sin, and that those given to Christ are indeed 'as the sand which is upon the sea-shore' for multitude?

It may be replied, however, that though such a bright future is possible in terms of the character of God, yet one is prevented from believing it by God's purposes as revealed in the prophetic word of Scripture. The key issue here is whether Scripture prompts us yet to expect any time of wider blessing for the Church before the Advent. I had many hesitations on this point,

* *The Journal of the Rev. John Wesley*, Standard Edition, vol. 3, 13.

conscious that there is much in the symbolic Old Testament descriptions of a period of world-wide blessing which may already be fulfilled, and also that some of the exalted anticipations of the prophets may well have more to do with the eternal state than with any period in time. Is there any event predicted by Scripture to take place in history of which one can say with any certainty that it is yet unfulfilled? In considering this question I came to believe that there is at least one event, namely, a great revival, which is both promised and, as yet, unaccomplished.

The predictions of Scripture concerning Israel's conversion, particularly those of Romans 11, cannot be said to be already fulfilled. Still less can they be referred to the eternal state. They must await fulfilment in history. This conclusion is not a detail which can be treated apart from our general view of the future of the Church of Christ, for Paul himself points to the spiritual repercussions of Israel's future conversion upon the world (Romans 11. 12, 15) and, by referring to Isaiah 59. 20 as a scriptural confirmation of his own apostolic testimony respecting the salvation of the Jews (Romans 11. 26), he teaches us that we are to look for a larger fulfilment in history of some of the grandest Old Testament predictions. When I saw this, like Bunyan's Pilgrim I was ready to emerge from Doubting Castle. Men have spoken too soon in claiming that the world has now entered a post-christian era and we have been fools to believe them.

The mention of John Bunyan leads me to say something on the school of Christians to which he belonged and of which we speak more largely in subsequent pages. J. C. Ryle in 'An Estimate of Thomas Manton' written in 1870 says, 'The Puritans, as a body, have done more to elevate the national character than any class of Englishmen that ever lived.' The source of this influence was their theology and within that theology there was an attitude to history and to the world which distinguished them as men of hope. In their own day this hope came to expression in pulpits and in books, in Parliaments and upon battlefields, but it did not end there. The outlook they had done so much to inspire went on for nearly two hundred years after their own age and its results were manifold. It coloured the spiritual thought of the American colonies; it taught men to expect great outpourings of the Holy Spirit; it prepared the way to the new age of world-missions; and it contributed largely to that sense of destiny which came to characterize the English-speaking Protestant nations. When nineteenth-century Christian leaders such as William Wilberforce viewed the world not so much as a wreck from which individual souls must escape, but rather as the property of Christ, to whose kingdom the earth and the fulness thereof must belong, their thinking bore the genuine hall-mark of the Puritan outlook.

A hope which led to such world-wide results is surely worth examining. In the light of history we can hardly say that matters prophetic are too secondary to warrant our attention. The fact is that what we believe or do not believe upon this subject will have continual influence upon the way in which we live. The greatest spiritual endeavours and achievements in the past have been those energized by faith and hope. By comparison how small are our efforts! And can we disregard the possibility that this stands related to the smallness of our anticipations and to the weakness of our faith in the promises of God? As one of the last great representatives of Puritan theology, J. H. Thornwell, wrote more than a century ago:

'If the Church could be aroused to a deeper sense of the glory that awaits her, she would enter with a warmer spirit into the struggles that are before her. Hope would inspire ardour. She would even now arise from the dust, and like the eagle, plume her pinions for loftier flights than she has yet taken. What she wants, and what every individual Christian wants, is faith – faith in her sublime vocation, in her Divine resources, in the presence and efficacy of the Spirit that dwells in her – faith in the truth, faith in Jesus, and faith in God. With such a faith there would be no need to speculate about the future. That would speedily reveal itself. It is our unfaithfulness, our negligence and unbelief, our low and carnal aims, that retard the chariot of the Redeemer. The Bridegroom cannot come until the Bride has made herself ready. Let the Church be in earnest after greater holiness in her own members, and in faith and love undertake the conquest of the world, and she will soon settle the question whether her resources are competent to change the face of the earth'.*

*   *   *

This book grew out of an address which I gave at the Puritan Conference in London in 1967. At that date I knew few volumes which credited the Puritans with the beliefs which were theirs upon unfulfilled prophecy. Most writers attributed the rise of the expectation of far-reaching and world-wide blessing not to the seventeenth century at all but to Daniel Whitby who published his 'Treatise of the True Millennium' as an appendix to his *Paraphrase and Commentary on the New Testament* in 1703. Christopher Hill in his *Puritanism and Revolution* published in 1958, gives the impression, as do other writers, that the Puritans far from being characterized by hope expected the imminent end of the world! The reason for these mistakes lies partly in the diffusiveness of the seventeenth-century literature which renders it difficult to assess which view-points predominated. It was not a feature of the mainstream Puritan divines – those whose theology is represented by the Westminster Confession (1647) and *The Savoy Declaration* (1658) – that they produced books specially dealing with unfulfilled prophecy. The seventeenth-century volumes which deal exclusively with prophecy are more often than not the products of men of acrobatic imaginations or of half-crazy fanatics. They are by no means a safe guide to Puritan thought and when they are treated as though they were the error to which I have referred easily occurs.†

In the following pages I have sought, when dealing with Puritan belief upon prophecy, to base conclusions on evidence

* *Collected Writings*, 1871, vol. 2, 48.
† I am thinking, particularly, of such authors as John Archer and Robert Maton whose books I purposefully do not consider in this volume.

drawn from a considerable number of the mainstream Puritans. This evidence has to be searched out from their sermons and commentaries, and though it has been the work of some years to garner the material I have used in this book, the field is so large that much has inevitably been left unturned. I hope, however, that I am not wrong in thinking that most of the conclusions I have drawn are broadly based upon evidence which is substantial. I say this not to impress anyone with the idea that views supported by so many spokesmen must necessarily be true, but simply as a comment upon the method I have employed in seeking to formulate what the majority of the Puritans actually believed.

I wish that I could have gone further in tracing the development of English Puritan thought, and in particular its relationship to that of the other Reformed Churches of the seventeenth century. For this reason I have included some treatment of the Scottish Church in these pages and from this there emerges the important fact that by the 1640s there was a common belief upon unfulfilled prophecy both in England and North of the Border. Had this been observed by some recent writers it might have prevented them concluding that this belief belonged more to the Independents than to the Presbyterians. In the same way I do not doubt that if more attention can be given to the thought of the Reformed Churches of the Netherlands, and to the Latin literature of such divines as Gisbertus Voetius (1589–1676) of Utrecht, the belief which I have termed 'the Puritan hope' would be found to be more international than my phrase suggests.

I make no apology for treating the Scots under the general term 'Puritan'. It is sufficient justification that the word was used in reference to the Scots in the seventeenth century itself. For example, Robert Boyd, Principal of the Glasgow College, was charged with being a Puritan in 1621* and Samuel Rutherford preaching in Scotland, probably in the 1630s, says, 'Many are ashamed to own Christ, and to profess him,

* H. M. B. Reid, *The Divinity Principals in the University of Glasgow*, 1545–1654, 1917.

they will not be called Puritans'*. Peter Heylyn was therefore not creating a precedent when in his *History of the Presbyterians*, published in 1670, he speaks of 'the Presbyterian or Puritan Faction in the realm of Scotland'.

*   *   *

It only remains for me to remember the many friends – some of them now in a better world – to whose assistance and encouragement I owe so much. Ministers of the gospel to whom I am particularly indebted include Erroll Hulse, the late J. Marcellus Kik, Kenneth J. MacLeay and John R. de Witt. As always I have been greatly aided by the support of Geoffrey Williams and his staff of the Evangelical Library, London. The literary advice and general guidance of S. M. Houghton of Charlbury has been invaluable and as his views on prophecy do not, in certain respects, correspond with my own I have appreciated the help all the more. In a real sense this book has grown out of a team spirit among those who have shared in the work of the Banner of Truth Trust. Iron has sharpened iron and my colleagues have helped me from the early stages in my thinking, some years ago, to the final work of turning a manuscript into a book.

* *Fourteen Communion Sermons*, reprinted 1876, 341.

REVIVAL CHRISTIANITY:
ENGLAND

qui obiit 14 Decemb 1677 Ætatis 84.
F.H.Van.Houe.sculp:

Samuel Fairclough

'It may here be observed, that from the fall of man to our day, the work of redemption in its effect has mainly been carried on by remarkable communications of the Spirit of God. Though there be a more constant influence of God's Spirit always in some degree attending his ordinances, yet the way in which the greatest things have been done towards carrying on this work, always have been by remarkable effusions, at special seasons of mercy, as may fully appear hereafter in our further prosecution of our subject.'

JONATHAN EDWARDS

A History of the Work of Redemption, 1774, period 1, part 1
(Edwards' *Works,* 1840, vol 1, 539)

'What can be the reason of this sad observation, That when formerly a few lights raised up in the nation, did shine so as to scatter and dispel the darkness of popery in a little time; yet now when there are more, and more learned men amongst us, the darkness comes on apace? Is it not because they were men *filled with the Holy Ghost, and with power*; and many of us are only filled with light and know-ledge, and inefficacious notions of God's truth? Doth not always the spirit of the ministers propagate itself amongst the people? A lively ministry, and lively Christians.'

ROBERT TRAILL (1642–1716)

By What Means May Ministers Best Win Souls to Christ, 1682
(Traill's *Works,* 1810, vol 1, 250)

FOLLOWING as it did so closely upon the Reformation it is not surprising that the Puritan movement in England believed so firmly in revivals of religion as the great means by which the Church advances in the world. For the Reformation was itself the greatest revival since Pentecost – a Spring-time of new life for the Church on such a scale that the instances recorded in the apostolic era of three thousand being converted on one day, and of a 'great multitude of the priests' becoming 'obedient to the faith', no longer sounded incredible.

The Reformation, and still more, Puritanism, have been considered from many aspects but it has been too often overlooked that the main features of these movements, as, for instance, the extensiveness of their influence, the singular position given to Scripture and the transformation in character of the morally careless, are all effects of revival. When the Holy Spirit is poured out in a day of power the result is bound to affect whole communities and even nations. Conviction of sin, an anxiety to possess the Word of God, and dependence upon those truths which glorify God in man's salvation, are inevitable consequences.

Today men may wonder at the influences which changed the spiritual direction of England and Scotland so rapidly four hundred years ago, making them Bible-reading nations and witnesses to a creed so unflattering to human nature and hateful to human pride.

Innumerable writers have attempted to explain the phenomena by political and social considerations. They have supposed that the success which the Reformers and Puritans achieved occurred through a curious combination of historical circumstances which cannot be expected to happen again. To the Christians of that era, however, the explanation was entirely different. They read in Scripture that when the Spirit is poured from on high then the wilderness becomes a fruitful field (Isa. 32.15). They read also, 'Not by might, nor by power, but by my Spirit, saith the Lord of Hosts' (Zech. 4.6), and they attributed all the spiritual renewal of their age to the mercy of God. In taking this view they understood at once that all the successes of the Reformation were repeatable – as repeatable as the victories of the apostolic age – for Scripture places no limitation upon the Spirit's work of glorifying Christ and extending his kingdom. Thus there was recovered at the time of the Reformation belief in what may be called revival Christianity, and the attention which the Puritans who followed gave to this area of truth profoundly influenced the following centuries and gave to the English-speaking world what may be called the classic school of Protestant belief on revival. So prevalent indeed did this outlook become that until the nineteenth century all who wrote specifically upon the subject represented the Puritan standpoint. Of these writers the most notable who treated the subject of revival at length were Robert Fleming (1630–1694) in his *The Fulfilling of the Scripture*, Jonathan Edwards (1703–1758) in several works, and John Gillies (1712–1796) in his *Historical Collections Relating to Remarkable Periods of the Success of the Gospel*.

*   *   *

The commencement of the Reformation in England and Scotland was marked by a thirst for Scripture among the people. Tyndale's version of the New Testament circulated in both realms from 1526 onwards and soon a train of preachers appeared, at first small in number, whose ministry was attended by effects which had not been commonly seen for many long centuries. Of George Wishart, the Scottish reformer, martyred in 1546, we have this account of his open-air preaching: 'He came to a dyke in a moor edge, upon the south-west side of Mauchline, upon the which he ascended. The whole multitude stood and sat about him (God gave the day pleasing and hot). He continued in preaching more than three hours. In that sermon God wrought so wonderfully with him that one of the most wicked men that was in that country, named Laurence Rankin, laird of Shiel, was converted. The tears ran from his eyes in such abundance that all men wondered. His conversion was without hypocrisy, for his life and conversation witnessed it in all times to come.'[1]

Scenes like this were soon to become common in the northern kingdom. In May, 1556, John Knox, running the gauntlet of the Catholic powers who still controlled the country, preached for ten consecutive days in Edinburgh. When he returned to Scotland again, in 1559, the spiritual revival became general. 'God did so multiply our number', Knox writes of the growth of the Protestant cause, 'that it appeared as if men had rained from the clouds.'[2] In a letter to an English friend written on June 23, 1559, he says: 'Now, forty days and more, hath my God used my tongue in my native country, to the manifestation of His glory. Whatsoever now shall follow, as touching my own carcass, His holy name be praised. The thirst of the poor people, as well as of the nobility here, is wondrous great, which putteth me in comfort that Christ Jesus shall triumph for a space here, in the north and extreme parts of the earth.'[3]

Looking back on this glorious period the Scottish Church historian, Kirkton, later wrote: 'The Church of Scotland hath been singular among the churches. And, first, it is to be admired that, whereas in other nations the Lord thought it enough to convict a few in a city, village, or family to himself, leaving the greater part in darkness, in Scotland the whole nation was converted by lump; and within ten years after popery was discharged in Scotland, there were not ten persons of quality to be found in it who did not profess the true reformed religion,

[5]

and so it was among the commons in proportion. Lo! here a nation born in one day.'[4]

Even when allowance is made for the number who were carried by outward persuasion rather than by inner spiritual conviction the history of the Scottish Reformation bears eloquent record to the vast success which the Gospel then had. It was a great revival.

The same holds true of England. Despite the severest penalties against the possession of Scripture, and against unauthorized preaching, spiritual concern spread rapidly in the later years of Henry VIII, after the appearance of Tyndale's New Testament. During the reign of the boy King, Edward VI (1547–1553), the public preaching of the gospel by Latimer, Hooper, Bradford and others was attended with remarkable success. An entry in the records of St. Margaret's, Westminster, bears its own witness to the way in which people pressed to hear the Word of God; it notes that one shilling and sixpence was expended, 'for mending divers pews that were broken when Doctor Latimer did preach'. Speaking of a few years later, John Jewel writes thus of open-air gatherings in the City of London: 'Sometimes at Paul's Cross six thousand persons were sitting together, which was very grievous to the papists.' Details like these show that the English Reformation was much more than a series of legislative Acts executed by the authorities. Political decisions certainly entered in, but the policy of burning which claimed nearly three hundred Protestants in the reign of Mary Tudor (1553–1558) served to demonstrate that convictions were planted in many hearts which no force could uproot. Upon the death of Mary the last English Catholic monarch of Tudor days passed from the scene, and two years later, in 1560, the Scottish Parliament formally abolished the Catholic religion in Scotland.

The storm of persecution which blew itself out in Mary's reign did more than test the roots of the new faith. By driving into temporary exile a number of the younger spiritual leaders it brought them into closer contact with the Reformed churches of the Continent. The influence of the two Continental theologians, Martin Bucer and Peter Martyr, had already been felt as they had taught at Cambridge and Oxford respectively in the days of Edward VI, but now, as a congregation of some two hundred exiles gathered at Geneva, the full weight of Calvin's ministry – as mighty in the pulpit as in the lecture hall – was experienced at first hand. From this haven in the Swiss Alps Knox and Christopher Goodman went to Scotland, while the others returned to England after the accession of Elizabeth I in 1558. Thereafter the two groups in England and Scotland developed along parallel lines, like two streams originating at one fountain. The fountain was not so much Geneva, as the Bible which the exiles newly translated and issued with many marginal notes in 1560. Between that date and 1644 no less than 140 editions of the Geneva Bible were to be issued and, as a modern writer says, 'it was read in every Presbyterian and Puritan home in both realms'. When these two streams came together again at the convening of the Westminster Assembly in 1643, their unanimity was given peerless expression in the great truths of evangelical religion set down in the Confession of Faith and in the Larger and Shorter Catechisms. In their understanding of the gospel and in practical divinity the Christians of England and Scotland were then one, and the expositions of the Scottish divines were as eagerly read in London as were the writings of the English Puritans north of the Border.

The problem which confronted the English and Scottish evangelicals in 1560 was basically the same, namely, the need to spread the gospel at the parish level in countries which had become formally Protestant. In England the main hindrance to this endeavour was the dead-weight of the Church, which though 'reformed' by Acts of Parliament, remained in many areas in its old pre-Reformation spiritual condition. For the next century the 'Puritans', as they were first nicknamed in the 1560's, gave themselves to the work of renewal in the national Church – a work which was terminated by the ejection of most of them after the passing of the Act of Uniformity in 1662. The Puritan age proper spanned these hundred years.

In Scotland, from the outset, the Church of Scotland was

C   [7]

free from the entanglements which the semi-reformed state
of the Church caused in England. At one blow the old priesthood and episcopal hierarchy lost their places, except in the
still Catholic Highlands, and the leadership of the Reformed
Church was in the hands of Knox (c. 1514–1572) and his brethren. Yet the presbyterial form of church government, which
set them free from the corruption of prelacy and made possible
the exercise of a scriptural church discipline, was not long allowed to continue unimpeded. James VI of Scotland had no
more enthusiasm for experimental godliness than his mother,
Mary Queen of Scots, who was deposed from the throne in
1567, and shortly he came to set himself against Knox's successors, an activity in which he could engage with all the more
power when he also became James I, King of England in 1603.
Thereafter, aided by willing bishops, he worked to shackle the
independency of the Scottish Church and to suppress the
English Puritans. This was the policy which led at length to the
Civil War of 1642 and the defeat of his son, Charles I.

Despite the force exerted against both Puritans and Covenanters (the term usually attached to the Scots brethren because of their national covenants affirming the Reformed religion) they both prospered and that because the rising tide of
spiritual life could not be effectively countered. A school of
preachers arose in both realms of whom it could truly be said
that their gospel came not in word only, 'but also in power,
and in the Holy Ghost, and in much assurance'. (1 Thess. 1.5)

In England the University of Cambridge was the nursery
for this school. Thomas Cartwright gave the movement its
momentum in the late 1560's when his preaching in Great
St. Mary's became so popular that 'the sexton was fain to take
down the windows, by reason of the multitudes that came to
hear him'. Cartwright and others were soon deposed for their
boldness, but the watchword of the movement continued to be,
'Pray for reformation by the power of the word preached'.[5]
From the 1570's onward, friends of Cartwright, such as Richard
Rogers, John Dod and Arthur Hildersham, began to put this
into practice at the parish level. In the next thirty years the few

[8]

swelled to a flood, partly through the foundation of Emmanuel College at Cambridge by Sir Walter Mildmay in 1584 ('to render as many as possible fit for the administration of the Divine Word and Sacraments'), and partly by the conversion of William Perkins.

Perkins, born in the year of Elizabeth's accession, became a student at Christ's College, Cambridge, in 1577 when he was without any spiritual concern. The great change came while he was still a student. At the age of twenty-four he was made a Fellow of his college and later, for over fifteen years until his early death in 1602, preached at St. Andrew's Church in the same university city. In these capacities Perkins had enormous influence. Even in 1613, when Thomas Goodwin went up to Cambridge, he tells us that 'the whole town was filled with the discourse of the power of Mr. Perkins' ministry'.[6] 'Master Perkins,' says Samuel Clarke, 'held forth a burning and shining light, the sparks whereof did fly abroad into all the corners of the kingdom.'[7]

A similar power rested upon the ministry of Laurence Chaderton (c. 1536—1640), the first Master of Emmanuel College, a position he resigned in favour of another Puritan, John Preston, in 1622. For fifty years Chaderton was also lecturer at St. Clement's, Cambridge, and when he laid down this charge in 1618, at the age of seventy-two, it is said that forty ministers begged him to continue, attributing their conversion to him. Thomas Goodwin reports the words of a Cambridge friend who, speaking of the conviction of sin which accompanied Chaderton's preaching, declared that 'when he heard Mr. Chaderton preach the gospel, his apprehension was as if the sun, namely Jesus Christ, shined upon a dunghill'.[8] On one occasion when Chaderton had preached for two hours and promised to stop, he was interrupted by a cry from the congregation, 'For God's sake, Sir, Go on, go on!'

By the end of the sixteenth century Cambridge was beginning to reap results from the work done by the first generation of Puritans at the parish level. Richard Rogers, for instance, who toiled with much success at Wethersfield, Essex, from

1574 to 1618, saw Paul Baynes, one of the former pupils at his parish school, become Perkins' successor in the lectureship in St. Andrew's Church in 1602. Not wishing to have another like Perkins, the authorities later suspended Baynes, but not before he had been an instrument in the conversion of many, including Richard Sibbes who himself became one of the most successful preachers of the Puritan era. When Sibbes was appointed lecturer at Holy Trinity, Cambridge, in 1610, additional galleries had to be built to accommodate the crowded congregation. After 1615 he was 'preacher' at Gray's Inn, London, but he returned to Cambridge as Master of St. Catherine's Hall in 1626 and combined this with his London post until his death in 1635. One of the Fellows at St. Catherine's Hall during this period was Thomas Goodwin, who in a sermon preached at this time reflected thus on the great work of God in Cambridge: 'If in any age or in any coast it is or hath been full tide, it is now in England. . . . And this gospel hath made this kingdom and this town as a "crown of glory in the hand of the Lord;" and "the glory of the whole earth", as Jerusalem is called.'[9]

It is when one looks at some of the ministries produced from this nursery of preachers in Cambridge that the Puritan age as an age of revivals reveals itself. We can here only pause to give a few illustrative examples.

William Gouge (1575—1653), a student at Cambridge in Perkins' day, became minister of the church at Blackfriars, London, in 1608; here he remained for forty-five years and six months. His general practice was to preach twice on Sunday and once every Wednesday forenoon to a crowded church. His expository sermons on Hebrews numbered more than a thousand, a work which save for half a chapter he had completed for publication by the time of his death. Of this man we read, God made him 'an aged father in Christ . . . for thousands have been converted and built up by his ministry'.[10] His son, Thomas Gouge, followed him in the ministry, and after his ejection in 1662 did much to establish the gospel in the Principality of Wales.

Samuel Fairclough (1594—1677) left Cambridge in 1623 for Barnardiston in East Anglia. Six years later he moved to Kedington, seventeen miles from Cambridge, where he remained until the Great Ejection. At the time of his settlement the place was characterized by profanity and ignorance, but 'when he had been there sometime so great was the alteration that there was not a family in twenty but professed godliness'. Many would ride from Cambridge to hear Fairclough's Thursday 'lecture' and not till long after were those days of spiritual blessing forgotten. Kedington Church, Samuel Clarke tells us, was 'so thronged, that (though, for a village, very large and capacious, yet) there was no getting in, unless by some hours' attending before his exercise began; and then the outward walls were generally lined with shoals and multitudes of people, which came (many) from far, (some above twenty miles), so that you could see the Church yard (which was likewise very spacious) barricaded with horses, tied to the outward rails, while their owners were greedily waiting to hear the word of life from his mouth'.[11]

It is plain that scenes like this were far from rare in East Anglia in the first half of the seventeenth century. Samuel Fairclough's own father, Lawrence Fairclough, had seen spiritual prosperity in his ministry at Haverhill, Suffolk, before his death in 1603. The successor to his work in Haverhill was one of the most 'awakening' of all Puritan preachers and one whose ministry was attended with a power which was still being spoken of in the mid-eighteenth century. This was John Rogers, nephew of Richard Rogers of Wethersfield, by whose financial support he studied at Emmanuel from 1588 until 1592. In 1605 he was called from Haverhill to be 'lecturer' in the beautiful vale of Dedham, later to be known to the world by the paintings of John Constable but famous in the seventeenth century for the great spiritual harvest which took place under Rogers' ministry. 'Let us go to Dedham to get a little fire' became a common saying among his contemporaries.

One who went to Dedham was Thomas Goodwin, while a student at Cambridge, and many years later when he was

Dr. Goodwin and President of Magdalen College, Oxford, he reported his memory of it to John Howe who recorded it as follows:

'He told me that being himself, in the time of his youth, a student at Cambridge, and having heard much of Mr. Rogers of Dedham, in Essex, purposely he took a journey from Cambridge to Dedham to hear him preach on his lecture day. And in that sermon he falls into an expostulation with the people about their neglect of the Bible (I am afraid it is more neglected in our days); he personates God to the people, telling them, "Well, I have trusted you so long with my Bible; you have slighted it; it lies in such and such houses all covered with dust and cobwebs. You care not to look into it. Do you use my Bible so? Well, you shall have my Bible no longer." And he takes up the Bible from his cushion, and seemed as if he were going away with it, and carrying it from them; but immediately turns again and personates the people to God, falls down on his knees, cries and pleads most earnestly, "Lord, whatsoever thou dost to us, take not thy Bible from us; kill our children, burn our houses, destroy our goods; only spare us thy Bible, only take not away thy Bible". And then he personates God again to the people: "Say you so? Well, I will try you a little longer; and here is my Bible for you, I will see how you will use it, whether you will love it more, whether you will value it more, whether you will observe it more, whether you will practise it more, and live more according to it." But by these actions (as the Doctor told me) he put all the congregation into so strange a posture that he never saw any congregation in his life. The place was a mere Bochim, the people generally (as it were) deluged with their own tears; and he told me that he himself, when he got out and was to take horse again to be gone, was fain to hang a quarter of an hour upon the neck of his horse weeping, before he had power to mount, so strange an impression was there upon him, and generally upon the people, upon having been thus expostulated with for the neglect of the Bible.'[12]

Another eye-witness of John Rogers' ministry was John

Angier, who was under his supervision for a period while he completed his preparation for the ministry. 'Mr. Rogers', says Angier, 'was a prodigy of zeal and success in his ministerial labours' and he recalled how a sense of the greatness of eternal issues would at times overcome the crowded church at Dedham; on one such occasion Rogers took hold of the supports of the canopy over the pulpit with both hands, 'roaring hideously to represent the torments of the damned'. At another time when Rogers was taking a wedding service he preached on the necessity of the wedding garment: 'God made the word so effectual that the marriage solemnity was turned into bitter mourning, so that the ministers who were at the marriage were employed in comforting or advising those whose consciences had been awakened by that sermon.'[13]

When the 'Great Awakening' began in America in 1740 and its critics complained of the novelty of the outward signs of grief and conviction to be witnessed in many congregations, the aged Timothy Edwards reminded them of how common this had once been in the days of John Rogers.

We shall content ourselves with one further example of the extraordinary measure of the Holy Spirit which rested upon much preaching in England in the Puritan period. This time we can quote from one of the few personal ministerial narratives which survive from three hundred years ago, the autobiography of Richard Baxter (1615–1691).

Baxter was born and spent his youth in Shropshire, a part of England then comparatively little influenced by the Puritan movement. In childhood he heard the word 'Puritan' only as a term of scorn in his neighbourhood, the villagers spending Sunday, except for the brief time in which Common-Prayer was read, 'dancing under a May-Pole and a great tree, not far from my father's door'. Books, however, did penetrate where there was no worthy preacher. About the age of fifteen Baxter was awakened and went 'many a-day with a throbbing conscience' through a reading of Edmund Bunny's *Resolution*. Another book, obtained from a travelling pedlar, resolved this state of sorrow: it was Richard Sibbes' *Bruised Reed*, 'which opened more the *Love of God* to me, and gave me a livelier apprehension of the Mystery of Redemption, and how much I was beholden to Jesus Christ'. In these new convictions he was further confirmed by the loan of part of William Perkins' *Works* from a servant of his father.

Baxter's theology never reached the full scriptural maturity of the school of Sibbes and Perkins, partly, perhaps, because he did not share the opportunities enjoyed by the many who trained at Cambridge in these years. Nevertheless, as an awakening preacher to the conscience, with constant emphasis on the need for personal godliness, Baxter attained to the front rank among the later Puritans. The most memorable part of his ministry was exercised in Kidderminster, Worcestershire, first for two years preceding the Civil War of 1642–6; then resuming in the late 1640's when peace was again restored, and continuing until 1660. Looking back on the great change which had been wrought in Kidderminster, Baxter wrote about the year 1666:

'When I came thither first, there was about one family in a street that worshipped God and called on his Name, and when I came away there were some streets where there was not past one Family in the side of a street that did not so; and that did not, by professing serious godliness, give us hopes of their sincerity. . . .

'And God was pleased also to give me abundant encouragement in the Lectures which I preached abroad in other places; as at Worcester, Cleobury, etc., but especially at Dudley and Sheffnal; at the former of which (being the first place that ever I preached in) the poor Nailers and other Labourers would not only crowd the Church as full as ever I saw any in London, but also hang upon the windows and the leads without . . . so that I must here, to the praise of my dear Redeemer, set up this pillar of remembrance, even to His praise who hath employed me so many years in so comfortable a work, with such encouraging success!'

Baxter goes on to write of the general spiritual success which marked the Commonwealth period and refutes the sneers of those in the days of Charles II who attributed the 'godliness' of the former age to the material profit which men obtained by their hypocrisy:

'I know in these times you may meet with men that confidently affirm that all religion was then trodden down, and heresy and schism were the only piety; but I give warning to all ages that they take heed how they believe any . . . I must bear this faithful witness to those times, that as far as I was acquainted, where before there was one godly profitable Preacher, there was then six or ten; and taking one place with another, I conjecture there is a proportionable increase of truly godly people, not counting heretics or perfidious rebels or church-disturbers as such: But this increase of godliness was not in all places alike: For in some places where the ministers were formal, or ignorant, or weak and imprudent, contentious or negligent, the parishes were as bad as heretofore. And in some places, where the ministers had excellent parts, and holy lives, and thirsted after the good of souls, and wholly devoted themselves, their time and strength and estates thereunto, and thought no pains or cost too much, there abundance were converted to serious godliness. And with those of a middle state, usually they had a middle measure of success. And I must add this to the true information of posterity, that God did so wonderfully bless the labours of his *unanimous faithful ministers*, that had it not been for the faction of the Prelatists on one side that drew men off and the factions of the giddy and turbulent Sectaries on the other side, (who pull'd down all government, cried down the ministers, and broke all into confusion, and made the people at their wits' end, not knowing what religion to be of); together with some *laziness* and *selfishness* in many of the ministry, I say, had it not been for these impediments, England had been like in a quarter of an Age to have become a Land of Saints, and a pattern of holiness to all the world and the unmatchable paradise of the earth.'[14]

The testimony of Philip Henry (1631–1696) may also be cited in regard to the prevalence of evangelical religion in the Commonwealth period. Henry went up to Christ Church,

Oxford, in 1647, and within a few years when Thomas Goodwin became President of Magdalen College and John Owen
Dean of Christ Church, the university enjoyed a period of
spiritual life comparable to that known in Cambridge in earlier
years. Others then studying or teaching at the university included Joseph Alleine, John Howe and Stephen Charnock.
In the early eighteenth century, when the spiritual blight
which accompanied the Restoration had done its work, the
fashionable *Spectator* diverted its readers with a tale describing
how Goodwin examined applicants at Magdalen not so much on
Latin and Greek as on the state of their souls. The examination
of one nervous college applicant, 'bred up by honest parents,
was summed up in one short question, namely, Whether he
was prepared for death?'[15] Ridiculous this might seem to the
Spectator's readers, but Matthew Henry learned differently of
the Oxford of those days from his father:

'He would often mention it with thankfulness to God, what
great helps and advantages he had then in the University, not
only for learning, but for religion and piety. Serious godliness
was in reputation, and besides the public opportunities they
had, there were many of the scholars that used to meet together
for prayer, and christian conference, to the great confirming of
one another's hearts in the fear and love of God, and the preparing of them for the service of the church in their generation.
I have heard him speak of the prudent method they took then
about the University sermons on the Lord's day in the afternoon; which used to be preached by the fellows of colleges in
their course; but, that being found not so much for edification,
Dr. Owen and Dr. Goodwin performed that service alternately,
and the young masters that were wont to preach it, had a lecture on Tuesday appointed them.'[16]

Philip Henry spent the first eight years of his ministry at
Worthenbury in Flintshire, and thereafter at Broad Oak,
Flintshire, until his death in 1696. In those later years the great
benefit which England had formerly enjoyed became the more
apparent. 'He would sometimes say,' writes his son, 'that during
those years between forty and sixty [i.e. 1640–1660], though on

civil accounts there were great disorders, and the foundations
were out of course, yet, in the matters of God's worship, things
went well; there was freedom, and reformation, and a face
of godliness was upon the nation, though there were those that
made but a mask of it. Ordinances were administered in power
and purity; and though there was much amiss, yet religion, at
least in the profession of it, did prevail. This, saith he, we know
very well, let men say what they will of those times.'[17]

II

REVIVAL CHRISTIANITY:
SCOTLAND

The Glasgow College

'Old Mr. Hutcheson, minister at Killellan, used to say to Mr. Wodrow, author of the *History of the Church of Scotland*, "When I compare the times before the restoration [1660] with the times since the revolution [1688], I must own that the young ministers preach accurately and methodically; but there was far more of the power and efficacy of the Spirit and grace of God went along with sermons in those days than now: and, for my own part (all the glory be to God), I seldom set my foot in a pulpit in those times, but I had notice of some blessed effects of the Word".'

JOHN GILLIES

Historical Collections, 1754, vol 1, 315

'Scotland has since the Reformation sent more saints to heaven than any country in Europe of the same population.'

DAVID BOGUE

Discourses on the Millennium, 1818, 362

THE spiritual prosperity which accompanied the Puritan movement in England was paralleled by the revivals which occurred north of the Border during the same period. Here also the instrument was a powerful ministry stemming from colleges under the influence of faithful teachers of the Word. Andrew Melville, fresh from Geneva and twenty-nine years of age, led the way by reorganizing the moribund University of Glasgow in the years 1574–1580.

In 1583 Robert Rollock was appointed the first Principal of the Town's College of Edinburgh, and under his leadership the college soon began to supply the churches with men well qualified for the gospel ministry. Rollock was a forceful teacher and not afraid to see some emotion in his classes. He would pray with his students daily, says an old writer, and once a week expound some passage of Scripture to them, 'in the close of which he was frequently very warm in his exhortations; which wrought more reformation upon the students than all the laws which were made, or the discipline which was exercised'.[1] Besides his college work, we read that 'he preached every Lord's day in the church, with such fervency and evident demonstration of the Spirit, that he was the instrument of converting many to God'.[1]

Robert Boyd was one student who, as he tells us, first began 'to learn Christ' under that 'happy and glorious soul', Robert Rollock. Others who were under him at this memorable period include John Welch and Edward Brice – both greatly used in later revivals – and Charles Ferme and David Calderwood, best remembered for their books. Ferme became a regent, or professor, under Rollock in 1589, and with his *Logical Analysis of the Epistle of Paul to the Romans* (a commentary which runs to 378 pages in the last-century reprint) he followed the practice which his mentor had commenced of preparing expository material to aid the pulpit. Rollock issued many commentaries, the worth of which was noted by J. C. Ryle when he wrote: 'Of our old writers, Rollock, the Scotch divine, is incomparably the best. In fact, I do not know such a "buried treasure" as his Latin Commentary on St. John.'[2]

Another factor which made Edinburgh a conspicuous centre of spiritual light at this time was the ministry of Robert Bruce, who in the late 1580's came direct from studying under Melville at St. Andrews to John Knox's old pulpit of St. Giles. At the very outset of his ministry there was an 'extraordinary effusion of the Spirit when he first dispensed the Sacrament of the Supper'.[3] Thereafter Bruce's ministry was a constant witness to the fact that preaching does not depend upon the energy of human gifts for its success. Of this ministry Robert Fleming writes:

'Whilst he was in the ministry at Edinburgh he shined as a great light through the whole land, the power and efficacy of the Spirit most sensibly accompanying the word he preached . . . his speech and his preaching was in such evidence and demonstration of the Spirit that by the shining of his face, and that shower of divine influence, wherewith the word spoken was accompanied, it was easy for the hearer to perceive that he had been in the mount with God . . . he preached ordinarily with such life and power, and the word spoken by him was accompanied with such a manifest presence, that it was evident to the hearers he was not alone at the work . . . some of the most stout-hearted of his hearers were ordinarily made to tremble, and by having these doors which formerly had been bolted against Jesus Christ, as by an irresistible power broke open, and the secrets of their hearts made manifest, they went away under convictions and carrying with them undeniable proofs of Christ speaking in him.'[4]

The freedom which the students of Bruce and Rollock enjoyed did not last long. By the 1590's the conflict between King James and the Church was apparent, and the royal policy aimed at fettering the presbyterian system by the introduction of 'commissioners' (alias a new episcopacy) who would be as dependent upon the King's favour as were the bishops south of the Border. The last free General Assembly of the Church of Scotland in the sixteenth century met at Edinburgh in 1596, and thereafter all such gatherings were either packed and bribed, or simply put down and forbidden, until the famous Assembly which met in Glasgow in 1638.

Many set-backs were endured in these forty years. Rollock died in 1599 in his forty-third year; it speaks much for the faithfulness of the men whom he trained that they were soon proved ready to endure so much. Robert Boyd departed an unwilling exile to France in 1597; John Welch, protesting against the silencing of Bruce in 1605, was himself imprisoned and banished for life in 1606. Charles Ferme was confined for some years, as also was David Calderwood. Andrew Melville was summoned to London in 1605 and, after four years in the Tower, was banished to France, where he died in 1622.

The list of sufferers could be greatly extended; yet the fact is that it was in this same period that the gospel spread far and wide in Scotland, constantly registering new successes until loyalty to the faith of the Reformation became characteristic of a great part of the land. The one explanation for this is that the Holy Spirit in revival power was sovereignly dissipating the darkness and building a Church whose testimony was to be a beacon for succeeding centuries. Often the old records give us no more than a glimpse of what occurred, but what they tell us is enough to make us understand why, despite the persecution, it was an age of great spiritual prosperity.

We hear, for example, of John Davidson preaching to fellow-ministers at the General Assembly of 1596 on the need for repentance: 'In this he was so assisted by the Spirit working

D   [23]

upon their hearts, that within an hour after they had convened, they began to look with another countenance than at first, and while he was exhorting them to these duties, the whole meeting was in tears, whereby that place might have justly been called Bochim.' Commenting upon this day's work in St. Giles, which had repercussions throughout the land, the modern biographer of Bruce writes: 'Unquestionably there was a profound religious revival afoot, and behind the strivings of parties there was operative a great spiritual work such as cannot be recorded in the bald narrative of history.'[5]

Similarly we read of a great revival under John Welch's preaching in the south-west, in Kirkcudbright and at Ayr, before his banishment. When Samuel Rutherford settled in the same area, at Anwoth, in 1627, the results of the spiritual harvest in the time of Welch were in plentiful evidence. Rutherford refers to the former pastor of Kirkcudbright as 'that Apostolicke, heavenly, and Propheticall man of God' and reports, 'from the godly witnesses of his life I have heard say, of every twenty four hours, he gave eight to prayer, except when the public necessities of his calling did call him to preach, visit, exhort in season and out of season'.[6]

Even more remarkable was the effect which followed Bruce's ministry in Inverness, in the wild and Catholic Highlands, when he was banished there for the second time in 1622. No great results appear to have marked his first stay there from 1605 to 1613, but during the second period in the northern capital a new day of blessing dawned in the North. Bruce sensed it even as he made the difficult and weary ride for the second time. On one of the last stages of the journey he stood so long, rapt in meditation, beside his horse one morning before mounting that his companion later asked him the reason for the delay. Bruce replied, 'I was receiving my commission from my Master to go to Inverness, and He gave it me Himself, before I set my foot in the stirrup, and thither I go to sow a seed in Inverness that shall not be rooted out for many ages.' More than two centuries later Christians in the Highlands still spoke of the days when multitudes walked and took ferries from the counties of Ross and Sutherland to hear Bruce preach in Inverness. Speaking of Bruce's ministry in general, his contemporary, David Calderwood, says he 'gained to Christ many thousands of souls'. Kirkton mentions one instance: 'A poor Highlander, hearing him, came to him after sermon and offered him his whole substance (which was only two cows) upon condition Mr. Bruce would make God his friend.' This was the first of the many revivals which were to make north-east Scotland one of the most Christian areas of the world.[7]

Among others converted under Bruce was Alexander Henderson, when he was minister of Leuchars; he later took a leading part at the Westminster Assembly.

With the suppression of the General Assembly, the universities and colleges passed entirely under royal control, and the banishment of those best able to influence students was cleverly designed to prevent the training of such men as Edinburgh had produced in the late sixteenth century. But in 1614 King James misjudged his man when he appointed thirty-six-year-old Robert Boyd to be Principal and Professor of Divinity in the University of Glasgow. Boyd, as noted earlier, was a pupil of Rollock. He was of noble family, reserved, polished and a brilliant scholar. Having been long absent in France, and therefore uninvolved in the developing conflict between presbytery and episcopacy in Scotland, James evidently judged that the man's mildness and his dependence on the royal favour for his office would make him sufficiently pliable. It was one of the many mistakes which King James made, for within a few years the royal party in Scotland was complaining that Boyd had joined the 'Puritans'.

In 1621 Boyd was compelled to lay down his post, but not before he had left his impress on a series of younger men whose calibre was not a whit less than those who trained under Rollock.[8] One of these men was Robert Blair. Blair had recently been made a Master of Arts when Boyd took office at Glasgow, and in his *Autobiography* he tells us of the memorable first address which the new Principal gave. What moved him to take up this work, Boyd asked his hearers to consider, 'seeing he was a gentleman of a considerable estate, whereupon he might live competently enough?' 'His answer', writes Blair, 'was, that considering the great wrath under the which he lay naturally, and the great salvation purchased to him by Jesus Christ, he had resolved to spend himself to the utmost, giving all diligence to glorify that Lord who had so loved him. I thought within myself, There is a man of God, there is one of a thousand!'[9]

Boyd's great love was practical divinity and the study of matters pertaining to the conscience. He would take his pupils through such themes as the Christian's conflicts with the Devil, and when they came to him to speak of their own spiritual experience he was a wise counsellor. Another of his students was John Livingstone, who says how Boyd was 'one of ane austere-like carriage, but of a most tender heart. . . . I always found him soe kind and familiar as made me wonder.'[10] Robert Baillie, one of the five Scots ministers appointed to the Westminster Assembly in 1643, was also at Glasgow under Boyd, and thirty years after his student days were over he spoke of the spirit of repentance and of joy sometimes stirred within them as their master prayed. For Baillie, who himself became Principal at Glasgow in brighter days, Boyd was among the most eminent of the Reformed Divines.[11]

One more future leader who as a regent, or professor, in the university was associated with Boyd was David Dickson. It is to Dickson that the English-speaking world owes the conception of a whole series of commentaries which for many years served to make the study of the Bible a common household employment. Boyd produced a *Commentary on the Epistle to the Ephesians* of stupendous size; as James Walker writes, this 'led to the calamitous result of a great divine being buried under his own erudition'.[12] The series of popular volumes which Dickson envisaged avoided this pitfall as the subsequent reprinting of a number of them has proved. To the series Dickson contributed expositions of *Hebrews*, 1635, *Matthew*, 1647, and *Psalms*, 1653–1654. George Hutcheson followed with rich folios on *The Minor Prophets*, 1653–1655, *John*, 1657, and *Job*,

1669. James Fergusson, 'after the pattern held forth by those reverend brethren, Mr. David Dickson and Mr. George Hutcheson', added his *Brief Exposition of the Epistles of Paul* (Galatians to Thessalonians), and Alexander Nisbet supplied *A Brief Exposition of the First and Second Epistles General of Peter*. The manuscript of Samuel Rutherford's work on *Isaiah* was lost and never printed. James Durham's volumes on *The Song of Solomon, Revelation*, and *Job*, were not designed as part of the same series, being published posthumously, as was the fine work of John Brown of Wamphray on *Romans*. 'Nor are Dickson and his fellow-interpreters to be despised,' writes James Walker. 'They want the scholarship of the present day, though they were scholars. But though they want our scholarship, they were more than our equals in theology.' C. H. Spurgeon reached a similar verdict in his *Commenting and Commentaries*.

In his own day, however, Dickson was best known as a preacher and few were granted more success. Giving up his professorship at Glasgow in 1618, he became minister of Irvine in Ayrshire. Soon persecution was again on the increase and he was deprived of his charge and banished to the Highlands in 1622. Yet the mood of Dickson and his brethren was one of great confidence. At a prayer meeting held near Edinburgh in 1621 such enlargement of heart was given as petitions were presented to God that the ministers separated from each other with the assurance 'that yet hereafter the work of God would flourish in the land more than formerly'.[13] Dickson himself prayed for two hours that day, so John Livingstone tells us, and in a manner which convinced all present that God was hearing the pleas for 'the present sad case of the Church'. In 1623, through the intervention of the Earl of Eglinton, Dickson was permitted to return to Irvine, and about the same time a great revival commenced. Robert Fleming reports it in these words:

'I must here instance a very solemn and extraordinary out-letting of the Spirit, which about the year 1625, and thereafter was in the west of Scotland, whilst the persecution of the church there was hot from the prelatic party; this by the profane rabble of that time was called the Stewarton-sickness, for in that parish first, but after through much of that country, particularly at Irvine, under the ministry of famous Mr. Dickson, it was most remarkable, where it can be said (which divers ministers and Christians yet alive can witness) that for a considerable time, few sabbaths did pass without some evidently converted, and some convincing proofs of the power of God accompanying his Word; yea, that many were so choaked and taken by the heart, that through terror the Spirit in such a measure convincing them of sin, in hearing of the Word they have been made to fall over, and thus carried out of the church, who after proved most solid and lively Christians. . . . Truly, this great spring-tide, which I may so call of the gospel, was not of a short time, but for some years' continuance, yea, thus like a spreading moor-burn the power of godliness did advance from one place to another, which put a marvellous lustre on these parts of the country, the savour whereof brought many from other parts of the land to see the truth of the same.'[14]

Such was the hunger to hear the Word of God preached in these times that week-day services became common. Dickson, for instance, held a service on Monday mornings before the opening of the market which on that day drew many from the surrounding area to Irvine. For this market-day sermon, it is said, the church was even more crowded than on the Lord's Day. About the same time, on Monday, June 21, 1630, to be precise, a service was held at Shotts, a parish midway between Glasgow and Edinburgh. It was at the conclusion of a week-end of communion services at which seventy-five-year-old Robert Bruce and others had been ministering the Word. By the Sunday evening, such was the sense of the presence of God that many were unwilling to go away, and thus, after a night spent by a number in prayer, a further service was held in the morning. The preacher was young John Livingstone and the occasion he later remembered as 'the one day in all my life wherein I got most presence of God in publick'. Thirty years after that communion Robert Fleming recalled the results of those four days at the Kirk of Shotts. A 'down-pouring of the Spirit', he says, accompanied the ordinances, 'especially that sermon on the Monday, the 21st of June, that it was known, which I can speak on sure ground, near five hundred had at that time a discernible change wrought on them, of whom most proved lively Christians afterward: it was the sowing of a seed through Clydsdale, so as many of most eminent Christians in that country could date either their conversion, or some remarkable confirmation in their case from that day'.[15]

Equally memorable was the work now done in the plantation of Ulster which became a haven for both English and Scots ministers of Puritan conviction. In the 1620's several such men who had settled in Ireland began to work together with much unity and affection. In 1623 Robert Blair arrived, newly dismissed from his professorship at Glasgow, and he in turn encouraged another of Boyd's former regents, Josias Welch, to come over to Ireland. This was the son of John Welch and as Blair noted, 'A great measure of that spirit which wrought in and by the father rested on the son'. They were joined in the late summer of 1630 by John Livingstone.

The moral state of Ireland had been hitherto deplorable. Atheism and sin abounded and the ministry of a large part of the clergy was not only ineffectual but worse than nothing. As in Jeremiah's day, 'from the prophets of Israel profaneness went forth into all the land'. Livingstone was not the only newcomer to be dismayed at the ignorance of the people, and on his settlement in the parish of Killinshie, he said, 'I saw no appearance of doing any good among them.' Yet to a population so generally sunk in carelessness the power of divine grace was now manifested. The first ministry to be attended with evidence that an awakening was at hand was that of the eccentric James Glendinning of Carrickfergus. Blair, recognizing this man's limitations, advised him to seek a less exacting charge. He also urged upon him the duty of dealing more plainly and directly with the consciences of his hearers and advised him to seek to awaken them by the searching style of preaching which had been so largely blessed in Scotland. This counsel brought a turning point in Glendinning's ministry; he moved to Oldstone, near the town of Antrim, and, amidst a people characterized by their licence and indifference, he preached the law of God and the terror of the divine wrath. Glendinning's limitations were now unnoticed by a people who could only think of the message they heard. Andrew Stewart, a contemporary who witnessed what happened at Oldstone, later wrote with amazement of the change which was wrought:

'Behold the success! For the hearers finding themselves condemned by the mouth of God speaking in His Word, fell into such anxiety and terror of conscience that they looked on themselves as altogether lost and damned; and this work appeared not in one single person or two, but multitudes were brought to understand their way, and to cry out, Men and brethren, what shall we do to be saved? I have seen them myself stricken into a swoon with the Word; yea, a dozen in one day carried out of doors as dead, so marvellous was the power of God smiting their hearts for sin, condemning and killing. And of these were none of the weaker sex or spirit, but indeed some of the boldest spirits, who formerly feared not with their swords to put a whole market-town in a fray; yet in defence of their stubbornness cared not to lie in prison and in the stocks, and being incorrigible, were as ready to do the like the next day.'[16]

This revival, which commenced about the year 1626, was known after the name of the nearby river, the Six-Mile Water, which flows through the towns of Ballynure, Ballyclare and Templepatrick. Soon, however, the work spread far beyond the locality in which it commenced. In the reaping-time which followed, Robert Blair, Robert Cunningham, James Hamilton, the elderly Edward Brice – whom we noted at Edinburgh in Rollock's day – Josias Welch, and several others, were all engaged. At the suggestion of John Ridge, an English minister of Antrim of the Puritan school, a meeting was held at Antrim on the first Friday of each month and to this all the ministers engaged in the awakening came for prayer and conference.[17] On these Fridays a great congregation would gather and generally two ministers would preach in the morning and two in the afternoon. Speaking of this gathering, Livingstone writes: 'We used to come together on the Thursday night before, and stayed the Fryday night after, and consult about such things as concerned the carrying on the work of God, and these meetings among ourselves were sometimes as profitable as either presbytries or synods.' Some of Robert Blair's words are worthy of quotation, particularly as he had so much of the leadership of the work:

'This monthly meeting thus beginning, continued many years, and was a great help to spread religion through that whole country.' After naming nobility and ministers who gave their aid, he continues: 'So mightily grew the Word of God, and his gracious work prospered in the hands of his faithful servants. . . . There were many converts in all our congregations. That blessed work of conversion was now spread beyond the bounds of Down and Antrim, to the skirts of neighbouring counties, whence many came to the monthly meetings, and the sacrament of the Lord's supper. The Lord was pleased to bless his Word, the people had a vehement appetite for it that could not be satisfied: they hung upon the ministers, still desirous to have more; no day was long enough, no room large enough.'[18]

John Livingstone tells us this about the spirit of those days:

'Among all these ministers there was never any jar or jealousie, yea, nor among the professors, the greatest part of them being Scots, and some good number of gracious English, all whose contention was to preferr others to themselves; and although the gifts of the ministers was much different, yet it was not observed that the hearers followed any to the undervaluing of others. Many of those religious professors had been both ignorant and prophane, and for debt and want, and worse causes, had left Scotland, yet the Lord was pleased by his Word to work such change. I doe not think there were more lively and experienced Christians any where than were these at that time in Ireland, and that in good numbers, and many of them persons of an good outward condition in the world. Being but lately brought in, the lively edge was not yet gone off them, and the perpetual fear that the bishops would put away their ministers, made them with great hunger wait on the ordinances.

I have known them that have come severall myles from their own houses to communions, to the Saturday sermon, and spent the whole Saturday night in severall companies, sometimes an minister being with them, sometimes themselves alone in conference and prayer, and waited on the publick ordinances the whole Sabbath, and spent the Sabbath night likewise. . . . In these dayes it was no great difficultie for ane minister to preach or pray in publick or private, such was the hunger of the hearers; and it was hard to judge whether there was more of the Lord's presence in the publick or private meetings.'[19]

'That solemn and great work of God, which was in the church of Ireland,' says Fleming, 'was a bright and hot sun-blink of the gospel; yea, may with sobriety be said to have been one of the largest manifestations of the Spirit, and of the most solemn times of the down-pouring thereof, that almost since the days of the apostles hath been seen, where the power of God did sensibly accompany the Word with an unusual motion upon the hearers, and a very great tack,* as to the conversion of souls to Christ. . . . I remember amongst other passages what a worthy Christian told me, how sometimes in hearing the Word, such a power and evidence of the Lord's presence was with it, that he hath been forced to rise and look through the church and see what the people were doing, thinking from what he felt on his own spirit, it was a wonder how any could go away without some change upon them.'[20]

This day of exceptional visitation passed away in the 1630's. Some of the ministers were called home by death. Josias Welch died in 1634, his friends Blair and Livingstone being present on that triumphant day in June when he passed over. The son of John Welch 'clapped both his hands, and cryed out, "Victory! Victory! Victory for evermore!" and within a short while thereafter he expired'. Another who departed about this time was Edward Brice, who 'in all his preaching insisted most on the life of Christ in the heart'. He died in 1636, having been in Ireland since 1613. The remainder of the evangelical leaders were silenced by the episcopal opposition which was at its

* A Scots word for a draught of fishes.

height in these days when Archbishop Laud hounded many Puritan ministers out of their pulpits. Robert Blair, for instance, was excommunicated by the Bishop of Down in 1634. After the sentence was pronounced, Blair rose and cited the bishop to appear before the tribunal of Jesus Christ to answer for his deed. Upon this the bishop expressed his confidence that he would be able to appeal to the mercy of God, only to be told by the persecuted minister, 'Your appeal is like to be rejected because you act against the light of your own conscience.'*

Notwithstanding the comparative shortness of this 'sunblink' in Ulster, and despite the terrible massacre which occurred in 1641, claiming the lives of some forty thousand Protestants, J. S. Reid could write of this time in his *History of the Presbyterian Church in Ireland*, published in 1833: 'The Gospel shot forth its branches in Ulster with wonderful rapidity, till, like the grain of mustard, from being the least of all seeds, it became a great and noble tree, which after the lapse of two centuries and the beating of many bitter storms, stands, at the present day, more firm and vigorous than ever.' Meanwhile in Scotland Bruce had died in 1631. Shortly before his death there had been one of those prayer meetings, in his home, which were so characteristic of the period, and from which much spiritual energy and confidence was derived. The aged Bruce prayed 'with such an extraordinary motion upon the hearts of all present, and so sensible an out-pouring of the Spirit, as scarce any present were able to contain themselves'.[21]

In the years which immediately followed, the episcopal party made a last desperate attempt to stem the rising tide of allegiance to the evangelical faith. Robert Blair and his associates, Livingstone, Cunningham and Ridge, were harried out of Ireland by persecution, only to find a similar situation prevailing in Scotland. We are not surprised to learn that it was David Dickson and the people of Irvine who at risk to them-

---

* Shortly after this the bishop fell seriously ill. When his physician, Dr. Maxwell, came to enquire what was wrong, 'he was long silent, and with great difficulty uttered these words, "It is my conscience, man". To which the doctor replied, "I have no cure for that".'

selves sheltered these fugitives. The work of the two older men, Cunningham, the Scot, and Ridge, the Englishman, was done, and here at Irvine they died in peace.[22] They had already proved in this world what Rutherford anticipated of heaven, 'When we come up to our father's house the higher Jerusalem, I trust we shall not stand in a vicinity to, or a distance from his face who sits on the throne and the Lamb, as *English and Scottish*'. Blair and Livingstone survived the storm and were leaders of the Scottish Church in the new age which was at hand.

It is against this background that the great political events of the late 1630's in Scotland are to be understood – the rejection of Laud's liturgy, the rallying of the people to sign the National Covenant, the abolition of Episcopacy at the General Assembly of 1638, leading in turn to the two Bishops' Wars, so called because of Charles I's intervention to support his falling party in Scotland. The story of the events between 1638 and 1660, with the Civil Wars, the Solemn League and Covenant uniting the Puritans in England and Scotland, the Westminster Assembly, and the work of Cromwell, has often been told. But with all the political confusion of that period it is often forgotten that for the churches these were years of peace and of much prosperity. The seed sown in tears was indeed reaped with joy. James Kirkton's words on the spiritual state of Scotland before the Restoration of Charles II in 1660 are a fitting testimony with which to close this sketch of a great revival period:

'At the king's return every parish had a minister, every village had a school, every family almost had a Bible. . . . Every minister was a very full professor of the reformed religion, according to the large confession of faith framed at Westminster by the divines of both nations. Every minister was obliged to preach thrice a week, to lecture and catechise once, besides other private duties wherein they abounded, according to their proportion of faithfulness and abilities. None of them might be scandalous in their conversation, or negligent in their office, so long as a presbytrie stood; and among them were many holy in conversation and eminent in gifts . . . nor did a minister satisfy himself except his ministry had the seal of a divine approbation, as might witness him to be really sent from God. Indeed, in many places the spirit seemed to be poured out with the Word, both by the multitude of sincere converts, and also by the common work of reformation upon many who never came the length of a communion. . . . I have lived many years in a parish where I never heard an oath, and you might have ridden many miles before you heard any: Also, you could not for a great part of the country have lodged in a family where the Lord was not worshipped by reading, singing and publick prayer. No body complained more of our church government than our taverners, whose ordinary lamentation was, their trade was broke, people were become so sober.'[23]

David Dickson's Church at Irvine

UNFULFILLED PROPHECY:
THE DEVELOPMENT OF THE HOPE

*Richard Sibbes, Puritan leader in
Cambridge and London*

'That God in his appointed time will bring forth the kingdom of the Lord Christ unto more glory and power than in former days, I presume you are persuaded. Whatever will be more, these six things are clearly promised:

1. *Fulness of peace* unto the gospel and the professors thereof, Isa. 11.6, 7, 54.13, 33.20, 21; Rev. 21.15.

2. *Purity and beauty of ordinances* and gospel worship, Rev. 11.2, 21.3. The tabernacle was wholly made by appointment, Mal. 3.3, 4; Zech. 14.16; Rev. 21.27; Zech. 14.20; Isa. 35.8.

3. *Multitudes of converts*, many persons, yea, nations, Isa. 60.7, 8, 66.8, 49.18–22; Rev. 7.9.

4. *The full casting out and rejecting of all will-worship*, and their attendant abominations, Rev. 11.2.

5. *Professed subjection of the nations* throughout the whole world unto the Lord Christ, Dan. 2.44, 7.26, 27; Isa. 60.6–9; – the kingdoms become the kingdoms of our Lord and his Christ (Rev. 11.15), amongst whom his appearance shall be so glorious, that David himself shall be said to reign.

6. *A most glorious and dreadful breaking of all that rise in opposition unto him*, Isa. 60.12 – never such desolations, Rev. 16.17–19.'

JOHN OWEN

'The Advantage of the Kingdom of Christ in the Shaking of the Kingdoms of the World', A sermon to the Commons assembled in Parliament, 1651 (*Works*, vol 8, 334)

IN the turmoil of ideas which accompanied the Reformation of the sixteenth century it was inevitable that the question of unfulfilled prophecy should be reopened. The restoration of the Bible in pulpits and homes was in itself enough to make this certain. For long years the evangelical meaning of the Second Advent of Christ, and truths concerning the last things in general, had lain out of sight with the removal of the Scriptures from the common people. The future, both with respect to history and to eternity was a dark unknown. Purgatory cast its shadow upon life from the cradle to the grave. Anti-Christ remained unidentified, except in the convictions of some few Lollards or Waldensians. The Jews, despised and downtrodden, heard no word of hope from the professing Church, and the unevangelized world lying beyond the narrow borders of Christendom received no messengers of the gospel of peace.

None of these things could last once the Scriptures were uncovered. Prophecy was again examined and the onset of persecution caused believers to dwell all the more upon the prospects which that subject brought before them. Not without reason did John Knox describe the Christians of England, suffering in the reign of Mary Tudor, as those 'that love the Coming of our Lord'. And yet it must at once be said that the Reformation period, save for restoring the certain hope of Christ's Second Coming, did not establish for Protestantism a

E

commonly accepted view of the unfulfilled prophecies which are to precede that coming. No unanimity was arrived at here as it was in many other areas of biblical truth. Luther, for example, regarded himself as living at the very close of history, with the Advent and Judgment immediately at hand. Others, on the outer fringe of orthodox Protestantism, 'drew out of its grave' (as a Puritan later complained against them) the belief common among some of the early Fathers, that Christ would appear and reign with his saints a thousand years in Jerusalem before the Judgment. From their emphasis on the word 'thousand' (Greek, *chilias*; Latin, *mille*), taken from Revelation, chapter 20, they were anciently called 'chiliasts' or 'millenaries'. Calvin deemed this view 'too puerile to need or to deserve refutation'[1]. He has in turn been accused in more modern times of failing to animate 'his fellow-Christians by preaching and instruction to await patiently and in faith the establishment of the kingly rule that Jesus had promised in connexion with His Parousia'.[2] This charge is true in so far as Calvin believed that Christ's kingdom is *already* established, and, unlike Luther, he expected it to have a yet greater triumph in history prior to the consummation, but it is false if it is understood to mean that Calvin did not proclaim the joyful expectation of Christ's return. The latter he most certainly did, as one characteristic statement of the reformer's is enough to show. Preaching in the great cathedral of St. Peter's, Geneva, from the text, 'The Lord grant unto him that he may find mercy of the Lord in that day' (2 Tim. 1.18), he dwells on the words 'in that day':

'Let us learn to stretch out our hope, even to the coming of our Lord Jesus Christ. . . . For if this hope do not reign in our hearts and sit as mistress there, we shall faint every minute of an hour. Will we therefore walk equally in God's service? Before all things let us learn to fasten our eyes and stay them upon this last day, and upon this coming of our Lord Jesus Christ, and know we that then there is a crown prepared for us, and let it not grieve us to be in great distress in the mean season, and to have many discommodities, to lead a painful and troublesome life, let us pass over all this, casting our eyes always upon this latter day, whereunto God calleth us, and indeed we see how Saint Paul speaks, *In that day*, saith he. No Christian man can read this text, but he must needs be touched to the quick. For we see that St. Paul was as it were ravished, when he spake of this coming of Jesus Christ and of the last resurrection. . . . Saint Paul, I say, spake not of these things coldly, nor according to man, but he was lifted up above all the world, that he might cry out, That day, That day!'[3]

This central hope, then, the Reformers clearly asserted. It was in regard to other subjects bearing on unfulfilled prophecy that they left no united testimony. Several of these subjects received little attention from the first generation of Reformers and, with one exception, they were left for their successors to take up. The exception was the unanimous belief that the Papal system is both the 'man of sin' and the Babylonian whore of which Scripture forewarns (2 Thess. 2; Rev. 19). In the conviction of sixteenth-century Protestants, Rome was the great Anti-Christ, and so firmly did this belief become established that it was not until the nineteenth century that it was seriously questioned by evangelicals.

One of the first developments in thought on prophecy came as further attention was given to the Scriptures bearing on the future of the Jews. Neither Luther nor Calvin saw a future general conversion of the Jews promised in Scripture; some of their contemporaries, however, notably Martin Bucer and Peter Martyr, who taught at Cambridge and Oxford respectively in the reign of Edward VI, did understand the Bible to teach a future calling of the Jews. In this view they were followed by Theodore Beza, Calvin's successor at Geneva. As early as 1560, four years before Calvin's death, the English and Scots refugee Protestant leaders who produced the *Geneva Bible*, express this belief in their marginal notes on Romans chapter 11, verses 15 and 26. On the latter verse they comment, 'He sheweth that the time shall come that the whole nation of the Jews, though not every one particularly, shall be joined to the church of Christ.'

The first volume in English to expound this conviction at some length was the translation of Peter Martyr's *Commentary upon Romans*, published in London in 1568. The probability is strong that Martyr's careful exposition of the eleventh chapter prepared the way for a general adoption amongst the English Puritans of a belief in the future conversion of the Jews. Closely linked as English Puritanism was to John Calvin, it was the view contained in Martyr's commentary which was received by the rising generation of students at Cambridge.

Among those students was Hugh Broughton (1549–1612) who had the distinction of being the first Englishman to propose going as a missionary to the Jews in the Near East, and also the first to propose the idea of translating the New Testament into Hebrew for the sake of the Jews. Broughton's ardour for the conversion of the Jews found no sympathy, however, with the English bishops whom he had early offended by his Puritan leanings. Though given no preferment in the English Church he was so well known in the East on account of his learning that the Chief Rabbi of Constantinople wrote to him in 1599 and subsequently invited him to become a public teacher there! This early possibility of a mission to the Jews was thwarted by the Church authorities, but Broughton's writings – of which the best known was probably his *Commentary on Daniel*, 1596 – stimulated further study of the whole question.[4]

Broughton was too much an individualist ever to become a leader of the Puritan movement. Two years before he was ejected from his fellowship at Christ's College, Cambridge, in 1579, William Perkins had entered the same college, a man whom we noted earlier as doing so much to influence the thinking of many who were to preach all over England. Perkins speaks plainly of a future conversion of the Jews: 'The Lord saith, *All the nations shall be blessed in Abraham:* Hence I gather that the nation of the Jews shall be called, and converted to the participation of this blessing: when, and how, God knows: but that it shall be done before the end of the world we know.'[5] The same truth was opened by the succession of Puritan leaders at Cambridge who followed Perkins, including

Richard Sibbes and Thomas Goodwin. In his famous book, *The Bruised Reed*, mentioned earlier in connection with Baxter's conversion, Sibbes writes:

'The Jews are not yet come in under Christ's banner; but God, that hath persuaded Japhet to come into the tents of Shem, will persuade Shem to come into the tents of Japhet, Gen. 9.27. The "fulness of the Gentiles is not yet come in", Rom. 11.25, but Christ, that hath the "utmost parts of the earth given him for his possession", Psa. 2.8, will gather all the sheep his Father hath given him into one fold, that there may be one sheepfold and one shepherd, John 10.16.

'The faithful Jews rejoiced to think of the calling of the Gentiles; and why should not we joy to think of the calling of the Jews?'[6]

This note of joy is significant. It had already been struck by Peter Martyr. If a widespread conversion of the Jews was yet to occur in the earth then the horizons of history were not, as Luther feared, wholly dark. Maintaining the truth that *the* great day for the Church would be the day of Christ's appearing at the end of time, Sibbes nevertheless saw warrant for expecting what he calls 'lesser days before that great day'. He continues:

'As at the first coming of Christ, so at the overthrow of Anti-Christ, the conversion of the Jews, there will be much joy. . . . These days make way for that day. Whensoever prophecies shall end in performances, then shall be a day of joying and glorying in the God of our salvation for ever. And therefore in the Revelation where this Scripture is cited, Rev. 21.4, is meant the conversion of the Jews, and the glorious estate they shall enjoy before the end of the world. "We have waited for our God," and now we enjoy him. Aye, but what saith the church there? "Come, Lord Jesus, come quickly." There is yet another, "Come, Lord", till we be in heaven.'[7]

From the first quarter of the seventeenth century, belief in a future conversion of the Jews became commonplace among the English Puritans. In the late 1630's, and in the national upheavals of the 1640's – the period of the Civil Wars – the subject not infrequently was mentioned by Puritan leaders.

As a ground for hopefulness in regard to the prospects of Christ's kingdom it was introduced in sermons before Parliament or on other public occasions by William Strong,[8] William Bridge,[9] George Gillespie[10] and Robert Baillie,[11] to name but a few. The fact that the two last-named were commissioners from the General Assembly of the Church of Scotland at the Westminster Assembly, which was convened by the English Parliament in 1643, is indicative of the agreement on this point between English and Scottish divines. Some of the rich doctrinal formularies which that Assembly produced, bear the same witness. *The Larger Catechism*, after the question, 'What do we pray for in the second petition of the Lord's Prayer?' (Thy Kingdom come), answers: 'We pray that the kingdom of sin and Satan may be destroyed, the gospel propagated throughout the world, the Jews called, the fulness of the Gentiles brought in . . . that Christ would rule in our hearts here, and hasten the time of his second coming.' *The Directory for the Public Worship of God* (section on Public Prayer before Sermon) stipulates in similar language that prayer be made 'for the conversion of the Jews'.

This same belief concerning the future of the Jews is to be found very widely in seventeenth-century Puritan literature. It appears in the works of such well-known Puritans as John Owen, Thomas Manton and John Flavel, though the indices of nineteenth-century reprints of their works do not always indicate this. It is also handled in a rich array of commentaries, both folios and quartos – David Dickson on the Psalms, George Hutcheson on the Minor Prophets, Jeremiah Burroughs on Hosea, William Greenhill on Ezekiel, Elnathan Parr on Romans and James Durham on Revelation: a list which could be greatly extended.

Occasionally the subject became the main theme of a volume. Perhaps the first in order among these was *The Calling of the Jews*, published in 1621 by William Gouge, the eminent Puritan minister of Blackfriars, London; the author was a barrister, Sir Henry Finch. A slender work, *Some Discourses upon the Point of the Conversion of the Jews*, by Moses Wall, appeared in 1650,[12] and nineteen years later Increase Mather, the New England divine of Boston, issued his work, *The Mystery of Israel's Salvation Explained and Applied*. 'That there shall be a general conversion of the Tribes of Israel is a truth which in some measure hath been known and believed in all ages of the Church of God, since the Apostles' days. . . . Only in these late days, these things have obtained credit much more universally than heretofore.' So Mather wrote in 1669.

By this latter date, however, divergencies of view had also become established within Puritan thought on prophecy, and to these we must now turn. They centre around those scriptural prophecies which appear to speak of a general conversion of the nations. The first expositors of a future conversion of Israel, Peter Martyr and William Perkins for instance, had placed that event very close to the end of time. Martyr interpreted the word 'fulness' in Paul's statement, 'blindness in part is happened to Israel, until the fulness of the Gentiles be come in' (Rom. 11.25) to mean that Christ's kingdom among the Gentiles will have reached its fullest development, indeed its consummation, by the time that Israel is called. By the conversion of the Jews, he says, the churches will 'be stirred and confirmed', but the thought that thereafter many more Gentiles will be converted is not possible, Martyr argues, for 'it is said, that the Jews shall then be saved and enter in, when the fulness of the Gentiles hath entered in. And if the calling of the Gentiles shall be complete, what other Gentiles shall there be remaining to be by the conversion of the Jews brought unto Christ?'[13]

Thomas Brightman (1562–1607) seems to have been one of the first divines of the Puritan school to reject the argument that the Jews' conversion must be placed at the very end of history. Brightman was a contemporary of Perkins at Cambridge and a fellow of Queens' College before his appointment to the living of Hawnes, Bedfordshire, in 1592. With his Commentary on the Revelation of St. John, *A Revelation of the Apocalypse* (first published in Latin in the year of his death and later in English) he stands at the head of the long line of subsequent English commentators on that book. For Brightman the Revelation gives a chronological outline of church history: events up to the 14th chapter he considered were already fulfilled; the 15th commences to deal with things yet to come; while the 20th gives a summary in which 'the whole history is repeated'. In the course of this exposition the Elizabethan Puritan gives considerable attention to the future prospects of the Jews: 'I have set down these things with more store of words, because I would give our Divines an occasion of thinking more seriously of these things.'[14]

Brightman's work confirmed the view that the Jews would be called, but in addition it brought forward considerations concerning the time of their conversion which tended to show that the matter was not so conclusively settled as Martyr had considered. Though there would be a certain fulness of the Gentiles made up before the salvation of Israel, this does not necessitate the belief that no more Gentiles can be added; Paul himself, Brightman argues, implies the contrary in verse 15 of Romans 11.[15] The Jews' calling, he believed, would be part of a new and brighter era of history, and not the end.

In the earliest and most popular Puritan exposition of Romans, the *Plain Exposition* of Elnathan Parr, published in 1620, it is interesting to note a development in the same direction. Parr was educated at Eton, graduated B.A. at Cambridge in 1597 and exercised a powerful ministry at Palgrave, Suffolk, dying about the year 1632. In handling chapter eleven he is in major agreement with Martyr and refers to his work. But over the prospects for the world at the time of Israel's future calling he does not accept the Continental divine's interpretation that the 'fulness of the Gentiles', preceding the Jews' call, means that God's saving work among the Gentiles will then be complete:

'The casting off of the Jews, was our Calling; but the Calling of the Jews shall not be our casting off, but our greater enriching in grace, and that two ways: First, in regard of the company of believers, when the thousands of Israel shall come in, which shall doubtless cause many Gentiles which now lie in ignorance, error and doubt, to receive the Gospel and join with them. The world shall then be a golden world, rich in golden men, saith

Ambrose. Secondly, in respect of the graces, which shall then in more abundance be rained down upon the Church.'[16]

In 1627, seven years after Parr's commentary appeared, further impetus was given to the expectation of world-wide blessing connected with the calling of the Jews, by the appearance of a Latin work by John Henry Alsted, *The Beloved City*. Alsted poses his main question in these words, 'Whether there shall be any happiness of the Church here upon earth before the last day; and of what kind it shall be?' From a consideration of some sixty-six places in the Scriptures he resolves this question in the affirmative and gives the following outline of the Church's history during the course of the Christian era:

1. From Christ's birth to the Council of Jerusalem, A.D. 50.
2. The second period is of the Church spread over the whole world and contains the calling and conversion of most nations.
3. From the beginning of the thousand years to the end thereof. And it shall contain, as well as the martyrs that shall then rise, the nations not yet converted, and the Jews; and it shall be free from persecutions.
4. From the end of the thousand years to the last judgment. In which the estate of the Church shall be very miserable . . .[17]

It will be seen immediately that Alsted identifies the period of the Church's highest development on earth, when the Jews will be called, with the millennium of Revelation 20. The most prevalent view hitherto was that the thousand years' reign of Christ was his spiritual rule over the Church in this world – a symbolic picture of the whole period between Christ's first and second advents. According to this traditional view, Christians of every generation share in Christ's spiritual reign; they have 'part in the first resurrection' (Rev. 20.5), that is to say, they are people who have been quickened in regeneration. This spiritualization of the word 'resurrection' is not without support from other Scriptures. For instance, Christ, speaking of the present gospel era, says, 'The hour is coming, and now is, when the dead shall hear the voice of the Son of God: and they that hear shall live' (John 5.25).

This interpretation, popularized by Augustine, was now being challenged. In Alsted's view the thousand years was literal – not simply a symbolic figure – and the resurrection to mark its commencement was likewise to be literal. This new position on Revelation 20 soon gained influence in England, particularly through the writings of Joseph Mede (1586–1638), a learned Fellow of Christ's College, Cambridge. Mede, like Alsted who influenced him, argued that the millennium is a future period of time, and he went further with the suggestion that it would be ushered in by a personal appearing of Christ – a 'pre-millennial' coming.[18]

Despite the general cautiousness of these two scholars, they both encouraged the practice of date-fixing and in the general excitement of the 1640's – the Civil War period – the question whether Christ's coming to establish a 'millennial kingdom' was near at hand was agitated by men of considerably less competence than Mede and Alsted. The end product was 'the Fifth Monarchy' party, so called because they believed that Christ's monarchy, succeeding the four spoken of by Daniel, was shortly to be set up, with the Jews converted and the millennium brought in. Thomas Fuller, in his *Worthies of England*, published in 1662 when this party was thoroughly discredited, comments pithily: 'I dare boldly say that the furious factors for the Fifth Monarchy hath driven that nail which Master Mede did first enter, farther than he ever intended it; and doing it with such violence that they split the truths round about it. Thus, when ignorance begins to build on that foundation which learning hath laid, no wonder if there be no uniformity in such a mongrel fabric.'[19]

*　　*　　*

We have traced in these last few pages a sequence and development of ideas which may be enumerated as follows: (1) the Jews to be converted; (2) their calling to be associated with a further expansion of the Church and therefore not to be at the end; (3) a fuller development and future prosperity of the Church to be identified with the thousand years' peace of Revelation 20; and (4) Christ himself to inaugurate this future reign and raise his saints.

It is important now to notice that these beliefs are not so necessarily related as to stand or fall together. The majority of Puritan divines believed that the scriptural evidence was broad enough to warrant an acceptance of points one and two above. Some considered that point three was correct, but that the 'resurrection' to usher in the millennium was not to be taken literally; it refers, they thought, to the spiritual resurrection of the Church's influence in the world which will then be witnessed.[20] This identification of the Church's time of highest development with a spiritual millennium was to command very wide support in eighteenth- and early nineteenth-century Protestantism. Whether right or wrong, no major difference exists between those who accepted this refinement of point three and those who only went as far as point two. Sometimes those who accepted point three, in the sense just given, have been termed 'millenaries' or 'chiliasts',[21] but Millenarianism proper is the view represented by point four and it is here that a radical difference is involved. According to this teaching the Church's brightest era is to differ from the present not simply in terms of *degree* but in *kind*. That is to say, it will be more than a larger measure of the spiritual blessings already given to the church; by Christ's personal appearing and the resurrection of saints an altogether new order of things is to be established. Christ will then reign in a manner not now seen or known. To this conclusion Mede's teaching pointed and from it Puritanism, generally, diverged.

The reason for this divergence was the unwillingness of the majority to be committed to a prophetic scheme which virtually made Revelation 20, a notoriously difficult chapter, the axis of interpretation. Thus Elnathan Parr, while speaking of the future blessing promised in Romans 11, declines to employ Revelation 20 on account of its obscurity, though he notes that some have done so.[22] Likewise John Owen with characteristic caution writes:

'The coming of Christ to reign here on earth a thousand years is, if not a groundless opinion, yet so dubious and uncertain as not to be admitted a place in the analogy of faith to regulate our interpretation of Scripture in places that may fairly admit of another application.'[23]

We must therefore note that is was not upon a Millenarian basis that the Puritan movement in general believed in the conversion of the Jews and a period of world-wide blessing. The belief was already common long before the challenge of Millenarianism became noticeable in the 1640's,[24] and, while the two sides held common ground in that both believed there are various passages in the Old and New Testaments warranting the expectation of future blessing for the world, men of the main Puritan school were quick to assert in answer to that challenge that those scriptures needed no pre-millennial interpretation of Revelation 20 to make their sense clear. Thus Robert Baillie answers a pre-millennial writer who had appealed to Romans 11.12 (where Paul writes of the Jews, 'If the fall of them be the riches of the world, and the diminishing of them the riches of the Gentiles; how much more their fulness?) in this way:

'There is nothing here for the point in hand: we grant willingly that the nation of the Jews shall be converted to the faith of Christ; and that the fulness of the Gentiles is to come in with them to the Christian Church; also that the quickening of that dead and rotten member, shall be a matter of exceeding joy to the whole Church. But that the converted Jews shall return to Canaan to build Jerusalem, that Christ shall come from heaven to reign among them for a thousand years, there is no such thing intimated in the Scriptures in hand.'[25]

Thomas Hall in his pungent little book, *A Confutation of the Millenarian Opinion*, 1657, makes this same point in dealing with a certain Dr. Homes whose argument he summarizes and answers in the following terms:

'Those things which are prophesied in the Word of God

and are not yet come to pass, must be fulfilled, (very true.) But the great sensible and visible happiness of the Church on earth before the Ultimate Day of Judgement is prophesied in the Word of God, which is the Old and New Testament (very true,) *ergo*, it shall come to pass; who ever denied it? But what is this to the point in hand? Or what Logick is this? Because in the last dayes the Jews shall be called, and because the Glorious Spiritual Priviledges of the Church shall then be advanced, *Ergo*, Christ and the saints alone shall reign on earth a thousand years. This is the Drs Logick you see from first to last.'[26]

*　　　*　　　*

We are now in a position to see how this somewhat prolonged discussion of Puritan thought on prophecy relates to the subject of revival. If the calling of the Jews and a wider conversion work in the world is to occur without such cataclysmic acts as the personal descent of Christ and the resurrection of saints, by what means will these blessings be brought to pass? The answer of the main Puritan school became a most important part of the heritage which they left to posterity. It was that the kingdom of Christ would spread and triumph through the powerful operations of the Holy Spirit poured out upon the Church in revivals. Such periods would come at the command of Christ, for new Pentecosts would show him still to be 'both Lord and Christ'. Their whole Calvinistic theology of the gospel, with its emphasis on the power given to Christ as Mediator for the sure in-gathering of the vast number of his elect, and on the person of the Holy Spirit as the One by whom the dead are quickened, dovetails in here. They rejected altogether a naturalistic view of inevitable progress in history – so common in the nineteenth century – but asserted that the sovereign purpose of God in the gospel, as indicated by the promises of Scripture yet unfulfilled, points to the sure hope of great outpourings of the Spirit in the future. It was upon such central beliefs as these that the Puritans based their expectations. John Howe, for instance, exemplifies their common attitude when he dealt with unfulfilled prophecy in a series of fifteen sermons on Ezekiel 39.29: 'Neither will I hide my face any more from them: for I have poured out my Spirit upon the house of Israel, saith the Lord God.' The series was posthumously published under the title, *The Prosperous State of the Christian Interest before the End of Time by a Plentiful Effusion of the Holy Spirit*. As Howe's emphasis on the work of the Saint is so characteristic of Puritan thought I have included a lengthy extract from these sermons at the end of this book, though it may help the reader to appreciate what follows if it is read after this present chapter.

Throughout Puritan literature, embracing authors who followed 'the independent way' in church government and those who were of Presbyterian convictions, and as common in Scotland as in England, there is this emphasis upon the kingdom of Christ advancing through revivals. We shall later seek to show how the transmission of this belief to the eighteenth and nineteenth centuries became one of the most powerful influences in the spiritual history of Britain and America.

In conclusion, it may be helpful to attempt a summary of the different views on unfulfilled prophecy which were current among the main-line Puritans;

1. A small number continued the view current among the early Reformers that the Scriptures predict no future conversion of the Jews and that the idea of a 'golden age' in history is without biblical foundation. The most able spokesmen for this position were Alexander Petrie and Richard Baxter.[27]

2. A larger number appear to have held the belief of Martyr and Perkins that the conversion of the Jews would be close to the end of the world. This was probably the dominant view at least until the 1640's.[28]

3. The attention drawn by such writers as Mede and Alsted to the millennium of Revelation 20, and to the Old Testament prophecies which appear to speak of a general conversion of the nations, led to a revived expectation of a pre-millennial appearing of Christ, when Israel would be converted and Christ's kingdom established in the earth for at least a thousand years before the day of judgment. Stated in its more

moderate form this belief commanded the support of some of the Westminster divines (notably, William Twisse, Thomas Goodwin, William Bridge and Jeremiah Burroughs);[29] in its wilder form it became identified with the Fifth Monarchy party. In all its forms, however, its influence seems to have been short-lived in the seventeenth century, and pre-millennial belief gained no general recognition in Protestantism until its revival two hundred years later.

4. The fourth group, like the second, believed in a future conversion of Israel and opposed the idea of a millennium to be introduced by Christ's appearing and a resurrection of saints. But, like the third group, they regarded Romans 11 and portions of Old Testament prophecy as indicating a period of widespread blessing both attending and following the calling of the Jews. The Confession of the Independents, *The Savoy Declaration* of 1658, summarizes this in its chapter 'Of the Church':

'We expect that in the later days, Antichrist being destroyed, the Jews called, and the adversaries of the Kingdom of his dear Son broken, the Churches of Christ being inlarged, and edified through a free and plentiful communication of light and grace, shall enjoy in this world a more quiet, peaceable and glorious condition than they have enjoyed.'

This statement has been attributed to the millenarianism current among Independents in the late 1640's, but it should be noted that the Savoy divines, among whom was John Owen, declined to identify this period of the Church's highest development with the millennium. Moreover, this same belief was maintained by staunch Presbyterians as, for instance, Thomas Manton[30] (author of the 'Epistle to the Reader' in the Westminster Confession), David Dickson[31] and Samuel Rutherford. Before Rutherford met any of the English Independents he wrote from St. Andrews in 1640: 'I shall be glad to be a witness, to behold the kingdoms of the world become Christ's. I could stay out of heaven many years to see that victorious triumphing Lord act that prophesied part of his soul-conquering love, in taking into his kingdom the greater sister, that kirk of the Jews, who sometime courted our Well-beloved for her little sister (Cant. 8.8); to behold him set up as an ensign and banner of love, to the ends of the world.'[32] This was no millennialism as Rutherford was careful elsewhere to say, 'I mean not any such visible reign of Christ on earth, as the Millenaries fancy.'[33]

Forty years later this same belief was the common testimony of the Covenanting field-preachers who upheld the confession of the Church of Scotland in its purity during 'the killing times'. Richard Cameron preached on July 18, 1680, just three days before his violent death on the moors at Ayrsmoss, from the text, 'Be still, and know that I am God: I will be exalted among the heathen: I will be exalted in the earth.' (Psa. 46.10). To his hearers, gathered with him under the shadow of eternity, Cameron declared:

'You that are in hazard for the truth, be not troubled: our Lord will be exalted among the heathen. But many will say, "We know He will be exalted at the last and great day when He shall have all the wicked on His left hand." Yes; but says He, "I will be exalted in the earth." He has been exalted on the earth; but the most wonderfully exalting of His works we have not yet seen. The people of God have been right high already. Oh, but the Church of the Jews was sometimes very high, and sometimes the Christian Church! In the time of Constantine she was high. Yea, the Church of Scotland has been very high, "Fair as the moon, clear as the sun; and terrible as an army with banners." The day has been when Zion was stately in Scotland. The terror of the Church of Scotland once took hold of all the kings and great men that passed by. Yea; the terror of it took hold on Popish princes; nay, on the Pope himself. But all this exalting that we have yet seen is nothing to what is to come. The Church was high, but it shall be yet much higher. "There is none like the God of Jeshurun." The Church of Christ is to be so exalted that its members shall be made to ride upon the high places of the earth. Let us not be judged to be of the opinion of some men in England called the Fifth-Monarchy men, who say that, before the great day,

Christ shall come in person from heaven with all the saints and martyrs and reign a thousand years on earth. But we are of the opinion that the Church shall yet be more high and glorious, as appears from the book of Revelation, and the Church shall have more power than ever she had before.'[34]

The above four classifications cannot be taken as exact; they are an approximation. The Puritans, apart from the Fifth Monarchists – if they can be classed as Puritan at all – had no party divisions determined by prophetic beliefs. Yet the seventeenth century was the formative period of the differing schools of thought on prophecy which at a later date are more sharply identifiable. The fact that a present-day classification of evangelical prophetical belief would prove very similar seems to show that few new considerations have entered into the debate in the last three hundred years.

Having thus looked in general at Puritan thought on prophecy we shall now turn to a chapter of Scripture which lay at the heart of the matter.

IV

APOSTOLIC TESTIMONY:
THE BASIS OF THE HOPE

'*The Description of the Holie Land*', a print in the New
Testament of the Geneva Bible, *1576*

'There awaits the Gentiles, in their distinctive identity as such, gospel blessing far surpassing anything experienced during the period of Israel's apostasy, and this unprecedented enrichment will be occasioned by the conversion of Israel on a scale commensurate with that of their earlier disobedience.'

JOHN MURRAY

The Epistle to the Romans, chapter 11, vv. 11–12

THERE are several reasons why the future of the Jews was a subject of importance in the minds of so many Christians in the seventeenth century. For one thing they considered that a concern for the welfare of that scattered nation is a necessary part of Christian piety. Of the Jews, concerning the flesh, Christ came; to them first was the gospel preached, and from them was it received by the Gentiles: 'Which should teach us', writes Edward Elton, 'not to hate the Jews (as many do) only because they are Jews, which name is among many so odious that they think they cannot call a man worse than to call him a Jew; but, beloved, this ought not to be so, for we are bound to love and honour the Jews, as being the ancient people of God, to wish them well, and to be earnest in prayer to God for their conversion'.[1]

We shall later note how this awareness of duty towards the Jews did enter into the day-to-day living of many Christians in the seventeenth century. And yet their interest in Israel was always set in a wider context than the particular future of that nation; it was Israel's future *within* the kingdom of Christ and the relation between their incoming and the advancement of Christ's glory that was uppermost in their thinking. The future of the Jews had decisive significance for them because they believed that, though little is clearly revealed of the future purposes of God in history, enough has been given us in Scripture to warrant the expectation that with the calling of the Jews there will come far-reaching blessing for the world. Puritan England and Covenanting Scotland knew much of spiritual blessing and it was the prayerful longing for wider blessing, not a mere interest in unfulfilled prophecy, which led them to give such place to Israel.

We shall be concerned, firstly, in this chapter, with what was claimed as New Testament evidence for a future general conversion of the Jews. The two gospel texts, Matthew 23.38, 39 and Luke 21.24 were sometimes cited. In these Christ appears to place a limit to the period during which a general judgment will rest upon the Jews and, by implication, to suggest that a brighter day for them would subsequently follow: 'Jerusalem shall be trodden down of the Gentiles, until the times of the Gentiles be fulfilled'; 'For I say unto you: ye shall not see me henceforth, till ye shall say, Blessed is he that cometh in the name of the Lord'. The words 'Blessed is he that cometh' remind us of the greeting and welcome given to Jesus upon his entry into Jerusalem, (Matt. 21.9) and the reference to their future use by the Jews suggests that their long continued hardness as a nation is one day to end – 'the cordial welcome is *contrasted* with the factual position at the time' when Jesus spoke.[2] The fact that Jesus did not entirely dismiss the question put to him by the disciples before his ascension, 'Wilt thou at this time restore again the kingdom to Israel', may also be suggestive. Another passage more often quoted by the Puritans was 2 Corinthians 3.15, 16: 'But even unto this day, when Moses is read the veil is upon their heart. Nevertheless when it shall turn to the Lord, the veil shall be taken away.' 'Alas,' writes Increase Mather, 'there is a veil of miserable blindness upon their hearts that they cannot, they will not, see the Truth: But, saith the Apostle, "This shall be taken away". And (saith he) "it shall turn". What is this? I answer: "It", there may note the body of the Jewish nation, or the words may be read, "They shall turn" (i.e. the blinded minds of the Jews shall turn) "unto the Lord".'[3]

Another New Testament text sometimes cited by seventeenth-century divines was Revelation 16.12, which speaks of the dry-ing up of the river Euphrates 'that the way of the kings of the east might be prepared'. It was suggested that 'kings of the east' is a reference to the Jews scattered in the East beyond the Euphrates.

Much might be said on these texts but it must be confessed that in the case of each a considerable amount of obscurity remains, and even taken together they scarcely amount to definite evidence of a future conversion of the Jews as a people. It was not, however, upon these texts that Puritan expositors placed the weight of the case. With reference to those who expected 'a large and visible addition of Jews to Christ's church', Johannes Wollebius (1586–1629) the Reformed theologian of Basel, noted that 'nothing that would uphold this idea may be found in the Apocalypse'. But he adds, 'Those who teach it look to Romans 11.25–26 for their chief authority'.[4] There can be no doubt that Wollebius' last assertion is correct and that the Puritan view of Israel's future, as far as the New Testament is concerned, rests principally upon their exposition of that chapter. 'I know not any Scripture containing a more pregnant and illustrious testimony and demonstration of the Israelites' future vocation,' says Mather, 'it being a main scope of the Apostle in this chapter to make known this Mystery unto the Gentiles.'[5] Similarly the eminent Scottish divine, James Durham, writes: 'Whatever may be doubted of their restoring to their land, yet they shall be brought to a visible Church-state. Not only in particular persons here and there in congregations; but that multitudes, yea, the whole body of them shall be brought, in a common way with the Gentiles, to profess Christ, which cannot be denied, as Romans 11 is clear and that will be enough to satisfy us.'[6] In the eighteenth century Jonathan Edwards was a spokesman for the same conviction when he wrote, 'Nothing is more certainly foretold than this national conversion of the Jews in Romans 11.'[7] To this chapter, therefore, and its interpretation, we must now turn.

The verses referred to by Wollebius read:

v. 25. *'For I would not, brethren, that ye should be ignorant of this mystery, lest ye should be wise in your own conceits; that blindness in part is happened to Israel, until the fulness of the Gentiles be come in.*

v. 26. '*And so all Israel shall be saved: as it is written, There shall come out of Sion the Deliverer, and shall turn away ungodliness from Jacob.*'

A number of questions are involved in the interpretation of these two verses:

1. The blindness spoken of in verse 25 clearly belongs to Israel as a race, with the exception of a believing remnant – hence the qualification of the Apostle, 'blindness *in part* has happened to Israel'. Does the salvation of verse 26 likewise designate a blessing which will belong to the Jewish people as a whole and as a race? Who are the 'all Israel' who shall be saved?

Some Reformation commentators, notably Calvin, took the view that the 'all Israel' of verse 26 refers to the sum total of the complete Church, including both Gentile Christians and the remnant of believing Jews. It does not, they thought, designate national Israel at some future point in history. This spiritualization of the term 'Israel' is not as strained as some have alleged. Two chapters earlier Paul is careful to show that race *as such* does not make a true Israelite (Rom. 9.6), and elsewhere Gentile believers are acknowledged as being of Abraham's seed (Gal. 3.29); in the New Testament perspective, national privileges in regard to salvation have ended and on at least one occasion the term 'Israel of God' is taken to describe the whole Church of Christ (Gal. 6.16). But there are strong reasons for not accepting this interpretation of the word 'Israel' in Romans 11.26.

(i) It would involve a violent transition from the literal meaning of the term in verse 25 to a spiritual one in verse 26, and the passage gives no indication that such a sudden difference of meaning is being introduced. On the contrary, it may be argued that Paul's usage of the term 'Israel' in this whole section is consistent and uniform. As Doekes observes: 'In these three chapters (Rom. 9–11) the term "Israel" occurs no less than eleven times. And in the preceding ten cases it refers indisputably to the Jews, in contrast with the Gentiles. What compelling reason can there be, therefore, to accept another meaning here? Not, to be sure, the context, for the differentiation between Jews and Gentiles does not cease in verse 25 but is continued in the verses which follow.'[8]

(ii) If the 'all Israel' of verse 26 refers to the final salvation of all believers, Jew and Gentile, why does Paul call it a mystery? Elnathan Parr's objection is relevant: 'Paul saith that he would not have the Gentiles ignorant; of what? That all the elect should be saved? Whoever doubted it? But of the calling of the Jews there was a doubt. He calls it a secret or mystery; but that all the elect shall be saved is no secret.'[9]

Accepting that Israel in verse 26 means Jewish people and not the Church as such, we must now proceed to a further question.

*　　*　　*

2. Is the salvation of 'all Israel' something that is progressively realized through the ages? Does it refer to the complete number of individual Jews who through the centuries have been added to the Church by faith in Christ, as for example Paul in the first century, Emmanuel Tremellius at the Reformation, Adolph Saphir in the nineteenth century, and so on? Some commentators have answered this in the affirmative and argued that Paul, in verses 25 and 26, is not speaking about a still-future conversion of the Jews as a nation. The apostle does not, they say, teach a temporal sequence in the order of events – not 'after the incoming of the fulness of the Gentiles *then* all Israel shall be saved'. 'Paul,' says a recent writer holding this view, 'is not thinking about the *time* but about the *way* or *manner* in which "all Israel" is saved.'[10] According to this interpretation, the hardening judicially inflicted upon Israel as a body will continue until the last of the elect Gentiles are saved, that is, until the very end; nevertheless through all the centuries a portion of elect Jews will escape that hardening, and this body – the entire Jewish remnant – is the 'all Israel'

who are to be united for ever with Gentile believers in the fold of God.

If this view is correct, then Romans 11 gives us no grounds for expecting any saving work of conversion among the Jews surpassing what has yet been seen in history: there is no prediction of a great revival among the Jews still to come. This exposition of Romans 11 was apparently common in the early seventeenth century, but it was almost uniformly rejected by English and Scottish exegetes of the Puritan school. Charles Ferme, for example, mentioned earlier as one of Robert Rollock's students in Edinburgh in the 1580's who later became eminent in his witness and suffering for the gospel, gives this comment on verses 25 and 26:

'As some, reserved of God through the election of grace, owned Christ as Lord in the days of Paul, so when the fulness of the Gentiles shall have been brought in, the great majority of the Israelitish people are to be called, through the gospel, to the God of their salvation, and shall profess and own Jesus Christ, whom, formerly, that is, during the time of hardening, they denied. . . . This interpretation of the passage is most pertinent to the scope of the present discussion; but because that recall of the Israelites is not yet witnessed in respect to the majority, most interpreters explain the passage differently, and understand what the apostle here says – "all Israel shall be saved", of Israel in spirit, and also of all Israelites according to the flesh, who at any time have believed, whether in times of apostasy, as were those of Ahab and Paul, or of open profession, as that of David, or of reformation, as those of Hezekiah and Josiah. In this way the meaning will be – "that the Gentiles having been added, through the gospel, to the people of God, that is, to the Israelites, who are Israelites in spirit, as well as according to the flesh, 'all Israel', viz. Israel in the spirit, consisting of the elect from among Jews and Gentiles, 'shall be saved' at the second coming of Christ".'[11]

Ferme's valuable work on Romans lay unpublished until 1651, but long before that date the interpretation he held to be 'most pertinent' had obtained general acceptance. As we noted in the previous chapter, it had been advanced in the notes of the Geneva Bible as early as 1560 and expounded in Peter Martyr's commentary on Romans published in English eight years later.

The argument against 'all Israel' being interpreted as 'the entire remnant of Israel' involves a wider consideration of the whole chapter. In summary form it may be stated as follows: Paul, in putting the question 'Hath God cast away his people?' (v.1), opens the subject of the cast-off condition of Israel and the problem how that condition is consistent with the promises and purposes of God. It is true, he says, that as a body they have fallen, but there is a remnant who believe in accordance with God's sovereign determination (vv. 2–10). The grace of God has prevented the apostasy of Israel being total and universal. The question, however, remains: Has God finished with the Jews collectively considered as a people? 'I say then, have they stumbled that they should fall?' Did their fall fulfill God's *ultimate* purposes towards them? 'God forbid!' (v. 11). We do not, Paul affirms, see the conclusion of God's design in Israel's fall because that fall is overruled for the salvation of Gentiles; which salvation is, in turn, intended to prompt Israelites to repentance and faith ('provoke them to jealousy'). Grace, not judgment, is thus God's *ultimate* purpose. Israel's stumbling is made the occasion for salvation coming to the Gentiles and that is not the end, for, as the apostle goes on to show, God has further planned the salvation of Israel on a scale which will enrich the Gentiles to a degree hitherto unprecedented:

v. 12. *'Now if the fall of them be the riches of the world, and the diminishing of them the riches of the Gentiles; how much more their fulness?*

v. 13. *'For I speak to you Gentiles, inasmuch as I am the apostle of the Gentiles, I magnify mine office:*

v. 14. *'If by any means I may provoke to emulation them which are my flesh, and might save some of them.'*

The effect upon Paul personally of the truth declared in verse 12, he wishes his Gentile hearers to know, is to quicken him in his Gentile ministry so that the success of that ministry may serve to awaken Jews. But along with his concern for his fellow countrymen there is a greater end in view because the interests of the Gentiles themselves are bound up with God's design towards Israel.

v. 15. '*For if the casting away of them be the reconciling of the world, what shall the receiving of them be, but life from the dead?*'

Concluding the parenthesis of verses 13 and 14 on his present ministry with its hope of saving 'some of them', Paul reverts to the prospect already envisaged in verse 12. According to the view we are here opposing, the prediction of verses 12 and 15 has to do with the aggregate of individual Jews saved through the ages and not a future national conversion. But the verses cannot bear that meaning for it ignores a vital part of Paul's argument, namely that the parallel drawn between the 'casting away' and 'the receiving of them' requires the subject to be the same in both instances. The people who were rejected are to be readmitted.

The remnant of believers never fell nor were cut off, and it cannot therefore be of them that Paul says they will be 'received' and grafted in again (v. 23). Thus Elnathan Parr, answering those who denied that 'any other calling of the Jews to be expected than in these days, now and then one', asserts: 'the very reading of the words of the 11, 12 and this verse, make the contrary manifest: *If the casting away of them:* of whom? Of the nation, say learned men: What shall the *receiving of them*? Of whom? Of them which are cast away; that is the nation: or else we make the Apostle say he knows not what: not that the same individuals of the nation which are cast away shall be received, but the body of the people to be understood.'[12]

The sense of verses 12 and 15, according to the common Puritan interpretation, points to a vast addition to the Church by Israel's conversion with resulting wider blessing for the world. There is a great revival predicted here!

John Brown, minister of Wamphray, Scotland, gives the following exposition in his *Exposition of Romans*, 1666, and it may be taken as typical of the whole school to which he belonged.

In verse 12, Brown says, the apostle meets a difficulty which might arise in the minds of Gentiles following the disclosure of verse 11 that the hardening of the Jews was not the final dispensation of God towards them. If room has been made in God's kingdom by the casting out of the Jews, the thought might occur that the restoration of the Jews would lead to the Gentiles being cast out. 'To this the apostle answereth, that, on the contrary, the Gentiles shall have braver days then, than ever they had; for if *their fall*, or stumbling, was the occasion by which the Gentiles dispersed up and down the world, enjoyed the riches of the gospel and of the knowledge of God in Christ, and their diminishing (to the same purpose, and explicating what is meant by *their fall*) that is, their rejecting of the Messias for the most part, so as there were but few behind, and that nation was worn to a thin company and a small number of such as embraced the gospel, *be the riches of the Gentiles*, the same with *the riches of the world; how much more shall their abundance be*? that is, How much more shall their inbringing and fulness, or the conversion of the body and bulk of that nation (for it is opposed to their diminishing) tend to the enriching of the Gentile world in the knowledge of Christ; and so the Gentiles need not fear that the conversion of the Jews shall any way prejudice them; but they may expect to reap advantage thereby.'

On verse 15, the minister of Wamphray continues: 'In this verse the apostle doth further explain and illustrate that argument set down, verse 12, and useth other expressions to the same purpose; *If the casting away of them*, that is, if the slinging away of the Jews, and casting them out of the church, *be the reconciling of the world*, that is, be the occasion whereby the gospel should be preached to the Gentile world, that thereby they might be reconciled unto God, *what shall the receiving of them be, but life from the dead*? Will there not be joyful days thro' the world, and among the Gentiles, when they shall be received into favour again? Will it not be like the resurrection from the

[67]

dead, when Jew and Gentile shall both enjoy the same felicity and happiness? Seeing out of the dead state of the Jews, when cast without doors, God brought life to the Gentiles, will he not much more do so out of their enlivened estate? will it not be to the Gentiles as the resurrection from the dead?'[13]

In the verses which follow there are three further reasons why the Jews' conversion is to be expected: because of the holiness of the first-fruits and the root, v 16; because of the power of God, 'God is able to graft them in again', v 23; and because of the grace of God manifested to the Gentiles, v 24, who would in turn be the means of salvation to the Jews, 'that through your mercy they also may obtain mercy' v. 31. Matthew Henry illustrates the last reason thus, 'If the putting out of their candle was the lighting of yours, by that power of God who brings good out of evil, much more shall the continued light of your candle, when God's time is come, be a means of lighting theirs again'.[14]

All these considerations lead to the conclusion that in verses 25 and 26 Paul is speaking of the realization in future history of what the predictions of the earlier verses point towards, namely the termination of the long period of Israel's blindness, and the resulting salvation of a large mass of that people. The 'all Israel' is not the believing remnant of all centuries but the body of the Jews received again at a particular period in history. The mystery of which Paul would not have them ignorant is, in Parr's words, 'that when the fulness of the Gentiles is come in, there shall be a famous, notorious, universal calling of the Jews'. This is not to say that every individual Israelite will then be converted; despite the thousands of believing Jews in the apostolic period the casting away of the Jews was so general that it permitted the assertion that Israel was cast off, so, despite those who will remain unbelieving, the number to be ingathered will be of an extent which justifies the expression 'all Israel shall be saved'.

*   *   *

3. We have already in part anticipated and answered a

third and last question, but it now needs closer attention. In the last chapter we noted that a number of seventeenth-century expositors believed in a future general conversion of Israel but placed the event at the very end of history. This view has contemporary upholders, one of whom writes, 'All Israel can be saved only as the last rays of the sun fade away for ever and light celestial takes their place'.[15] Justification for this belief is taken from two statements in Romans 11 which we must now consider.

First, Paul's words on the incoming of 'the fulness of the Gentiles' (v. 25), are taken to mean the conclusion of the kingdom of God in the world – 'the fulness' being equated with the complete number of the elect from among the Gentiles. If this is so, then the salvation of 'all Israel' which is to attend this fulness of the Gentiles must take place on the verge of eternity and signal the end of Gospel blessing for the world.

Paul's use of the word 'fulness' earlier in Romans 11 does not, however, necessitate this meaning. The period of Israel's fall in verse 12 is contrasted with her changed condition at the time of her 'fulness'; fulness, then, for Israel cannot mean the sum total of elect Jews because there were obviously elect Jews at the time of her fall. 'Fulness' in verse 12 means the large numerical increase of converted Jews, but not excluding the possibility of others being subsequently added. So in verse 25 it is not necessary to believe that 'fulness' means anything more than a large addition of Gentiles, 'a multitude of the Gentiles', says Matthew Poole's *Annotations*, 'greater by far, than was in the apostles' days'.[16] The verse says nothing which requires us to expect no further expansion of the kingdom of Christ thereafter. As a recent commentator writes, ' "The fulness of the Gentiles" denotes unprecedented blessing for them but does not exclude even greater blessing to follow.'[17]

A second statement quoted from Romans 11 to justify the belief that the conversion of the Jews will be at the end of the world is the phrase in verse 15, 'what shall the receiving of them be, but life from the dead?' In these words Paul is adding to what he has already said in verse 12. In that verse he did not say what the blessing would be which would accompany the incoming of the fulness of the Jews but left it in the form of an exclamation: 'If the fall of them be the riches of the world . . . how much more their fulness?' 'How much more?' comments Parr, 'as if he admired it and were not able to express or conceive.' In verse 15, however, Paul does specify something of the nature of the blessing, it will be 'life from the dead'. Some interpreters, including Origen and Chrysostom in the early centuries, take this phrase as referring to the physical resurrection of the dead, and so taken the verse would prove that the conversion of the Jews must be placed at the very end of time.

But there is no necessity for the phrase to be so taken in a literal sense. As Poole notes, life from the dead is 'a proverbial speech, to signify a great change'. Certainly in the Scriptures the idea of resurrection is frequently used with a spiritual and figurative meaning. It is so employed by the prophets as, for example in Hosea 6.2, 'the third day he will raise us up and we shall live in his sight', and in Ezekiel 37, where Israel's spiritual revival is forcefully described as their coming out of their graves. In Christ's teaching, conversion is likened to quickening the dead (John 5.21), and the restored prodigal is characterized as one who 'was dead and is alive again' (Luke 15.32).

Not only is a spiritual interpretation of the phrase 'life from the dead' possible, there are indeed good grounds for regarding it as preferable.

(i) Verses 12 and 15 speak of the interaction between Jews and Gentiles in the advancement of the kingdom of God, and the riches coming to the Gentiles on the occasion of the Jews' defection is represented as being exceeded by the blessing which would attend their restoration. While it is true that resurrection and glorification are the final and highest blessings belonging to the Church, they are benefits which do not naturally succeed to the Gentiles as a result of Israel's recovery. But taking 'life from the dead' figuratively, Paul's progression of thought advances smoothly: if Israel's fall and dishonour brought the gospel of reconciliation to the Gentiles, how much more will her renewal and restoration to honour bring revival to the world? 'For if the casting away of them be the reconciling of the world, what shall the receiving of them be, but life from the dead?' As Godet paraphrases it, 'When cursed, they have contributed to the restoration of the world; what will they not do when blessed?'

(ii) The second advent of Christ which will accomplish the resurrection of the dead will bring a consummation of blessing to the Church – not an extension of it to either Jew or Gentile (2 Thess. 1.9–10). If the conversion of the Jews were understood to be in any way linked with the resurrection day the uniform teaching of many other parts of Scripture would require some time lapse to occur between the two. As Parr observes: 'Though God can save men in an instant, yet he hath appointed means, which means cease at the resurrection, and therefore no calling to be then expected: for that is the time of revealing judgement, not of preaching Mercie.'[18] This qualification of a time lapse must therefore be introduced in the literal view, the conversion of sinners and the coming of Christ to judgment being two quite separate things. On the other hand, if 'life from the dead' be understood spiritually it is easily apparent, according to the analogy of other scriptures, how the conversion of a large mass of people – a nation – would at once contribute to far-reaching quickening in the world. 'And their seed shall be known among the Gentiles, and their offspring among the people: all that see them shall acknowledge them, that they are the seed which the Lord hath blessed. . . . For as the earth bringeth forth her bud, and as a garden causeth the things that are sown in it to spring forth; so the Lord God will cause righteousness and praise to spring forth before all nations' (Isa. 61.9–11).

(iii) Finally, as John Murray has carefully shown in his recent *Exposition of Romans*, the standard Pauline phrase to denote the resurrection of the body is 'resurrection from the dead': nowhere else does 'life from the dead' refer to the physical resurrection and its closest parallel, 'alive from the dead' (6.13) refers to spiritual life.[19]

For reasons such as these, Puritan exegetes (comparable in this to Ambrose the early Church Father) took 'life from the dead' figuratively. Thus the marginal note of the Geneva Bible gives this note on Romans 11.15: 'The Jewes now remain, as it were, in death for lack of the Gospel, but when both they and the Gentiles shall embrace Christ, the world shall be restored to a new life.'

This belief introduced a new perspective in the Puritan understanding of history. While some retained the view that Romans 11 taught a conversion of the Jews at the end of time, there is evidence that the main-stream of belief became committed to the view given above. In 1652, for example, eighteen of the most eminent Puritan divines, including men of presbyterial convictions as William Gouge, Edmund Calamy and Simeon Ashe, and Independents as John Owen and Thomas Goodwin, wrote in support of missionary labours then being undertaken in New England and affirmed their belief that: 'the Scripture speaks of a *double conversion* of the Gentiles, the first before the conversion of the *Jewes*, they being *Branches wilde by nature* grafted into the *True Olive Tree* instead of the *naturall Branches* which are broken off. This fulness of the *Gentiles* shall come in before the conversion of the *Jewes*, and till then *blindness* hath happened unto Israel, Rom. 11.25. The second, after the conversion of the Jewes . . .'[20]

*　　　*　　　*

Before we leave Romans 11 we must comment on one other issue of major significance which cannot be passed over. A great part of the differences among Christians over prophecy relates to the interpretation of Old Testament prophecy. Those who insist on what is called the literal principle of interpretation argue that the fulfilment of Old Testament prophecies respecting Israel's future blessing and the world-wide success of Christ's kingdom cannot be in the present age: the personal advent of Christ must intervene to introduce a new dispensation. According to this view certain of the grand predictions of Isaiah and the Prophets apply not to the Christian Church in her present form but to a future millennial kingdom.

It is difficult to understand how this opinion can be maintained in the light of the New Testament writers' own use of the Prophets. The fact is that the age of highest blessing predicted by the Prophets is spoken of by the apostles as already in being – God's gathering to himself a people (Hos. 2.23), Christ's reign over the Gentiles (Isa. 11.10), and the day of world-wide salvation (Isa. 49.8); these are all texts quoted by Paul as having a present fulfilment (cf. Rom. 9.26; 15.12; 2 Cor. 6.2). Similarly we find James in Acts 15.14, 16, referring the prediction of Amos 9.11, 'In that day will I raise up the tabernacle of David that is fallen', to the conversion of *Gentiles* in the apostolic era, and the writer of the Epistle to the Hebrews, far from restricting the great predictions of Jeremiah 31 to Israel in a future age, considers the privileges there described as already possessed in the New Testament Church (compare Jer. 31.31 and Heb. 8.8). There is here not a trace of the idea that the witness of the Prophets to an age of coming blessedness must be referred to a millennial kingdom introduced by the Second Advent. On the contrary there is plenty to warn us that the literal principle is a dangerously misleading guide to the interpretation of the Prophets. Paul is certainly not employing that principle in Galatians 4.26, 27 when he distinguishes the Jerusalem 'which now is, and is in bondage with her children', from 'Jerusalem which is above', and which he tells the Galatian believers 'is the mother of us all'. It is to this spiritual Jerusalem that he then proceeds to apply the glorious prediction of Isaiah 54.1. The assertion that prophecies spoken of 'Zion' or 'Jerusalem' in the Old Testament can only refer to national Israel is untenable.

Recognizing this, another school of prophetic interpreters has argued that *no* Old Testament predictions respecting Israel await fulfilment. The fulfilment has *already* occurred in the Christian Church. But this claim goes too far, for it leaves out of account Paul's use of the Prophets in the chapter of Romans now under consideration. Having opened, as we have seen, the divine mystery that the casting off of Israel was not final, he turns for confirmation to the inspired testimony of Scripture: 'blindness in part is happened to Israel, until the fulness of the Gentiles be come in. And so all Israel shall be saved: *as it is written*, There shall come out of Sion the Deliverer and shall turn away ungodliness from Jacob: For this is my covenant unto them, when I shall take away their sins' (v. 25b–27). This quotation, taken from Isaiah 59.20 and Jeremiah 31.34, would be valueless in this context were it not that the words quoted collaborate what Paul has already affirmed respecting Israel. The way he employs these texts is proof that the full scope of Old Testament prophecy has not yet been realized in history.[21]

This is of major significance. We have already noted that predictions of Christ's kingdom in Isaiah and in Jeremiah were considered applicable by the New Testament writers to the Church in the apostolic age. Paul's use of the same prophets in Romans 11.26, 27 now shows that the fulfilment was only initial and by no means exhaustive. A larger fulfilment still awaits the Church, when the same covenant faithfulness of God which has already brought gospel blessings to the Gentile world will be the cause of the removal of Israel's sins. Gentile and Jew are thus both contained in the same Old Testament predictions, and because these predictions admit of *successive* fulfilments and speak of the *same* salvation there is nothing to prevent what has already been referred to New Testament converts being applied to the future conversion of Israel. Jeremiah 31.34 has both been fulfilled (Heb. 8.8) and is yet to be fulfilled in a day of greater gospel blessing (Rom. 11.27).

If this is the right lesson to draw from Paul's use of the Prophets in Romans 11 then there is a key given to us for the interpretation of a number of Old Testament prophecies which are similar to the two particular texts which Paul quotes. The Puritans saw this clearly and used the key to good effect in their expositions of the Old Testament. An illustration of this can be taken from the works of the eminent Robert Leighton. In a sermon on Isaiah 60.1 entitled 'Christ the

Light and Lustre of the Church', preached when he was minister of Newbattle, Scotland, in January, 1642, he had no hesitation in applying the exhortation, 'Arise, shine; for thy light is come', to the whole Church. At the same time he knew that Isaiah 60.1–3 stands related to what is predicted in Isaiah 59.20, and that the latter verse is referred by the apostle particularly to Israel's salvation. He therefore gives to his text its full scope:

'This prophecy is, out of question, a most rich description of the kingdom of Christ under the Gospel. And in this sense, this invitation to *arise* and *shine* is mainly addressed to the mystical Jerusalem, yet not without some privilege to the literal Jerusalem beyond other people. They are first invited to *arise* and *shine*, because this Sun arose first in their horizon. Christ came *of* the Jews, and came first *to* them. . . . Undoubtedly, that people of the Jews shall once more be commanded to *arise* and *shine*, and their return shall be *the riches of the Gentiles* (Rom. 11.12), and that shall be a more glorious time than ever the Church of God did yet behold. Nor is there any inconvenience if we think that the high expressions of this prophecy have some spiritual reference to that time, since the great doctor of the Gentiles applies some words of the former chapter to that purpose, Rom. 11.26. They forget a main point of the Church's glory, who pray not daily for the conversion of the Jews.'[22]

George Hutcheson, in his valuable *Brief Exposition on the Small Prophets*, uses this same broad principle of interpretation. Expounding Hosea 2.23, 'And I will sow her unto me in the earth, and I will have mercy upon her that had not obtained mercy . . .' he writes: 'The Apostle doth apply this also, Rom. 9.25, to Israel in the spirit of Jew and Gentile, who were brought in to Christ even in his time, because the Covenant is the same with all the confederates, and there was then some accomplishment in part of this prediction. But the full accomplishment thereof is reserved for Israel (of whom this chapter speaks most expressly) at their Conversion as a Nation. And if we take it up as comprehending Jew and Gentile; yet the full accomplishment thereof is reserved for that time wherein the Conversion of Israel shall be accompanied with the coming in of the fulness of the Gentiles, and be as a life from the dead to the world, Rom.11.15, 25, 26.'

*   *   *

Concluding, then, this short survey of the Puritan treatment of Israel in Romans 11, the following points summarize the views which come to prevail:

1. The salvation now possessed by a remnant of believing Jews is yet to be enjoyed by far larger numbers of that race.

2. At the time when Paul wrote, this was not to be expected until a considerable number of the Gentiles had been evangelized and their evangelization would thus hasten the day of Israel's calling: 'blindness in part is happened to Israel, until the fulness of the Gentiles be come in'.

3. In the economy of salvation there is an interaction appointed by God between Jew and Gentile; gospel blessing came to the world by Israel's fall, a yet greater blessing will result from her conversion.

4. Nothing is told us in Romans 11 of the duration of time between the calling of the Jews and the end of history. 'The end of this world shall not be till the Jews are called, and how long after that none yet can tell' (Parr).

5. The quotations from Isaiah and Jeremiah, confirming Paul's teaching, indicate that the *full* extent of gospel blessing predicted by the Prophets is yet to be realized. 'As Isaiah, and other of the prophets, do put over this great flourishing of the church to the days of the gospel, the apostle, Rom. 11, doth point at a more precise time wherein this in a larger measure shall be made out' (Robert Fleming).

*   *   *

In modern times the acceptance of three beliefs have probably contributed largely to the assumption that the convictions just stated are merely of historic interest and not tenable for Christians today.

First, in the last hundred years the belief has held sway in

English-speaking Protestantism that Christ's advent must precede Israel's conversion and the subsequent blessing of the world. Because main-stream Puritan thought did not accept this pre-millennial view of the advent, their position has been represented as encouraging the expectation of 'a Christless and kingless millennium', and, not surprisingly, where this charge has been believed, disinterest in Puritan teaching has been the result. To this subject we shall return in a subsequent chapter.

Second, another influential school of prophetic thought has maintained that any general or national conversion of Israel in the future would be inconsistent with the overriding message of the New Testament. This school of thought stresses that Israel, geographically and physically considered, could have distinct spiritual significance only in the period *prior* to the breaking down of the middle wall of partition between Jew and Gentile. Now, in respect of the privileges of the gospel, there is no longer Jew or Gentile – the perspective is no longer national, but spiritual and universal. Jerusalem is no more to be the centre of worship as it once was (John 4.21). Pursuing this same line of thought in reference to Romans 11, William Hendriksen, writes: 'If here in Romans 11.26a Paul is speaking about a still-future *mass*-conversion of Jews, then he is overthrowing the entire carefully built up argument of chapters 9–11; for the *one* important point which he is trying to establish constantly is exactly this, that God's promises attain fulfilment not in the nation as such but in the remnant according to the election of grace.'[23]

Such statements as these are important and valid against any view of Israel's future which supposes she will receive salvation on terms other than those proclaimed in the Gospel, or that she will obtain spiritual privileges distinct from and above those possessed by Gentile Christians. But as we have already seen, this was not the Puritan view: Puritans did not believe that there are any special and unfulfilled spiritual promises made to Israel *apart from* the Christian Church. All that they asserted was that it was in no way inconsistent with the New Testament economy that there should be a great revival in the future, bringing Israel as a mass into the Church and thereby fulfilling, in John Murray's words, a '*particular* design in the realization of God's worldwide saving purpose'.[24] Hendriksen's assertion is not accurate enough: the burden of Paul's teaching in Romans 9–11 is that salvation is of grace alone, but it is surely no necessary consequence of grace that it be confined to a remnant. Divine sovereignty may indeed justly so confine it, as Israel's long-continued judicial blindness bears solemn witness, yet the same sovereignty may be displayed in a nation being born in a day and when converts are multiplied as the dew of the morning! There is no conflict between Paul's gospel and the belief that in the 'latter day glory' vast numbers of the natural descendants of Abraham will own and serve their Redeemer, and that Israel will then show forth the glory of that gospel as, to a lesser extent, the English-speaking nations visited with revival have done in times past. Certainly, as the late J. Marcellus Kik wrote in 1948, the idea must be repudiated that Israel is to have some unique place in a future kingdom of God, but this does not leave us without belief in their future blessing:

'Even in the present time there are some within the Church who simply cannot believe that the old dispensation has been terminated. They still look for a temporal Jewish kingdom whose capital, Jerusalem, will hold sway over all the earth. This was the carnal conception of this kingdom which Christ fought and the apostles opposed, and against which his Church must still fight. It is true that we look forward to the conversion of the Jewish nation, and that the whole world will be blessed by this conversion. But that is something entirely different from the idea of a temporal Jewish kingdom holding sway over all the nations of the world.'[25]

In this connection it needs to be added that though a number of the Puritans believed that the Jews would be restored to their own country[26] none supposed that the land of Israel would ever again have the theocratic and symbolic significance which it possessed during the Old Testament era. They would have agreed with the nineteenth-century Reformed author who, after stating the case for Israel's restoration, wrote: 'As to the question, then, what will the Jews do in the Holy Land? we reply that they will do just what the English do in England, or the Americans in America. They will traffic, will cultivate the soil, will fill professional and mechanical pursuits, and be a Christian people, in an interesting and important country.'[27]

A third commonly-accepted belief which militates against a consideration of the Puritan view is that Scripture witnesses to a steadily worsening world and thus demands from us a very different expectation with regard to the whole period which lies between us and the coming of Christ. 'Scripture certainly does not sustain the notion', writes Herman Hoeksema, 'that the Church will experience a period of great prosperity, antecedent to the coming of the Lord. The very opposite is true.'[28] If this assertion is correct then the exposition given of Romans 11 must *ipso facto* be erroneous.

There can be no doubt that both by alleged Scripture evidence and by appeal to the dark character of contemporary history, evangelical Christians have been long acclimatized to regard the opinion stated by Hoeksema as proven. We think, however, that it may be honestly questioned whether the Scripture passages appealed to can bear all that is deduced from them. Foremost among these passages is the Olivet discourse of Christ, recorded in Matthew 24, Luke 21 and Mark 13. This prophetic discourse followed Christ's announcement concerning the temple, 'There shall not be left one stone upon another, that shall not be thrown down' – clearly a reference to the destruction of the city which came about at the hands of the Romans in A.D. 70. In the discourse itself there is much that applies specifically to the 'breaking off' (Rom. 11.19) of the Jewish nation in the first century A.D. The convulsion of the Roman Empire, earthquakes, 'Jerusalem compassed with armies', 'the abomination of desolation . . . in the holy place', the exhortation to pray that flight from the city would not be necessary on the Sabbath day, the appearance of false Messiahs – all these things point to events which were shortly to take place and which are now past history. The great tribulation predicted for the Jews on account of their apostasy has been fulfilled. As Paul writes, 'the wrath is come upon them to the uttermost' (1 Thess. 2.16). And yet these texts and others in the Olivet discourse are often quoted as though they have had no fulfilment!

Nevertheless it is certainly true that the Olivet discourse looks forward to the second advent and it may well be that some of the 'signs' which preceded the overthrow of Jerusalem will recur on a grander scale as the world draws near its end; to accept this, however, is by no means the same as saying that the Olivet discourse comprehensively describes the whole *course* of world history between the first and second advents. The claim that what is in view is 'the course of This Age down to the time of the end', and that, therefore, 'until the very end, evil will characterize this Age',[29] is one which, we think, goes beyond the evidence of our Lord's own words.

Probably the next most frequently referred to passage in support of the view that the world will progressively darken is 2 Timothy, chapter 3, which commences, 'This know also, that in the last days perilous times shall come'. The popular citation of this text without a consideration of its precise import and context is an unhappy illustration of how debate on prophetic issues is too often conducted. The peril of which Paul speaks is the contagion liable to be received from the prevalence of such men as those described in the verses which follow. In particular, they are 'evil men and seducers' (v. 13), who were alive at the time when Paul wrote, hence the exhortation to Timothy in verse 5, 'from such turn away'. And while in their personal character they would go from bad to worse (v. 13), their public influence according to Paul was soon to pass. They resemble Jannes and Jambres who deceived Pharaoh and the Egyptians long ago, and like those two deceivers they were to have their day: 'Now as Jannes and Jambres withstood Moses, so do these also resist the truth: men of corrupt minds, reprobate concerning the faith. But they shall proceed no further: for their folly shall be manifest unto all men, as theirs also was' (v. 8–9).

Paul was thinking primarily of his own time! The only

wider bearing which we may legitimately give to the passage rests on verse one, where Paul says that during the whole period which he calls 'the last days' there would be a recurrence of perilous seasons or times. One such time had arrived even as Paul wrote this last letter to Timothy in the days of Nero; others were to follow – Paul does not say how many nor how often. All he does assert is that in the present dispensation (which is what the New Testament means by 'the last days'), there were to be some periods of grievous conflict for the Church. This is far different from the claim that Paul expected nothing but such seasons and anticipated nothing but ever-increasing wickedness! In fact the New Testament gives us other features of 'the last days'. It tells us that the full Pentecostal endowment of the Spirit belongs to 'the last days' (Acts 2.17), and that the 'last days' is the new era in which God has spoken by his Son (Heb. 1.2). The last days are the gospel age, ushered in by Christ's incarnation and death, and they are the last because no further earthly dispensation is to follow. The last has come!

Such is, we believe, the correct interpretation of 2 Timothy 3.1. In the words of Thomas Boston, in a sermon on 'Perilous Times in the Last Days', he says: 'Even in the days of the gospel, in which sometimes there are sweet and glorious times, yet at other times there come difficult and perilous times.'[30] Similarly B. B. Warfield, after referring to the same passage, writes: 'It would be manifestly illegitimate to understand these descriptions as necessarily covering the life of the whole dispensation on the earliest verge of which the prophet was standing . . . we must remember that all the indications are that Paul had the first stages of 'the latter times' in mind, and actually says nothing to imply either that the evil should long predominate over the good, or that the whole period should be marked by such disorders.'[31]

It only remains to be said that while the Scriptures seem to indicate a time of serious declension immediately preceding the advent, this provides no proof that a great era of revival cannot intervene between now and Christ's coming. One cannot argue logically from the evidence for a final apostasy – evidence sometimes overstated[32] – that a downward tendency must mark all future history

But the objection may be raised, 'If there is to be a great extension of Christ's kingdom in the future, with attendant spiritual prosperity, how can a state of declension immediately preceding Christ's appearing be harmonized with it?' This question only has force if the calling of the Jews is envisaged as being so close to the end that time would scarcely allow for such progress and such a reversal. No proof, however, is forthcoming to show that the period of time involved must be so limited in duration. As we have observed, Romans 11 says nothing on the length of the period between Israel's salvation and the second advent. Peter Martyr's answer to this same objection, written four hundred years ago, can therefore still stand:

'What shall we say unto the words of Christ wherein he sayth, *Doost thou thinke that when the sonne of man commeth he shall find faith upon the earth?* Verely if the Jewes be in such great plenty converted unto Christ, and that with the commodity of the Gentiles,* as we have before declared, then shall there remain much faith, which Christ when he returneth unto us shall find. But we may answere, that here is no contrariety . . . peradventure the Jewes shall return again and shall acknowledge their Messias, and shall confirm the Gentiles being wavering and seduced. It is possible also, that when the Jewes shall believe, and the Gentiles shall after a certayne tyme put to their help, then, as the nature of the fleshe is, may arise some security, and licentiousness, especially if Antichrist follow, by means whereof an infinite number both of the Jewes and of the Gentiles may be alienated from Christ: so that that shall be true, that Christ when he commeth shall find very few which purely and sincerely shall confess him.'[33]

---

* 'With the commodity of the Gentiles' is the translator's rendering of Martyr's 'et cum utilitate Gentium', literally, 'with the benefit (or advantage) of the Gentiles'. Martyr's Latin *Romans* was published the same year as the English version, 1568.

V

THE HOPE AND PURITAN PIETY

*The Seal of the Corporation for Promoting
the Gospel in New England which continued
the work done by the Society under
Puritan leadership from 1649 to 1660. The
emblem, which was earlier used by the
Massachusetts Bay Colony, depicts an Indian
with the Macedonian cry, above his head,
'Come over and help us'*

'Seeing God hath given us such a treasure and so inestimable a thing as his word is, we must employ ourselves as much as we can that it may be kept safe and sound and not perish. . . . First of all let every man see he lock it up fast in his own heart. But yet it is not enough for us to have an eye to our own salvation, but the knowledge of God must shine generally throughout all the world and every one must be partaker of it, we must take pains to bring all them that wander out of the way to the way of salvation: and we must not only think upon it for our life time, but for after our death.'

JOHN CALVIN

Sermons on the Epistles of St. Paul to Timothy and Titus, 1579, 746–7

'In Dr. Whyte's opinion, at no time has any land for its size, save Palestine, produced "so many men and women of a profoundly spiritual experience, and of an adoring and heavenly mind, as Scotland possessed in the sixteenth and seventeenth centuries". In his ecstasy he exclaims, "What minds and what hearts those men and women had! And how they gave up their whole mind and heart to the life of godliness in the land, and to the life of God in their own hearts! How thin and poor our religious life appears beside theirs!" To the causes which he suggests for this superiority – the persecution, the new Reformation doctrines, the masculine and Pauline preaching – other two at least may be added, the solid and serious books then in favour, and the place assigned to the inspired psalms, now too often usurped by frothy hymns.'

DAVID HAY FLEMING

'Dr. Whyte and Samuel Rutherford',
Critical Reviews Relating Chiefly to Scotland, 1912, 350

'Now, Christians, the more great and glorious things you expect from God, as the downfall of antichrist, the conversion of the Jews, the conquest of the nations to Christ, the breaking off of all yokes, the new Jerusalem's coming down from above, the extraordinary pouring out of the Spirit, and a more general union among all saints, the more holy, yea, the more eminently holy in all your ways and actings it becomes you to be.'

THOMAS BROOKS

The Crown and Glory of Christianity,
1662 (Complete Works, 1867, 444)

IN the two preceding chapters we have sought to show how mainstream Puritanism believed that the Church, despite all the odds set against her, was yet to be an instrument of blessing on a scale far surpassing all that has been previously seen in history. It is our present purpose to show the consequences of this outlook upon spiritual character in the seventeenth century.

At the outset it has to be admitted that an interest in unfulfilled prophecy is not always conducive to Christian piety. The Christians at Thessalonica were only the first among many in the course of Church history whose witness was marred by a feverish and misguided expectation upon this subject. In 1620 Elnathan Parr complained of 'certain foolish prophecies dispersed that the world shall end within these twenty years', while two centuries and a half later C. H. Spurgeon had still to bewail the influence of 'twopenny-halfpenny prophets all crying out as one man that He will come in 1866 or 1867'.[1] It is plain that attention to prophecy, instead of producing a moral and sanctifying effect, can merely promote speculative curiosities and intellectual pride. Towards the end of his life Richard Baxter made the pithy observation: 'We find it so easy to possess men with a fervent zeal for the Millenary Opinion, and so hard to make them zealous in holy love to God and man, and in heavenly conversation, as may make us suspicious that both sorts of zeal have not the same original.'[2]

Puritan pastors were alive to this danger and took steps to prevent aberrations developing in their own congregations. When they dealt with unfulfilled prophecy it was not as a 'special subject' of peculiar importance – as became the fashion in the nineteenth century – rather, their treatment almost invariably occurred in the ordinary course of expository preaching, and both by this example and by precept the people were warned of the danger of giving to prophecy a place disproportionate to its importance. Thus Peter Martyr says:

'It is a miserable thing, that whereas we have so many clear and manifest things in the holy scriptures, concerning faith, hope, charity, and the bonds of other virtues, wherein there is nothing obscure, we will leave those utterly neglected and with so great superstition follow other things which are uncertain and serve less unto salvation. This doth the devil endeavour, that we should earnestly occupy ourselves in questions which be infinite and unprofitable; laying aside other things, which should be necessarily kept.'[3]

In the same vein of warning John Howe taught his people to observe:

'That to have our minds and hearts more set upon the best state of things that it is possible the church should ever arrive to on earth, than upon the state of perfect felicity above, is a very great distemper, and which we ought to reckon intolerable by any means to indulge ourselves in. We know none of us can live in this world but a little while, and that there is a state of perfect rest, and tranquillity, and glory remaining for the people of God. We have, therefore, no pretence for being curious in our inquiries about what time such or such good things may fall out to the church of God in this world. It is a great piece of fondness to cast in our own thoughts, Is it possible that I may live to see it? For ought we know, there may be but a hand's breadth between us and glory, if we belong to God; tomorrow may be the time of our translation. We ought to live in the continual expectation of dying, and of coming to a better state than the church can ever be in here.

It argues a great infirmity, a distemper in our spirits, that we should reflect upon with severity, if we should be more curious to see a good state of things in this world, than to see the best that can ever be, and infinitely better than we can think, in heaven.'[4]

By such cautions as these the Puritans checked the kind of unbalanced spiritual character which prophetical interest has too often encouraged. At the same time their general view of unfulfilled prophecy was conveyed sufficiently to give a distinct tone to the spiritual character and outlook of the Church three hundred years ago. Their beliefs on this subject were not speculative areas of thought, disconnected from the everyday fundamentals of the Christian faith; on the contrary they were connected with that faith at some of its most vital points, as, for instance, with the Person of Christ, with the Church, and with prayer. These are the main themes which we shall now consider in their relation to what we have called the Puritan hope. Puritan piety, in its essentials, was of course no different from true Christian piety of all ages, yet in some respects it was distinctive; it possessed certain pronounced features which, in turn, gave to Puritan Christianity not a little of the force which it exercised upon the course of history. There can be no question that belief in regard to unfulfilled prophecy contributed significantly to this distinctiveness and, as we shall see, it was the way in which that belief combined with fundamentals that made it so influential.

In this chapter, therefore, we shall seek to show how their belief concerning Christ, the Church and prayer stood related to their understanding of unfulfilled prophecy.

*   *   *

Puritan beliefs as related to the work of Christ stood in direct succession to the beliefs of the Reformers and particularly to those of John Calvin. It was Calvin who recovered from the New Testament the whole concept of Christ's lordship and sovereign glory in the carrying out of man's redemption, and he brought to the fore the truth that the mediatorial work of

Jesus did not cease at his death and resurrection; that work, for the gathering and perfecting of his Church continues, and its ultimate success rests securely upon the position which Christ now occupies. Lordship is his present possession (Rom. 14.9); he has been given 'power over all flesh' (John 17.2), further, 'all power in heaven and in earth' (Matt. 28.18), so that in the interests of his mediatorial kingdom he governs the universe. Thus Ephesians 1.22 affirms that the Father 'hath put all things under his feet, and gave him to be the head over all things to the church, which is his body'. All this is richly expounded in the Westminster *Shorter Catechism* beginning with the statement, 'Christ, as our Redeemer, executeth the offices of a prophet, of a priest, and of a king, both in his estate of humiliation and exaltation.' (Answer to Question 23.)

The advancement of Christ's kingdom stands directly related to the work of his exaltation, in which he now exercises his rule by the Holy Spirit: thus the conversion of three thousand on the day of Pentecost, the 'great number' who believed at Antioch, and the whole magnificent success of the gospel in the apostolic era are spoken of as things which 'Christ hath wrought' (cf. Acts 2.33, Acts 11.21, Rom. 15.18, 19). These successes of the gospel were proofs that Christ's reign had begun. How triumphant that reign is to be in the earth before the end was the subject of many Old Testament prophecies. According to Psalm 2, the enthronement of the Messiah would lead to his receiving 'the uttermost parts of the earth' for his possession. Another psalm, after speaking of the vicarious sufferings of Christ, speaks in this way of the glory which was to follow: 'All the ends of the world shall remember and turn unto the Lord: and all the kindreds of the nations shall worship before thee. For the kingdom is the Lord's: and he is the governor among the nations' (Psa. 22.27, 28). In the New Testament, the realization of the Old Testament hope has commenced, Christ is now going forth 'conquering and to conquer' (Rev. 6.22), and it is his coming by his Spirit, among his enemies, in converting power, which explains all the revivals of Christian history. To this same activity of Christ, as we have already noted in Romans 11, Israel's future salvation is attributed: 'All Israel shall be saved: as it is written, There shall come out of Sion the Deliverer . . .'

Just as Calvin first recovered the New Testament emphasis on Christ as king and head of his Church, exercising his power by the Holy Spirit, so he also struck the note of confidence which was to sound through coming centuries. In his *Institutes of the Christian Religion*, published in 1536, he addresses the Preface to King Francis I of France, in an appeal for respite from the bitter persecution then being inflicted upon the scattered French believers. The gospel was then everywhere spoken against; and what would be its prospects if Francis I disdained all relief and the kings of the earth continued their rage against the cause of Christ? Of the answer to that question Calvin tells his sovereign he has not the slightest doubt. The outcome is certain:

'Our doctrine must stand sublime above all the glory of the world, and invincible by all its power, because it is not ours, but that of the living God and his Anointed, whom the Father has appointed king that he may rule from sea to sea, and from the rivers even to the ends of the earth; and so rule as to smite the whole earth and its strength of iron and brass, its splendour of gold and silver, with the mere rod of his mouth, and break them in pieces like a potter's vessel; according to the magnificent predictions of the prophets respecting his kingdom (Dan. 2.34; Isa. 11.4; Psa. 2.9).'[5]

A consideration of such texts as these quoted by the Reformer awakened afresh in the sixteenth century zeal for the world-wide acknowledgment of the claims of Christ and taught men to look with assurance for the progressive realization of his kingdom. Thus we find Calvin himself repeatedly using language which, were it not for the testimony of Scripture, might be judged as wildly beyond the realm of possibility. For example, in a prayer following a lecture on Malachi, chapter 1, he concludes, 'Undoubtedly Thy name shall be magnified and celebrated throughout the whole world',[6] and again, after speaking on Micah, chapter 7:

'May we daily solicit thee in our prayers, and never doubt but that under the government of thy Christ, thou canst again gather together the whole world, though it be miserably dispersed, so that we may persevere in this warfare to the end, until we shall at length know that we have not in vain hoped in thee, and that our prayers have not been in vain, when Christ shall exercise the power given to him for our salvation and for that of the whole world. Amen.'[7]

On the second petition of the Lord's Prayer, 'Thy kingdom come', Calvin writes: 'As the kingdom of God is continually growing and advancing to the end of the world, we must pray every day that it may come: for to whatever extent iniquity abounds in the world, to such an extent the kingdom of God, which brings along with it perfect righteousness, is not yet come.'[8] While the completion of what is involved in this petition awaits the final advent, as Calvin recognized, he also saw that the words warrant an expectation that much more of the kingdom of God is to be realized in history and on earth.

If Calvin did not consciously focus attention upon unfulfilled prophecy he certainly laid foundations in regard to the understanding of the mediatorial reign of Christ which governed Puritan thought in this area. The success of the gospel for which they yearned was bound up with their trust in Christ. They never gave way to the feeling that because the condition of the world was so deplorable the Second Coming of Christ was the only hope for mankind; in their mind, to have done so would have been to fall into unbelief in regard to the promised results of his first coming. If what was predicted seemed impossible, the remedy was to contemplate more closely the authority and glory which now belongs to the Head of the Church.

Innumerable examples could be given at this point from Puritan expositors, but I confine myself to two. First, let us hear George Newton (1602–1681), senior colleague of Joseph Alleine at Taunton, Somerset. After expounding the words of Christ in his great High Priestly prayer, 'I have declared unto them thy name, and will declare it' (John 17.26), Newton concentrates on the significance of the promise, *and will declare it:*

'Let our hearts be full of hope in reference to this business. Since Christ hath undertaken it, let us expect the execution of it. Our Saviour's words are a promise to the Father, what he will do in after times for his people: saith he, 'I will declare thy name" to them. And therefore as it is our duty to believe the promise, so to expect the good things promised. To be continually in a waiting frame, looking and hearkening after the accomplishment of this excellent work of his, spying if we can see the daybreak, and the Father's name shine forth to other nations who never had a glimpse of it by any gospel revelation, till in the end, "from the rising of the sun unto the going down of the same, his name be great among the Gentiles," according to that prophecy relating to these latter times and ages of the world, Mal. 1.11.

'Let us strive with Christ in prayer that he would make good the word that he hath spoken to the Father before so many witnesses. O my beloved, when ye look on many heathen nations that yet are overwhelmed in ignorance and Egyptian darkness, that yet know nothing of the Father's name . . . go to Jesus Christ and say, O Lord, thou hast professed that thou wilt declare the Father's name to other persons, and to other nations, to the end of the world . . .

'Let our hearts be full of joy while we are looking forward to the accomplishment of this work. Oh, let it cheer our spirits under all the sinking damps and deep discouragements that are upon them in relation to the church, to think in what blessed state and glorious posture she will be, when Christ shall have declared his Father's name to all the nations under heaven, when the Jews shall be converted, and when the fulness of the Gentiles shall come in. O my beloved, that will be a joyful time indeed! It is true, those times, my brethren, shall be very comfortable and full of gladness many ways. And this is not the least, that people shall be brought in to the knowledge of the Lord out of all quarters of the world, and that by heaps and multitudes. . . . There was never such a time since the foundation of the world, nor shall be till that blessed season come: and therefore let out souls rejoice in the foresight of it, though we never live to see it.'⁹

For a second example I quote Richard Sibbes. Preaching to students and townsmen at Cambridge, where he ministered with so much success until his death in 1635, he gives this application to the truth concerning Christ's power:

'Let no man therefore despair; nor, as I said before, let us despair of the conversion of those that are savages in other parts. How bad soever they be, they are of the world, and if the gospel be preached to them, Christ will be "believed on in the world". Christ's almighty power goeth with his own ordinance to make it effectual. . . . And when the fulness of the gentiles is come in, then comes the conversion of the Jews. Why may we not expect it? They were the people of God. We see "Christ believed on in the world". We may therefore expect that they shall also be called, there being many of them, and keeping their nation distinct from others.'¹⁰

With convictions such as these on Christ's present and future reign in the world English Puritanism was necessarily hopeful in outlook. This was a feature noted by the outstanding secular historian, S. R. Gardiner, who contrasts the difference between the Puritans and their religious contemporaries in the troubled years leading up to the Civil War of 1642. 'Like the other Puritans,' he writes, 'Sibbes is distinguished by his triumphant confidence in the issue of his activity. Herbert's melody, in its happiest tones, has always something sad and plaintive about it. Even Laud and Wentworth acknowledged to themselves, that the chances were against them. Eliot in his prison, Sibbes in his pulpit, are jubilant with exultation.'¹¹

Before leaving this consideration of Puritan belief on Christ's work and kingdom, it needs to be pointed out that the same belief gave rise to the first major missionary endeavour of English Protestantism. The persecution of the Puritans in England in the period prior to the Civil War led to the emigration of some 15,000 persons to the shores of New England between

1627 and 1640. Among the number were many ministers who had been at Cambridge in the time of Sibbes and they were not slow to see their spiritual responsibility towards the heathen in the New World. The seal of the colonists of Massachusetts Bay, who arrived and settled in 1628, had on it a North American Indian with the words proceeding from his mouth, 'Come over and help us'. 'This device on the seal of their colony,' observes Nehemiah Adams, 'published to the world the fact that they regarded themselves as foreign missionaries to North America. This was also the case with their brethren of the Plymouth Colony who arrived eight years before.'[12]

Best known of the missionaries to the Indians was John Eliot (1604–1690), whose biography, written by Cotton Mather, was to have far-reaching influence. Eliot crossed the Atlantic in 1631 to minister to English settlers. He was more than forty when he began to study Algonquin – the difficult language of the Indians of Massachusetts. At the end of his notebook, in which he had mastered the intricacies of the Indian grammar, he wrote, 'Prayers and pains through faith in Christ Jesus will do anything'. Mather comments, 'Being by his *prayers* and *pains* thus furnished, he set himself in the year 1646 to preach the gospel of our Lord Jesus Christ among these desolate outcasts.'[13]

Eliot's work – its thoroughness, hardships and Christ-centredness – became an epic story. Of his preaching, Mather says, 'there was evermore much of Christ in it'. He became also a pioneer Bible translator, completing Genesis in 1661. Answering the charge that Roman Catholics had been more diligent than Protestants in missions, his first biographer comments: 'Eliot was very unlike to that Franciscan who, writing into Europe, gloried much how many thousands of Indians he had converted; but added, "that he desired his friends would send him the book called the Bible; for he had heard of there being such a book in Europe, which might be of some use to him". No: our Eliot found he could not live without a Bible himself; he would have parted with all his estate, sooner than have lost a leaf of it; and he knew it would be of more than *some use* unto the Indians too; he therefore with a vast labour translated the Holy Bible into the Indian language.'[14]

Support for this missionary work increased steadily in England after the first of a series of missionary tracts had been published in 1643. In 1649 Parliament itself took action by establishing the Society for Propagation of the Gospel in New England, and between that date and the Restoration of 1660 no less than £15,910 15s. 6½d. was contributed from all parts of England towards this first evangelical misssionary society. Many set-backs were to occur after this commencement of missionary endeavour, but the Puritans had given a lead which was not to be forgotten and the missionary appeal with which Cotton Mather closed his book, *The Triumphs of the Reformed Religion in America: Or, The Life of the Renowned John Eliot*, published in 1702, was to be heard and acted upon by men who were not yet born: 'May sufficient numbers of great, wise, rich, learned, and godly men in the three kingdoms, procure well-composed *societies*, by whose united counsels the noble design of evangelizing the world may be more effectually carried on.'[15]

What should be noted now is the way in which the Puritan hope was so influential in the origins of what was to become, a hundred and fifty years later, world-wide missionary endeavour. The hope is prominent throughout the missionary tracts published in the 1640's and 1650's. It is expressed in characteristic terms in the Preface to Thomas Shepard's *The Clear Sunshine of the Gospel Breaking Forth upon the Indians in New England*, 1648, where twelve prominent English Puritans address their words 'To the Right Honourable the Lords and Commons, Assembled in High Court of Parliament'. The initial blessing upon the work among the Indians, they write, is only a pointer towards what is yet to come:

'The utmost ends of the earth are designed and promised to be in time the possessions of Christ. . . . This little we see is something in hand, to earnest to us those things which are in hope; something in possession, to assure us of the rest in promise, when the ends of the earth shall see his glory, and the kingdoms of the world shall become the kingdoms of the Lord and his Christ, when he shall have dominion from sea to sea, and they that dwell in the wilderness shall bow before him (Psa. 22.27; Rev. 11.15; Psa. 72.8–11). And if the dawn of the morning be so delightful, what will the clear day be? If the first fruits be so precious, what will the whole harvest be? If some beginnings be so full of joy, what will it be when God shall perform his whole work, when the whole earth shall be full of the knowledge of the Lord, as the waters cover the sea (Isa. 11.9, 10) and east and west shall sing together the song of the Lamb?'[16]

A recent writer, R. Pierce Beaver, in his *Pioneers in Mission*, comments upon this extraordinary confidence as it appeared among the New England Puritans:

'Men living in a relatively small community on the edge of an unexplored continent, remote from the great population centers, having some contacts with remote lands by sea trade but closely related only to the British homeland, having converted only a few hundreds of Indians, with one voice proclaim their certainty that the whole wide world belongs to Christ and is being brought to him! It is the universalism of the prophets which sustains this view, and due to their conviction about the inerrancy of the Scriptures and the faithfulness of God's promises, the New England Puritans were convinced as to the soundness of their expectation.'[17]

*   *   *

A second respect in which Puritan beliefs on prophecy gave a decided colour to their piety concerns their commitment to the Church. In our own day piety is too often thought of in a purely personal way and the Church is spiritualized into some vague concept of the communion of all believers each of whom is individually related to Christ; the Christian's duty towards the Church is something which comes well down

[95]

in the scale of priorities and is separable – in the common way of thinking – from loyalty to Christ.

The whole orientation of Puritan spiritual character was different at this point. The Church and her visible biblical structure, seen in her ordinances, her unity, her preaching and her discipline, was in the forefront of their thinking. Her strength and purity must take precedence over all other considerations because she is the Church of Christ. Her welfare is bound up with the honour of her Head in whose name, and according to whose will, all her work is to be performed. With the apostle Paul, the Puritans delighted to celebrate the truth that the power which is 'able to do exceeding abundantly above all that we ask or think', is to be exercised to his glory 'in the church by Christ Jesus throughout all ages, world without end' (Eph. 3.21). The Church is focal in God's eternal design to bring glory to his Son. This concept inspired the passion with which the Puritans and Covenanters threw themselves into the work of Church reformation, and it also lay behind international concern for the unity of the Church in doctrine and discipline. Their piety had a strong *corporate* emphasis; for the individualistic type of evangelical living they had no sympathy whatsoever.

It should be at once apparent that this viewpoint, connected with Puritan belief on unfulfilled prophecy, differs markedly in its practical effects from the view which, based on another scheme of prophetic interpretation, sees no future for the organized Church. The Puritans saw the Church as a divine institution, provided by her Head with laws, government and officers, sufficient by his blessing for the full realization in history of the promise that Christ 'shall have dominion also from sea to sea, and from the river unto the ends of the earth' (Psa. 72.8). If the Church is the God-appointed means for the advancement of this kingdom, then her future is beyond all doubt. 'Unto this catholick, visible church,' says the Westminster Confession, 'Christ hath given the ministry, oracles, and ordinances of God, for the gathering and perfecting of the saints in this life, to the end of the world; and doth by his own presence and Spirit, according to his promise, make them effectual thereunto.'[18]

With this belief in the Church's future the Puritans gained energy and resolution. Had they adopted the short-term view the problems of the Church in their day might justifiably have seemed hopeless, but they faced them with an unflinching sense of their duty towards posterity. Succeeding centuries would reap the advantage of an uncompromised witness to the Word of God. Their work could not be in vain for the testimony of Christ's Church was yet to encircle the world. Jonathan Edwards was to epitomize this forward-look when he wrote, 'It may be hoped that then many of the Negroes and Indians will be divines, and that excellent books will be published in Africa, in Ethiopia, in Tartary.'[19] The Church, after all, would be victorious!

Many illustrations could be given from the seventeenth century of how much conscious concern for the Church appeared in Puritan piety. Witness, for instance, the words of Samuel Rutherford. Writing to Lady Jane Kenmure from Anwoth in 1633, he says:

'Madam, think upon this, that when our Lord, who hath his handkerchief to wipe the face of the mourners in Zion, shall come to wipe away all tears from their eyes, he may wipe yours also, in the passing, amongst others. I am confident, Madam, that our Lord will yet build a new house to himself, of our rejected and scattered stones, for our Bridegroom cannot want a wife. Can he live a widower? Nay, he will embrace both of us, the little young sister, and the elder sister, the Church of the Jews; and there will yet be a day of it.'[20]

In a letter written on April 22, 1635, the Anwoth pastor, shortly to be sentenced to confinement at Aberdeen for his contendings for the Church, resumes the theme:

'The Antichrist and the great red dragon will lop Christ's branches, and bring his vine to a low stump, under the feet of those who carry the mark of the beast; but the Plant of Renown, the Man whose name is the Branch, will bud forth again and

[97]

blossom as the rose, and there shall be fair white flourishes again, with most pleasant fruits, upon that tree of life . . .

'In the name of the Son of God, believe that buried Scotland, dead and buried with her dear Bridegroom, shall rise the third day again, and there shall be a new growth after the old timber is cut down . . .

'O to see the sight, next to Christ's Coming in the clouds, the most joyful! Our elder brethren the Jews and Christ fall upon one another's necks and kiss each other! They have been long asunder; they will be kind to one another when they meet. O day! O longed-for and lovely day-dawn! O sweet Jesus, let me see that sight which will be as life from the dead, thee and thy ancient people in mutual embraces.'[21]

Twenty-six years later, when Rutherford lay dying at St. Andrews, in 1661, he spoke with the same anticipation. Though he had lived to see Christ's covenanted cause in Scotland reduced to near ruin with the restoration of Charles II, and though for himself he could say 'there is nothing now betwixt me and the resurrection but paradise', he had not lost sight of promises respecting the Church on earth: 'We cannot but say it is a sad time to this land at present, it is a day of darkness and rebuke and blasphemy. The royal prerogative of Christ is pulled from his head. Yet we are to believe, Christ will not so depart from the land, but a remnant shall be saved; and he shall reign a victorious conquering King to the ends of the earth. O that there were nations, kindreds, tongues, and all the people of Christ's habitable world, encompassing his throne with cries and tears for the spirit of supplication to be poured down upon the inhabitants of Judah for that effect.'[22]

In the same year as Rutherford died in Scotland, Elizabeth Heywood died at Denton in Lancashire. Her station in life had been very different from that of the eminent Westminster divine, for she had been a housewife and mother, married to Oliver Heywood. But her husband's record of her last words gives us the same characteristic spirit:

'On the Friday before she died, when she had been panting and struggling for breath, seeing the children of the family about her, she said, "Sirs, prepare for this time, for it will come to you that are young, as well as to me. I want breath to speak. O spend your breath well! not in idle and vain conversation but to God's glory. . . . If God do suffer those lordly spirited men to afflict his church for a time, I believe it will not be long: the church is dear to the Lord, and he will not suffer it always to be trampled upon. O sirs, let the church of God lie near your hearts, it lies near God's heart: 'They shall prosper that love Zion'; prefer Jerusalem before and above your chief joy."

'Then, after praying for ministers of the Gospel, and for her own family, she petitioned "for the church of God, that the Jews might be converted, and that the gospel might be preached to the remainder of the Gentile nations".'[23]

*　　*　　*

These words of Elizabeth Heywood lead us to the third area in which Puritan piety and their prophetic beliefs coalesced, namely the exercise of prayer. As we have seen, they believed that the world-wide success of the gospel was promised in Scripture, that it would be realized by repeated outpourings of the Holy Spirit, and yet that the Church was the divinely appointed means for the fulfilment of this end. In connection with the Church's responsibility in this regard, there was no duty higher in Puritan esteem than the duty of prayer. The seasons when the kingdom of Christ is rapidly to spread in the earth are not revealed, but they will come in answer to prayer.

We have already noted the place which the future of Jew and Gentile occupied in the directions for prayer in such representative church documents as *The Larger Catechism* and *The Directory for Public Worship*. A number of years before these were drawn up, the call to prayer for the conversion of the Jews and for the success of the gospel through the world was already a feature of Puritan congregations. At Plymouth, Devon, it was to be noted in the ministry of John Barlow,[24] just as it was on the other side of the country at Palgrave,

Suffolk, where Elnathan Parr preached his expositions of Romans from which we have already quoted.[25]

As the century advanced, so the tide of prayer seems to have risen. William Gurnall, in the beautiful cloth-weaving town of Lavenham, where he ministered for thiry-five years following his appointment in 1644, would plead thus with his people for prayer for the world:

'Let not the sea that divides thee and the other parts of the earth make thee think thou art not concerned in their happiness or misery. Let thy prayers walk over the vast ocean, and bring matter for thy devotions, like the merchant's ship her freight from afar. Visit the Churches of Christ abroad; yea, the poor Indians, and other ruins of mankind, that lie where Adam's sin threw them with us, without any attempt made as yet upon them by the gospel for their recovery, and carry their deplored condition before the Lord. Our Drake is famous for compassing the earth with his ship in a few years: Thou mayst by thy prayers every day, and make a more gainful voyage of it too than he did.'[26]

Sometimes the call to prayer had special reference to the Jews. John Owen, preaching before the House of Commons in 1649, speaks of 'the bringing home of his ancient people to be one fold with the fulness of the Gentiles . . . in answer to millions of prayers put up at the throne of grace, for this very glory, in all generations'.[27] At the same period, days of prayer and humiliation were kept in Scotland, one particular object being 'That the promised conversion of his ancient people of the Jews may be hastened'.[28]

This same yearning is to be found scattered in the long-forgotten records of Puritan diaries and biographical accounts. We read of John Pinckney, a typical Puritan pastor ejected from his church at Longstock, Hampshire, in 1662, that 'he ever discovered a most compassionate concern for the Jews, and did upon all occasions pray for their conversion with extraordinary earnestness'.[29]

Cotton Mather, the New England Puritan leader, notes in his diary:

'This Day, from the Dust, where I lay prostrate before the Lord, I lifted up my Cries . . . for the conversion of the *Jewish Nation*, and for my own having the Happiness, at some time or other, to baptise a *Jew* that should by my Ministry be brought home unto the Lord.'[30]

Oliver Heywood on August 2, 1663, jotted down that his 'soul mightily breathed after' these petitions; 'that God would promote his work in the world by subduing antichrist, converting Jews, enlightening blind nations'.[31]

The same thing is to be found in the Scottish Christian leaders of that period, as we have already seen in the case of Rutherford. One long-to-be-remembered example occurs in the life of Richard Cameron, the 'Lion of the Covenant'. On the open hills at Shawhead, Kirkcudbrightshire, Cameron preached on May 30, 1680, from the text 'And ye will not come to me, that ye might have life'. In the midst of this sermon, which has been described as one of the most remarkably blessed of the Lord preached in Scotland, Cameron fell into a 'rap of calm weeping', and his hearers wept with him. Compelled for the moment to stop, he 'prayed for the restoration of the Jews, for the fall of Antichrist, and for the hastening of the day when the Stuarts would be swept from the throne'. Two hundred years later, John Herkless tells us, the memory of those services had not died out among the people of the districts where Cameron spoke.[32]

Perhaps one of the most striking of these old records comes from the life of Walter Smith who died alongside Donald Cargill on the scaffold in Edinburgh on July 27, 1681: 'as he did cleave to him in love and unity in life,' writes Patrick Walker, 'so he died with his face upon his breast'. In 1679, Smith, himself a minister of the gospel, had drawn up some rules for the meetings of the praying societies in the south-west. In these we read:

'As it is the undoubted duty of all to pray for the coming of Christ's kingdom, so all that love our Lord Jesus Christ in sincerity, and know what it is to bow a knee in good earnest, will long and pray for the out-making of the gospel-promises to his Church in the latter days, that King Christ would go out upon the white horse of the gospel, conquering and to conquer, and make a conquest of the travail of his soul, that it may be sounded that the kingdoms of the world are become his, and his name called upon from the rising of the sun to its going down. (1) That the old offcasten Israel for unbelief would never be forgotten, especially in these meetings, that the promised day of their ingraffing again by faith may be hastned; and that dead weight of blood removed off them, that their fathers took upon them and upon their children, that have sunk them down to hell upwards of seventeen hundred years. (2) That the Lord's written and preached word [may be sent] with power, to enlighten the poor pagan world, living in black perishing darkness without Christ and the knowledge of his name. (3) That the damnable delusions of Mahomet, and errors of Antichrist, Arian, Arminian, Socinian and Quakers, may be discovered; that the blind may no more lead the blind, and go to hell wholesale, living and dying so; and the many errors abounding among many other sectaries may come to light.'[33]

It might seem today that the record of such prayers is no more than an historical curiosity, but the Puritans held no such view of prayer. For them prayers were 'laid up' with God to be answered in his time. 'Let us remember', says Lachlan Mackenzie, 'that the Church was 4,000 years praying for the appearance of the Messiah. We have not been praying the half of that time for the conversion of the Jews and the fulness of the Gentiles.'[34] And Thomas Goodwin enlarges upon this theme in his work *The Return of Prayers*:

'There may be some prayers which you must be content never yourselves to see answered in this world, the accomplishment of them not falling out in your time: such as those you haply make for the calling of the Jews, the utter downfall of God's enemies, the flourishing of the gospel . . . all which prayers are not yet lost, but will have answers: for as God is an eternal God, and Christ's righteousness an "everlasting righteousness", and therefore of eternal efficacy, Dan. 9. 24, so are prayers are also, which the work of the eternal Spirit of Christ, made to that God in his name, and in him are eternally accepted, and therefore may take place in after ages. So the prayer that St. Stephen made for his persecutors took place in Saul when St. Stephen was dead. So David's prayer against Judas, Psa. 109.8, 9, took effect above a thousand years after, as appears, Acts 1.20. So the prayers of the church, for three hundred years, in the primitive times, that kings might come to the knowledge of the truth, and they "lead peaceable and quiet lives, in all godliness and honesty," (which St. Paul, in Nero's time, exhorted unto, 1 Tim. 2.2) were not answered and accomplished till Constantine's time . . .

'There is a common treasure of the church, not of their merits, but of their prayers. There are bottles of tears a-filling, vials a-filling to be poured out for the destruction of God's enemies. What a collection of prayers hath there been these many ages towards it! And that may be one reason why God will do such great things towards the end of the world, even because there hath been so great a stock of prayers going for so many ages, which is now to be returned.'[35]

*   *   *

Is it any wonder, with these convictions, that for the Puritans the future was charged with hope? How this hope was retained through the dreary early years of the eighteenth century and how it joined with a new age of revival and with world-wide missions originated by Christians in the Puritan tradition, will be the theme of our next two chapters.

VI

THE EIGHTEENTH-CENTURY
AWAKENING:
THE HOPE REVIVED

*George Whitefield, born in 1714 – the year of
Matthew Henry's death. An evangelist to millions*

'I believe there is such a work begun, as neither we nor our fathers have heard of. The beginnings are amazing; how unspeakably glorious will the end be! In New England, the Lord takes poor sinners by hundreds, I may say by thousands. In Scotland, the fruits of my poor labours are abiding and apparent. In Wales, the word of the Lord runs and is glorified, as also in many places in England. In London, our Saviour is doing great things daily . . .'

GEORGE WHITEFIELD, April 6, 1742

'That which was deemed visionary at first, soon came to be regarded in a very different light; one after another of the dissenting ministers began to perceive that the work of reformation begun, was of God, and must prevail; while others felt themselves constrained to abstain from all formal opposition to it, lest haply they should be found fighting against God. In England, Wales, Scotland, and America, the great work of conversion was proceeding with amazing rapidity, and devout lookers-on, of every class, began to feel something like awe in contemplating the wonderful effects produced upon persons in almost every rank in life, from the princes and nobles of the land to the obscurest and most profligate of the people.'

JOHN MORRISON
The Fathers and Founders of the London Missionary Society,
1839, vol 1, 43

THE notion that the Church advances in the world by a steady and uninterrupted course of progress is one which cannot bear examination in the light of the period which followed the Restoration of Charles II in 1660. At that date evangelical Christianity stood on the threshold of some eighty years' declension. One cause of this was that almost all of the best-known Puritan preachers were now passing into old age; few were to live to see the accession of a Protestant monarch, William III, in 1688. Another reason was the repressive legislation employed by the government, commencing with the Act of Uniformity of 1662 which at one stroke displaced some 2,000 Puritan ministers from parish churches, schools and the two universities. Disorganized, shorn of all political favour and harried by persecution, the Nonconformist churches – as they now became – were soon but a shadow compared with the congregations of earlier years; and when toleration came at last in 1688 it was soon evident that something far more valuable had been in large measure lost, namely, the presence and power of the Spirit of God.

Gilbert Burnet, who became Bishop of Salisbury in 1689 and died in 1715, recorded the opinion of the 'great men of the Church' that Nonconformity would die out with the generation then existing. The prophecy was incorrect but there was no gainsaying that Nonconformity was a spent force. Between 1695 and 1730 it appears that only one new Non-

conformist Church was erected in London[1] and neighbourhood, while the existing congregations barely managed to hold
their own. No more did the common people crowd to hear the
preaching of the Word. The spirit of worldliness had done its
work and they now 'far preferred the chatty, easy-going, careless "parson" ', says Herbert Skeats, to the 'severe Presbyterian'
or 'godly Independent'.[2] In addition to this, the pulpit of these
two leading Nonconformist denominations was itself under-
going a change. When a union of the two groups was attempted
in London in the 1690's it foundered on the discovery of the
number of churches no longer committed to the old Calvinistic
orthodoxy. 'In less than half a century,' according to the opinion of Skeats who describes conditions around 1720, 'the doctrines of the great founders of Presbyterianism could scarcely
be heard from any Presbyterian pulpit in England'.[3] Robert
Traill, a representative of the old theology, writing in 1692,
asks: 'What can be the reason why the very Parliaments in the
reign of James I and Charles I were so alarmed with Arminianism, as may be read in history, and is remembered by old
men; and that now for a long time there hath been no talk,
no fear of it; as if Arminianism were dead and buried, and no
man knows where its grave is? Is not the true reason to be found
in its universal prevailing in the nation?'[4]

As is so often the case, this theological change took place in
the name of progress. Reason, it was said, must be respected
as well as revelation, and charity forbade an imposition upon
ministers of the old Confessions and Catechisms. How far this
new spirit had gone was illustrated in 1719 when, at a debate
at Salters' Hall, a majority of London Dissenters refused to
make it necessary for ministers to subscribe to the orthodox
doctrine of the Trinity. At that debate nearly all the Independents were on the side of the large minority, but even in
their ranks the coming years were to show a readiness to
compromise on the part of several of their leading ministers.
Speaking of the aftermath of the Salters' Hall dispute, Skeats
says:

'If, as was undoubtedly the case, breadth of thought and

charity of sentiment increased, and, to some extent, settled into a mental habit of the nation, religious activity did not increase. The zeal of Puritanism was almost as unknown as it was unimitated. It seems to have been impossible for the Christian men of this generation to fight with the old force of Christianity while they were being fitted into a new armour of thought.'[5]

This being the case with those who were, by tradition, the custodians of evangelical truth, little need be said of the state of the Established Church. The testimony of one Anglican writer sums up the position in these words:

'When the Puritans were expelled, they carried with them the spiritual light of the Church of England. . . . Religion in the Church of England was almost extinguished, and in many of her parishes the lamp of God went out. The places of the ejected clergy were supplied with little regard even to the decencies of the sacred office: the voluptuous, the indolent, the ignorant, and even the profane, received episcopal orders, and like a swarm of locusts overspread the Church.'[6]

Through the eighty years, 1660–1740, the spiritual history of the Establishment was largely one of dreary futility. The flight of James II in 1688 relieved the threat of a returning Roman Catholicism, but thereafter neither party in the Church – the 'High' with its sacerdotalism and divine right of king's theory, and the 'Low' with latitudinarian indifference to doctrine and its alliance with the Whigs in politics – could do anything to arrest the carelessness with which all religion soon came to be treated by the nation at large. Scarcely a greater contrast exists in English history than that between the honour publicly paid to Christianity in the mid-seventeenth century and the attitude of the 1730's when at court Queen Caroline talked politics with her husband, George II, during services in the royal chapel. When the Queen was dying in 1737 the court not surprisingly viewed Archbishop Potter's prayers at her bed-side as the empty farce that it was. 'It has come to be taken for granted', wrote Bishop Butler in 1736, 'that Christianity is no longer a subject of enquiry; but that it is now at length discovered to be fictitious. And accordingly it is treated as if, in the present age, this was an agreed point among all persons of discernment, and nothing remained but to set it up as a principal subject for mirth and ridicule.'[7]

*   *   *

North of the Border the train of events following the Restoration was very similar. The men who had been leaders in the revivals of the 1620's and 1630's were already passing from the scene when King Charles II betrayed the promises he had made earlier to the Church of Scotland. Rutherford died in 1661; David Dickson in 1662, 'sure that Jesus Christ would not long sit with such indignities done against his work and people'; and Robert Blair in 1666. John Livingstone, Blair's fellow-labourer in Ireland in brighter days, died in exile in Holland in 1672. Of the four hundred ministers ejected from their churches in 1662 only ninety survived to see the first General Assembly of the reconstituted Church in 1690. In the intervening years those who stood by the covenanted testimony of the Scottish Church endured the utmost severities; according to John Howie's figures, some 18,000 Christian people suffered either 'death, or the utmost hardships and extremities' until the last leader, the youthful James Renwick, went to the scaffold on February 17, 1688. When the persecution finally passed, many a moor and hillside in south-west Scotland, where an undaunted remnant had been faithful unto death, was marked by a martyr's grave.

The return of freedom and toleration at the accession of William III found the majority of the Church of Scotland – in which episcopal clergy intruded after 1660 were allowed to remain – ready to pursue a broader policy. The architect of the new policy was William Carstairs, a Christian man but one whom W. G. Blaikie could describe as 'a courtier and a diplomatist, and the great aim of his policy was to keep things quiet, to avoid commotion, and maintain the *status quo*.' The eighteenth century was not far advanced when the fruit of this accommodating spirit began to be seen. In 1712 Parliament passed an Act restoring Patronage in the Church of Scotland;

this Act, which was approved by the General Assembly, rendered it possible to place ministers in congregations contrary to the wishes of the people who were in many cases more evangelical than the clergy. Five years later John Simson, Professor of Divinity at Glasgow, and 'a master in the art of teaching heresy orthodoxly' was but gently handled by the General Assembly after a charge that he was teaching Arminianism, while on the other side, an old Puritan book, *The Marrow of Modern Divinity*, reissued through the influence of Thomas Boston, minister in the Selkirk parish of Ettrick, and some of his ministerial friends, was solemnly condemned by an Act of Assembly in 1720. In 1729 Boston stood alone in the General Assembly to protest when, after it was proved that Simson was now teaching Arianism, the decision was taken simply to suspend the professor from his duties and to permit him to continue to receive his salary.[8]

This spirit of laxity had two results. First, it led to the secession of four ministers from the Church of Scotland in 1733 – the year after Boston's death – and the formation of the Secession Church. By 1766 this church, which kept the gospel alive in many parts of Scotland, possessed 120 churches and 100,000 worshippers. Second, it gradually placed the leadership of the Church into the hands of 'the Moderates' whose religion was generally nothing more than dry morality. This was what greatly burdened Thomas Halyburton, Professor of Divinity at St. Andrews, at the time of his death in 1712. Speaking to some around his bed he said: 'O sirs! I dread mightily that a rational sort of religion is coming in among us; I mean by it, a religion that consists in a bare attendance on outward duties and ordinances, without the power of godliness; and thence people shall fall into a way of serving God which is mere deism, having no relation to Christ Jesus and the Spirit of God.'[9]

James Robe of Kilsyth, writing in 1742 of the state of the Church of Scotland, confirmed how justified Halyburton's fears had been:

'While the government, worship and doctrine, established in this church were retained in profession, there hath been an universal corruption of life, reaching even unto the sons and daughters of God. Former strictness as to holiness and tenderness of life was much relaxed among both ministers and people of the better sort: a formal round of professional duties was the religion of the professors, and in this they rested: as to the multitude, they were visibly profane, and without any sense of religion at all. Things were become so bad with us, that there were few whom we, the ministers of the Word, could comfort as believers in Christ, and exhort to rejoice in hope of the glory of God, when we found them a dying.'[10]

*　　*　　*

Everywhere in the English-speaking world, including Wales and the American colonies, a similar situation prevailed; formalism, coldness of heart, indifference to religion, and worldliness holding a general sway over the populations. 'Soul extinct, but stomach well alive', was Carlyle's apt description of the scene.

It has not been sufficiently observed, however, that during this period the evangelical ministers who maintained the old Puritan theology, sometimes in lonely and difficult situations, never questioned that a new spring-time of revival would be given from on high. Their inherited view of revivals and unfulfilled prophecy made the future progress and world-wide expansion of Christ's kingdom a certainty even at a time when, as Montesquieu claimed, the English had no religion at all. According to this Frenchman who visited England in 1729–31, 'If anyone spoke of religion, everybody laughed'.

Many examples of this attitude of confidence could be given. Matthew Henry ministered at Chester from 1687 to 1712 when he removed to London, where he died in 1714. Through his famous Commentary he was to have a vast influence in propagating the evangelical and Calvinistic faith so powerful in his father's day. In a sermon entitled 'England's Hopes,' preached on January 1, 1707, from Isaiah 63.4, 'The year of my redeemed is come', Henry speaks of a coming fulfilment of this prediction:

'The year of the revival of primitive Christianity in the power of it, will be the year of the redeemed. This we wish, we hope, we long to see, both at home and abroad. . . . When the bounds of the church will be enlarged by the conversion of Pagan and Mahometan nations to the faith of Christ, and the spreading of the gospel in foreign parts . . . Pray for the pouring out of the Spirit upon us from on high and then the year of the redeemed would soon come . . . But if the year of the redeemed should not come in our days; if the carcasses of this generation should fall in this wilderness, as justly they may for our unbelief and murmuring, and we should not go over Jordan to see that goodly mountain, and Lebanon: yet let it suffice us, that those who shall come after us shall enter into that rest. Joseph dies in Egypt, but lays his bones in confidence that God will surely visit Israel.'[11]

The faithful witness of Thomas Boston in the unsympathetic General Assembly of the Church of Scotland has already been mentioned. Dr. MacFarlan has observed how, in the Memoirs of Boston and the lives of several of the more faithful men of that period, 'we have laid open to us many of the hidden springs of a coming change'.[12] Like Matthew Henry, Boston worked on in hope during a dark day, and like him also he fed this hope to his people through the promises of Scripture. Thus in one sermon, preached in 1716, on 'Encouragement to Pray for the Conversion of the Jews', we find the pastor of Ettrick expounding this head of doctrine: 'There is a day coming in which there shall be a national conversion of the Jews or Israelites. The now blinded and rejected Jews shall at length be converted into the faith of Christ, and join themselves to the Christian Church.'

The application of this doctrine included the following words:

'Have you any love to, or concern for the Church, for the work of reformation, the reformation of our country, the reformation of the world? Any longing desire for the revival of that work now at a stand; for a flourishing state of the church, that is now under a decay? then pray for the conversion of the Jews.

[113]

'Are you longing for a revival to the churches, now lying like dry bones, would you fain have the Spirit of life enter into them? Then pray for the Jews. "For if the casting away of them be the reconciling of the world; what shall the receiving of them be, but life from the dead." That will be a lively time, a time of a great outpouring of the Spirit, that will carry reformation to a greater height than yet has been . . . '[13]

Across the Atlantic in New England the same expectation was kept alive and frequent reference to it is to be found in letters and sermons of the period. Samuel Danforth, minister of Taunton, New England, wrote in 1705, 'I think sometimes that the time of the pouring out of the Spirit upon all flesh may be at the door. Let us be earnest in prayer, that Christ's kingdom may come.'[14] In 1721, after a local revival at Windham, Connecticut, Mr. Adams of New London urged the continuance of prayer for the far wider blessing promised of God, 'Oh! that the Lord would arise and have mercy upon Zion, that the time to favour it, the set time may come, that the whole earth may be filled with the knowledge of the glory of the Lord, as the waters cover the sea!'[15]

*   *   *

Though a number, like the Simeons and Annas of another day, thus waited for a divine visitation, when the great revival of the eighteenth century at last began in the late 1730's, it was unexpected by the mass of nominal Christians. And even those who had long prayed for a new out-pouring of the Spirit were to be astonished at both the extent and power of the work. The first signs of the dawn of a new day occurred in places far distant from one another and among ministers who were quite unaware of how the hearts of others in different countries were also being stirred. Congregations in the Middle States of America were roused from slumber by the preaching of the Tennents. At Northampton, in New England, an awakening occurred in 1735 under the ministry of Jonathan Edwards, and the same year in Wales the two main leaders of the coming revival in that country were both converted, Daniel Rowland, a Cardiganshire curate ordained in 1733, and Howell Harris, a schoolmaster of Brecknockshire. 1735 saw also the conversion of George Whitefield while a student at Oxford, and it was his preaching in London in 1737 that was the first sign in England that a new work of God was commencing. For nearly three months in the autumn of that year 'there was', says Whitefield, 'no end of the people flocking to hear the Word of God. . . . The sight of the congregations was awful. One might, as it were, walk upon the people's heads; and thousands went away from the largest churches for want of room.'[16] In 1738, when Whitefield was away in Georgia, John Wesley had his evangelical experience in Aldersgate Street, London, and continuing the preaching work of Whitefield he could soon write, 'Great multitudes are everywhere awakened'.[17]

By 1739 it was beyond question that a great revival had commenced in England. New Year's Day witnessed the small group of leaders in London, including Whitefield and Wesley, met in a prayer meeting reminiscent of the private gatherings of ministers in the previous century. In the next five weeks Whitefield preached some thirty times in and about London, then moving to the Bristol area he took the momentous step on February 17 of preaching to some 200 colliers in the open-air at Kingswood, the use of a church having been denied to him. From this point onwards open-air preaching became an inescapable necessity as congregations gathered in thousands. In the bleak months of February and March Whitefield estimated that there were as many as ten thousand hearers on one occasion at Kingswood; and in London, on Moorfields and Kennington Common, during the following months still vaster crowds assembled for the preaching of a message which had so recently been generally dismissed with scorn. At a time when the population of the capital was only some 600,000, and when gin and gambling were the great public interests, it was an amazing phenomenon that a Christian preacher could now command far larger gatherings than any of the theatres or entertainments of the day. In July, 1739, Whitefield wrote from London, 'A great work of God is doing here. The Lord Jesus gets himself the victory every day.'[18] And in August: 'The Spirit of God is moving on the faces of thousands of souls in England. The word runs very swift, and Satan falls like lightning from heaven.'[19]

In March, 1739, Whitefield first visited Wales and met Howell Harris. At that date an awakening was already spreading rapidly in the south and west of Wales. Between 1735 and the summer of 1737 Harris had travelled some two thousand five hundred miles on foot speaking and exhorting, often only to handfuls of people. By the autumn of 1737 considerably larger numbers were assembling – nearly five hundred at Brooks, near Abergavenny, about four hundred at Merthyr Cynog, and in Llangeitho over fifteen hundred.[20]

Llangeitho, in Cardiganshire, and the adjacent parishes of Llancwnlle and Llandewibrefi, were served by Daniel Rowland who was curate to his absentee elder brother. Until his conversion Rowland was a typical clergyman of the age, serving 'An easy-going God'. Thereafter the change in his ministry was immense. 'He proclaimed', says his biographer, 'eternal perdition to a sinful world.' Notwithstanding the message of judgment, his churches were soon crowded and such were the overpowering effects of the Word preached that numbers stricken with conviction of sin lay prostrate on the ground in the churchyard of Llancwnlle. It was at this time, or soon after, that a movement of the Spirit, long to be remembered, occurred in Llangeitho church. One Sunday morning as Rowland read the words of the Litany, 'By Thine Agony and bloody Sweat; by Thy Cross and Passion; by Thy Precious Death and Burial; by Thy glorious Resurrection and Ascension; and by the coming of the Holy Ghost', many fell to the floor, suddenly seized by an awareness of their state as sinners, while others gave with tears the appointed response, 'Good Lord, deliver us.'

Physical side-effects resulting from intense conviction of sin were to follow the evangelical revival throughout its course. Especially was this the case in the American colonies where the local revivals witnessed in a few places during the previous decade became, in 1740, 'the Great Awakening'. Everywhere the reign of formality seemed to be broken and tears streamed down the faces of thousands under the preaching of the gospel. Before the end of that same year all parts of the eastern seaboard of America, from Boston in the north to Savannah in the south, were expressing a stirring of religious concern exceeding anything remembered from former days. In May, 1740, it was reported, 'There was never such a general awakening and concern for the things of God known in America before.'[21] In June, Whitefield, who had returned to America the previous autumn, wrote, 'O what wonderful things is God doing in America! . . . What the event of the present general awakening will be, I know not.'[22] In July, amazed at the spread of the work, he exclaimed, 'Surely our Lord intends to set the world in a flame.'[23]

The Great Awakening continued in America until 1743–44, bringing thousands into the kingdom of God and establishing a new spiritual and moral outlook in the colonies as a whole. 'It was estimated,' says Turnbull, an American writer who belonged to the generation immediately following the revival, 'that in two or three years, thirty or forty thousand souls were born into the family of heaven in New England, besides great numbers in New York, New Jersey and the more southern provinces.' Of the many whom he personally knew as having professed conversion during the Awakening he writes: 'They were constant and serious in their attendance on public worship, prayerful, righteous, and charitable, strict in the government of their families; and not one of them, so far as he knew, was ever guilty of scandal.'[24]

News of the Awakening in America spread quickly and in Scotland, in particular, it was heard with eager attention by those who had been long praying for a day of visitation from God. John Willison, Church of Scotland minister at Dundee from 1718 until his death in 1750, noted the information with gladness in his book *The Balm of Gilead*, published in January, 1742. At the same time he lamented over Scotland, 'How rare is conversion work now, in respect of former times!'[25]

Whitefield's visit to Edinburgh and Glasgow in the summer of 1741 had brought a quickening of spiritual concern and some conversions, yet this provided no evidence that a general revival was at hand. Within a month of the publication of Willison's book, however, an out-pouring of the Holy Spirit had occurred in the parish of Cambuslang, five miles south-east of Glasgow, and this was attended with such spiritual power that it was rightly judged that a new day of blessing had come to Scotland. In January of 1742, ninety heads of families in Cambuslang had requested their minister, William M'Culloch, to hold a week-night service for the exposition of Scripture, this type of address being termed a 'Lecture'. The night fixed was Thursday. On Thursday, February 18, after several days in which a spirit of prayer had been especially evident, some fifty people detained their minister through the night as they sought spiritual help and relief from conviction of sin. From this point onwards the influence and success which followed the ministry of the Word was such that preaching now became M'Culloch's daily work. The whole parish with its nine hundred inhabitants was profoundly moved as quarrels, swearing, drunkenness, and all the other characteristics of worldliness gave way visibly to a confession of wrongs, restitution, remorse and prayerfulness.[26] 'The report,' says a contemporary, 'spread like fire; vast multitudes were attracted thither. I believe that, in less than two months from its commencement, there were few parishes within twelve miles that had not more or less of their people awakened by resorting thither; and many who were awakened there came from places greatly more distant.'[27]

By April 28, 1742, M'Culloch believed that about three hundred souls had been awakened; within five months the figure had risen to five hundred, most of whom, he trusted, had 'been savingly brought home to God'. The testimony of many other ministers who visited Cambuslang was no less striking. John Willison wrote in April, 'The work at Cambuslang is a most singular and marvellous out-pouring of the Holy Spirit.' George Whitefield, who returned to Scotland in June, wrote after his first visit to Cambuslang, 'The awakening here

in Scotland is unspeakable . . . God seems to awaken scores together. I never was enabled to preach so before.'[28] A few days
later he returned again to Cambuslang 'to assist at the blessed
sacrament'. Of this communion season he reported: 'On Sabbath day, scarce ever was such a sight seen in Scotland. There
were undoubtedly upwards of twenty thousand people. . . .
All night in different companies, you might have heard persons praying to, and praising God. The children of God came
from all quarters: it was like the passover in Josiah's time.'[29]
At a second communion in August, Whitefield judged the numbers to be between thirty and forty thousand. After such a summer as this it is no wonder to find him writing to Howell Harris
from Edinburgh in September; 'We have had most blessed
days here. I and the people have been in the suburbs of heaven.
Blessed be God! I live in heaven daily.'[30]

The revival had clearly spread far beyond Cambuslang. In
May a parallel work had begun in the small parish of Kilsyth
where for twenty-nine years, since 1713, James Robe had
faithfully ministered. 'The good man', says MacFarlan, 'had
long been on the mount, as the prophet was on Carmel, plead-
ing with God; and many a weary look he cast towards the sea,
without observing any sign even of clouds. He preached also
much and long on the work of the Spirit, as if to bring the
people under its power; and yet, so far as for the time appeared,
his preaching was only *of* the work – it wanted evidence of the
Worker being himself there.'[31] On Sunday, May 18, the same
extraordinary power seen in Cambuslang appeared in this
parish also. A spirit of mourning and conviction came upon
multitudes and within a short time upwards of three hundred
were said to be awakened – two hundred belonging to the district and others who were strangers. At the sacrament held
at Kilsyth on October 3, there were nearly fifteen hundred
communicants. Speaking of the increase of unity which revival
brings, John Erskine pointed to the evidence this parish provided:

'As the Baillie of Kilsyth attests, so much of the Spirit of mildness and friendship prevails among the People in that Place,

that there have been no pleas before their Court for these several months past; whereas formerly a great many were brought before it every week.'[32]

James Robe lived until 1753, William M'Culloch until 1771, and both men testified to the permanency of the blessing which had been brought to their parishes. Nine years after 1742, of the two hundred Kilsyth parishioners mentioned above, 'upwards of a hundred had either died hopefully or continued to walk worthy of their profession'. M'Culloch and his elders gave detailed evidence of the state of Cambuslang in 1751, including mention of 'about four hundred persons, who were awakened here in 1742, and who, from that time to the time of their death, or till now, have been enabled to behave in a good measure as becometh the gospel'. M'Culloch also compiled two quarto volumes containing the experiences of one hundred and five of these persons in the hope that the material would one day be deemed worthy of publication.[33]

*   *   *

The revivals which, as we have seen, came to the English-speaking world from the late 1730's onwards, varied widely in their duration. In New England 'the Great Awakening' of 1740 was over by 1743, and not until 1791 did another age of extensive revivals commence in America. In England the same powerful influences which suddenly aroused thousands in London and around Bristol in 1739 were to be subsequently felt in Wiltshire, Cornwall, Yorkshire, Tyne-side and several other areas, though in the main it was in quieter ways that the tide of the gospel rose in the land. Whitefield's helper, John Syms, wrote to a New England friend in 1743, 'There are few or no counties in England or Wales where there is not a work begun. . . . The gospel in this day may be likened to a *fire set to well dried fuel*: it no sooner touches but a flame arises.'[34]

The most prominent revivals to occur in Scotland after 1742 were those by means of which large areas of the Scottish Highlands were transformed. In this northern area of Britain which until then had been largely a moral wilderness, a succession of gospel preachers whose lives are told in Dr. John Kennedy's *The Days of the Fathers in Ross-shire*, permeated the country with evangelical religion. Another Scottish writer speaking of the same period in the Highlands says: 'by the blessing of Heaven and the outpouring of the Holy Spirit attending their faithful exhibition of the truth to the consciences of their people, religion was seen to blossom as the rose. Their churches were crowded by arrested and deeply-affected audiences, and for a few years seldom a Sabbath passed without one or more being seriously impressed.'[35] Under these prolonged revivals, Dr. Kennedy judged the spiritual prosperity of Ross-shire to have reached its height in 1782, though for many years thereafter further times of awakening were known in the county as well as elsewhere in the Highlands.

The history of Wales parallels that of northern Scotland in the frequency and power of the revivals which were common for nearly a century after the voices of Rowland and Harris had broken the general slumber in 1737. From that date until his death in 1791, Rowland witnessed seven revivals in Cardiganshire, including the so-called 'Great Revival' of 1762 which seems to have spread throughout South Wales.

Until 1791 the gospel only had a very limited and partial success in North Wales, but in December of that year the sober-minded Thomas Charles wrote of the glorious work then taking place in Bala and its neighbourhood:

'General concern about eternal things swallowed up all other concerns. And a spirit of conviction spread so rapidly that there was hardly a young person in the neighbourhood but began to enquire, What will become of me? The work has continued to go on ever since with unabated power and glory, spreading from one town to another, all around this part of the country. A dispensation so glorious, I never beheld, nor indeed expected to see in my day. . . . The coming of the Lord amongst us has been with such majesty, glory, and irresistible power, that even his avowed enemies would be glad to hide themselves somewhere, from the brightness of his coming. . . . If the Lord God is graciously pleased to continue the work, as it has prevailed for some months past, for some months yet to come, the Devil's kingdom will be in ruins in our neighbourhood. Those who were foremost in wickedness and rebellion are now amongst the foremost in seeking for mercy and salvation in the blood of the Lamb. It is an easy and delightful work to preach the glorious Gospel here, in these days. Divine truths have their own infinite weight and importance in the minds of the people. Beams of divine light, together with irresistible energy, accompany every truth delivered. . . . I bless God for these days, and would not have been without seeing what I now see in the land. – No; not for the world.

'And I am not without hopes, but these are dawnings of the promised millennium, and showers that precede the storm which will entirely overturn the kingdom of darkness.'[36]

For the next forty years similar revivals occurred in several parts of North Wales, the preachers most singularly used in them being Ebenezer Morris, Robert Roberts and John Elias.

*   *   *

The evangelical revival in the English-speaking world two hundred years ago had vast influence in increasing the confidence that all the nations of the earth would yet be turned to the gospel of Christ. The great numbers who then simultaneously entered the kingdom of God, the many more who, though still unconverted, gave outward allegiance to the truth, and the moral change wrought upon the attitude of whole generations, gave Christians to understand that gospel preaching accompanied by future outpourings of the Spirit would be well able to transform the world.

This expectation was certainly based in part upon the extraordinary contrast, in terms of the numerical increase of the Church, between the earlier and later halves of the eighteenth century. We have already noted something of the numbers caught up in the revival but a little more must be said on this point. It was not the practice of any churches in those days to call for a public profession of faith after a sermon and then announce the number of 'converts'. What numbers we do have were based on quite different calculations. The size of open-air gatherings was estimated, and though the figures given were necessarily of varying degrees of accuracy, the testimony of independent witnesses not infrequently corroborated these estimates. The number of new churches is in many cases more exactly known. The numbers of new communicants and church members were also in many places recorded. These were not simply 'church-goers', it needs to be remembered, but those who generally had been carefully examined for a consistent Christian life before they were permitted to approach the Lord's table. Thus, at the second great communion at Cambuslang in the summer of 1742, when about 3,000 sat at the Lord's table, we read, 'if there had been access to get tokens, there would have been a thousand more communicants'. M'Culloch and his fellow-ministers knew that a revival was not the time to relax church discipline by admitting persons not previously examined and granted 'tokens'.

In England the influence of the revival was felt in almost all sections of the Church. Alongside but still inside the Established Church there were John Wesley's 'Methodist' Societies, the first of which was formed in 1739. By 1767 there were 25,911 persons in Britain belonging to these societies, the majority of these being located in English counties; in 1783, the number was 45,955 and in 1790 – the year before Wesley's death – 71,568. Wesley's societies held their meetings in all manner of places, though new meeting-houses became increasingly essential. From one chapel in 1739 the number grew to 359 by 1784, and the later multiplication of buildings was still more phenomenal.[37] By the year 1879 there were in Cornwall alone 385 preaching places able to seat a total of 100,290 people! The Methodist membership in that county was then 23,656.[38]

Inside the Church of England there was also a vast increase of evangelical influence. How small that influence was in the early days of the evangelical revival can be judged by the estimate that in the 1740's no more than six or seven clergy belonged to the evangelical school; yet this was the same party which in 1788 numbered over 500![39] As an example of growth on the parish level the case of Haworth in Yorkshire is striking. William Grimshaw had become the incumbent at this moorland village in 1742; in the same year, he says, 'our dear Lord was pleased to visit my parish'. Six years later, in 1748, Grimshaw was charged before the Archbishop of York with preaching outside his parish. Part of the interrogation went as follows: 'How many communicants had you at your quarterly sacraments, when you first came to Haworth?' 'Twelve, my Lord.' 'How many have you now at such solemnities?' 'In the winter from four to five hundred, and sometimes in the summer near twelve hundred.' This made no reference to the vast throngs which attended the communion seasons for the preaching of the Word. In 1749 Whitefield reckoned the number assembled in Haworth churchyard for this purpose to be about 6,000. Not long before his death in 1763, Grimshaw stood with John Newton on a hill near Haworth and gave this testimony to his younger friend:

'When I first came into this country, if I had gone half a day's journey on horseback towards the east, west, north, and south, I could not meet with nor hear of one truly serious person: and now, through the blessing of God, besides a considerable number whom I have seen or known to have departed this life rejoicing in the Lord's salvation, and besides five dissenting congregations of which the ministers, and nearly every one of the members, were first awakened under my ministry, I have still at my sacraments, according to the weather, from three to five hundred communicants, of the far greater part of whom I can give almost as particular an account as I can of myself. By my frequent visits, and converse with them, I am acquainted with their several temptations, trials, and exercises, both personal and domestic, both spiritual and temporal, almost as intimately as if I had lived in their families.'[40]

Grimshaw's work can be taken as representative of what happened in many other parishes in the Church of England. Of the numbers influenced under Whitefield it is quite impossible to conjecture. His ministry was more diffuse than that of

Wesley, and unlike his friend – who rarely worked with him after 1741 on account of his hostility to Calvinism – Whitefield laid no foundations for a new church organization. The harvest of revival under his preaching was consequently garnered by many – by Church of England parishes, by new congregations such as his own 'Tabernacle' at Moorfields, London, and by a number of the older Nonconformist congregations which came to benefit by the awakening. There is certainly evidence to show that the number of persons thus brought into the kingdom of God and not associated with the Arminian branch of Methodism was very great indeed. In 1742 Whitefield speaks of 350 'awakened souls' being received in one day at the Tabernacle and, after a period of open-air preaching in London in May of the same year, of a thousand notes given him by persons 'convinced, converted, or comforted'.[41] No wonder he wrote, 'We have had a glorious *Easter*, or rather a *Pentecost*.' His letters of later years give many similar details, as the following written from Kendal on June 21, 1750, will indicate:

'I arrived at Kendal this morning, where I shall preach this evening. An entrance is now made into Westmoreland. Pen cannot well describe the glorious scenes that have opened in Yorkshire, etc. Perhaps, since I saw you, seventy or eighty thousand have attended the word preached, in divers places . . . '[42]

Six years later Charles Wesley was preaching in Birstal, Yorkshire, and noted, 'My congregation was less by a thousand or two, through George Whitefield preaching today at Haworth.'[43]

Two preachers on the same day, in the same area of the country, drawing congregations which could be numbered in thousands gives some idea of the percentage of the population affected by the gospel! And these figures, it should be remembered, occurred in a century when, though the population increased from five and a half to over nine million, it was far smaller than at the present day. If the same percentage of today's population in England were so touched by revival it would be enough to make a majority of the nation attenders at evangelical churches. This is precisely what happened two hundred years ago. We read, for instance, of the Mayor of Liverpool writing to the Home Office in 1792 to urge the building of more Anglican churches in the villages of Merseyside. The reason he gave was this:

'In all these places are nothing but Methodist and other Meeting houses and as all the people in the country are in general dispos'd to go to some place of worship on the Sunday, they go to these places because there is none other . . .'[44]

Similar testimonies could be given to the habit of church-going which became characteristic of much of the country after the evangelical revival.

Hardly any figures seem to exist on the numbers reaped in the south and west of Wales during the revivals seen in the days of Rowland and his colleagues. It is said that by 1746 Rowland had three thousand communicants in his small Cardiganshire parishes, and that some hundred ministers owed their conversion to him. Edward Morgan was of the opinion that 'There are thousands, yea tens of thousands now in heaven, who acknowledge him as their father in Christ.' As Morgan himself, however, tells us, the truth is that though the revivals in South Wales extended generally over several counties, 'they were not recorded, except in heaven'.[45] The spread of these revivals to North Wales in 1791 has already been noted. For many years thereafter an extraordinary degree of blessing attended the preaching in the North. In August, 1793, Thomas Charles wrote: 'A very general awakening now prevails through the greatest part of the county of Caernarvon. Some hundreds have been effectually brought to the Lord. In some parts of Anglesey and Denbighshire a great work is going on.'

The effects of preaching in this period read like a page from apostolic history as once more it could often be said that 'fear came upon every soul'. The preaching of John Elias at Rhuddlan, Flintshire, in the summer of 1802, which cowed evil-doers for many years to come;[46] the revival at Beddgelert in 1818 which gave such an impetus to religion in the Arvon district of Caernarvonshire that existing chapels had to be enlarged and twelve new ones built;[47] the awakening through a sermon of Michael Roberts at Llanidloes in April, 1819, which added a thousand to the churches of Montgomeryshire;[48] the sermon of Elias on 'Let God arise, let his enemies be scattered', at Pwllheli in 1832, from which it is said there was a membership increase in the churches of Caernarvonshire of no less than 2,500 persons[49] – all these events and many more were long treasured in the memories of the Christians of North Wales.

In the case of Wales a further evidence exists to show that these numbers represented no mere temporary excitement. When the Society for Promoting Christian Knowledge brought out an edition of 10,000 copies of the Welsh Bible they were sold out in six months and it was judged that not one-fourth part of the need had been met! This demand had considerable influence in leading to the formation of the British and Foreign Bible Society, which in only fifteen years had to print seven editions of the Bible, and seven of the New Testament. Their first edition of the Welsh Bible ran to 20,000 copies, the quantity of the second and third is not recorded. The New Testaments amounted to 45,000 copies. And all these were sold almost as rapidly as they came out![50] It is no wonder that Thomas Charles could write in 1811, 'The whole country is in a manner emerging from a state of great ignorance and barbarity, to civilization and piety.'[51]

*   *   *

Of all the lessons which the eighteenth-century revival taught the Church, none was more important than the practical demonstration that scriptural preaching, accompanied by the power of the Spirit of God, is *the* divine means for extending the kingdom of Christ. This was to be the significant theme of Rowland Hill's sermon when he preached at the formation of the first interdenominational missionary society of modern times in 1795. Having spoken of the glorious revivals of the past, he declared: 'What has been done, shall be done. God will ever stand by his own truth, and if he be for us, who can be against us? Preaching the Gospel of the kingdom does all the work.'[52]

The leaders of the eighteenth-century awakening did not live to see the new missionary age which was dawning when Hill spoke, but in redirecting the Church to her true work they had recovered principles which were as relevant to the world as to the English-speaking nations. All that was needed was men of faith and prayer who, understanding these principles, would go out to apply them to all the world. The hope, nurtured in seventeenth-century Britain, recovered in the days of Whitefield, was about to penetrate the darkest places of heathendom.

Charles Wesley both celebrated the revival and anticipated what was to come when he wrote in 1749:

> *When He first the work begun,*
> *Small and feeble was His day:*
> *Now the word doth swiftly run,*
> *Now it wins its widening way:*
> *More and more it spreads and grows,*
> *Ever mighty to prevail;*
> *Sin's strongholds it now o'erthrows,*
> *Shakes the trembling gates of hell.*

VII

WORLD MISSIONS:
THE HOPE SPREADING

David Bogue whose proclamation of the duty to
evangelize all nations contributed largely to a
turning-point in Church history

'I well remember the late Rev. Andrew Fuller reporting, at my father's house, in the year 1792, the impression which had been made upon an association meeting of his own denomination, by Mr. Carey's sermon on the address to the church (Isaiah 54.2), *Lengthen thy cords, and strengthen thy stakes*; from which Mr. C. pressed the two propositions, that we should *expect* great things, and *attempt* great things. Hence originated the Baptist Missionary Society. The London Missionary Society followed; then the Church Missionary Society; then the Bible Society; and, in succession, various other institutions, all, we trust, destined to contribute their share to that great and blessed consummation,

> *'By prophecy's unerring finger mark'd*
> *To faith's strong eye.'*

JOHN SCOTT

The Life of Thomas Scott, 1836, 115

'If I should die, I shall be able to say to the rising generation, *God will surely visit you.* A work is begun that will not end till the world be subdued to the Saviour. We have done a little for him, accompanied with much evil; the Lord grant that that may not be laid to our charge in that day.'

ANDREW FULLER

in a letter, May, 1812.
Life of Andrew Fuller, John Ryland, 1816, 536

FOR a decade and more in the mid-seventeenth century England had appeared to be on the threshold of an era of worldwide missionary endeavour. But the vision – clear to the eyes of faith in the 1640's – was to recede. Cromwell's plans to divide the world into four great mission-fields were of no interest to the government which succeeded his, and a century and a half had to pass before the Churches were ready to take the gospel to all the ends of the earth. The indifference to doctrine in the Established Church together with the struggles and consequent decline of Nonconformity make it a matter of no surprise that missionary work practically stood still after 1660. John Eliot's name, instead of being found at the head of a succession of missionaries endowed with a common purpose, remained practically alone in missionary annals until eighty years later when the Great Awakening in New England saw his mantle passed on to David Brainerd.

Yet elsewhere in Protestantism there were already foreshadowings of what was to come. Amid the cold rationalism into which Lutheranism had fallen in Germany, Philipp Jacob Spener (1635–1705) relit the fire of evangelical piety and simultaneously called the Church to her missionary obligation. Spener was followed by August Hermann Francke, Professor of Theology at Halle, who sought to make that ancient university not only a 'seat of wisdom and piety'[1] but a centre for missionary purposes. When the King of Denmark required missionaries for Danish colonies in India in 1705 it was Francke who supplied two men of sterling worth – the first of a long line of eminent men who were to go overseas from Halle.

Of the disciples of Spener and Francke who were to remain at home, none was more eminent than John Albert Bengel (1687–1752). It is striking to find in Bengel both the same general views of the prophetic future of the Church of Christ as we have seen in the English Puritans and also a like insistence upon missionary endeavour. 'The approach of better times for Christianity', he writes, 'may be compared to the gradual peep of verdure through the dissolving snow, with here and there a green patch more or less conspicuous. The large wintry covering spread over all the nations, and which *we* are waiting to see dissolved, consists of Mohammedism, Popery and Infidelity. These are alike, as amounting to one and the same usurpation over immortal souls.'[2] All such obstacles to the incoming of the Gentiles 'will be broken through at the proper time', and when an abundance (Bengel's interpretation of 'fulness' in Romans 11.12 and 25) of the Gentiles have been converted 'the hardening of Israel will terminate'. The full conversion of Israel will then lead to the wider blessing of the world.[3]

'At present', he wrote in 1740, 'the age of missions to the heathen and to the Jews is not fully arrived. . . . But though it is too early for the *general* conversion of Jews and Gentiles, it appears a sin of omission on the part of Protestant churches, that they have not begun long ago to send missions to both. I, at least, cannot help thinking, that endeavours of this kind would have been far more noble, than the hitherto excessive painstaking of Protestants to settle every subtle question in polemical divinity, or rather, to gain themselves only credit and celebrity in controversy.'[4]

From Halle, however, a stream of missionary influence far wider than the Danish mission of 1705 was to ensue. As an infant in his grandmother's castle of Gross-Hennersdorf in Saxony, Count Zinzendorf met the saintly Spener. A few years later he heard read in the Great Room of the Castle reports from the Halle missionaries. 'There and then,' he later recorded, 'the first missionary impulse arose in my soul'[5] The impulse became a settled purpose during Zinzendorf's six years of studying at Francke's school at Halle (1710–16). He writes of a solemn covenant made with a friend in 1715, 'We resolved to do all in our power for the conversion of the heathen, especially for those for whom no one else cared.' In 1722 Zinzendorf gave shelter on his lands at Herrnhut to Moravian Christians expelled from Austria, and it was from the humble and fervent community then formed that ten years later the first Moravian missionaries left for the West Indies.

In 1736, as an unsuccessful missionary to Georgia, John Wesley first met the Moravians. After his return to England in 1738 – 'I went to America to convert the Indians; but oh, who shall convert me?' – it was from the Moravians that much of his new light came. At Herrnhut Zinzendorf told him: 'The word of reconciliation which the apostles preached, as the foundation of all they taught, was: That we are reconciled to God, not by our own works, not by our own righteousness, but wholly and solely by the blood of Christ.'

This was now the universal message which the Methodists were to preach, and of the distant consequences one of the most important was the departure of Dr. Thomas Coke in 1784 with the first Wesleyan missionaries to America. In 1813, at the age of sixty-six Coke was still working tirelessly for missions. In that year he laid before the Methodist Conference 'the grand duty of preaching the Gospel of the Grace of God to the perishing millions of the East' and proposed that he should lead a party of missionaries to India. The dissension of his brethren was countered with the burning words, 'If you will not let me go, you will break my heart!'[6] Leaving England the same year, Coke died on the last stage of the voyage to Bombay and was buried at sea. His companions, three missionaries for Ceylon, two for India and one for Java, laid the foundations of Wesleyan missions in the Far East.

Coke was used to turn others, outside his own denomination, to behold the world's need, one of the most important examples of his influence being Samuel Pearce, whose name will recur later in this story. Pearce writes:

'I do not remember any wish for foreign service, till I heard Dr. Coke preach at one of Mr. Wesley's chapels, from Psalm 68.31: "Ethiopia shall soon stretch out her hands unto God." Then it was that, in Mr. Horne's phrase, 'I felt a passion for missions.' Then I felt an interest in the state of the heathen world far more deep and permanent than before, and seriously thought how I could best promote their obtaining the know-ledge of the crucified Jesus.'[7]

Though Moravian–Wesleyan influence was thus an impor-tant contributing factor, in the rise of the new missionary era it was not, however, from this source that the great momentum for foreign missions came. For this we must look elsewhere and the facts are not hard to find.

*　　*　　*

In and after the 1790's there arose in Britain a series of new missionary societies, which were to be so strongly supported that for more than a century Britain was to remain in the foremost place in the world-wide spread of true Christianity. This small country down to 1900, and beyond, was to contri-bute more men and more money to the missionary cause than any other nation.* Reflecting on this position of leadership in his preface to Robe's *Narrative of the Revival of Religion*, reissued in 1839, Robert Buchanan spoke of the opportunity given to Britain 'to bring an influence to bear on the rest of the world, unexampled perhaps in the history of mankind'. He further writes:

'Britain is manifestly at this moment the citadel of the Christian world. . . . Britain's Christianity and Britain's singu-larly favoured position together, appear in the eye of the thoughtful Christian like the streak of light which glimmers at early dawn along the horizon's verge. Let the Spirit of God give

---

* Of the 13,607 Protestant foreign missionaries in 1900, 5,901 were from the British Isles, and 4,110 from the United States. In that same year, of the $17,161,092 contributed to Protestant foreign missions, $8,225,645 was from the British Isles and $5,403,048 from the United States. *Ecumenical Missionary Conference*, New York, 1900, vol. 2, 424. Quoted by K. S. Latourette, *A History of the Expansion of Christianity*, 1945, vol. 4, 95.

William Carey

Rowland Hill, 1744–1833, converted while a school-boy at Eton, became an evangelist in the footsteps of Whitefield and was, on that account, refused ordination to the priesthood of the Church of England. For fifty years after its opening in 1783 he ministered at the Surrey Chapel, London [below] and took a leading part in the formation of the London Missionary Society which he long continued to urge forward 'in its career of holy benevolent effort for the salvation of miserable and guilty millions of the human race'. An annual anniversary collection for the L.M.S. at the Surrey Chapel 'seldom averaged less than four hundred pounds'.

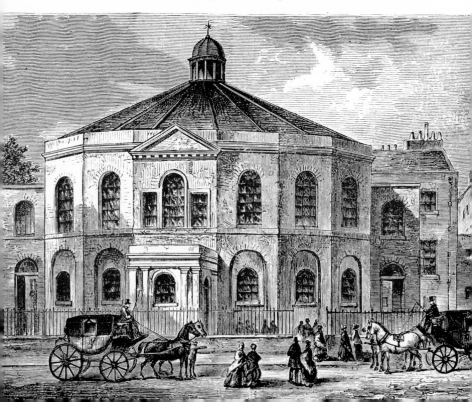

Alexander Duff at the age of thirty

John Love

The Albury Park Conference of 1826. This reconstruction of the
first prophetic conference of the nineteenth century drawn by H. Anderson,
shows Henry Drummond, the owner of Albury, addressing Hugh
M'Neile at the head of the table. Irving (also portrayed below) is facing
Drummond and on his right is Daniel Wilson, later Bishop of India.

the impulse to our Christianity, causing it to spread more widely, and burn more brightly here, and we can see nothing exaggerated or over sanguine in the hope that the light now gathering behind the mountains of Britain, shall arise like the morning sun, and pour out a flood of glory over the whole habitable earth.'

This attitude, shared by so many at the time Buchanan wrote, was not unconnected with a recognition of such providences as the advance of the Industrial Revolution and the spread of the Empire which had given Britain rule over many millions across the globe. Yet it was not from wealth, machines and commerce that the great momentum came. We believe it can be conclusively shown that the inspiration which gave rise to the first missionary societies of the modern era was nothing other than the doctrine and outlook which, revitalized by the eighteenth-century revival, had come down from the Puritans.

In the transmission of this inheritance from the seventeenth century to the pioneers of the new missionary age which dawned at the end of the eighteenth, the connecting links were, supremely, George Whitefield and Jonathan Edwards. In the late 1730's it was from such Puritan divinity as Matthew Henry's Commentary that Whitefield learned much of his theology; his subsequent thirteen crossings of the Atlantic, his preaching to Negroes and to all classes of hearers witnessed to his contemporaries and to the following generation what that theology could inspire. There is often to be found in Whitefield's letters such expressions as this: 'My soul is athirst for the salvation of poor sinners. These words, "Go ye into all the world, and preach the gospel to every creature, &c." have been particularly pressed upon my heart.'[8] Similarly, Edwards, not simply by his preaching in the Great Awakening in America, but more specifically by his books reasserting the experimental and doctrinal Calvinism of the Puritans, by his *Life and Diary of the Rev. David Brainerd* (1749), and by the witness of his last seven years spent as a missionary to the Indians and whites at a frontier settlement, gave a lead to posterity which was to be all-important.

L   [135]

The evangelical Anglican party which Whitefield did so much to establish, and which was born of revivals at the parish level, was characterized in its second generation by its attention to foreign missions. Thomas Haweis, Thomas Scott, John Venn and Charles Simeon were leaders among the many in the Established Church who shared Whitefield's outlook. And so united were they in doctrine that in 1786 Wesley's Methodist Conference acknowledged 'the fact that nearly all the converted clergymen in the kingdom were Calvinists'.[9] In that same year the Anglicans had designated a chaplain to Australia and India and sought, through the aid of the newly converted William Wilberforce, to gain government backing for a 'great official Church Mission to India'.[10] The bid failed. At about the same time the hopes of others were also meeting with disappointment, and in this connection mention must be made of the endeavours of David Bogue.

Bogue is one of the greatest of the forgotten figures of Church history. Born in Berwickshire in 1750, and converted while still a child, Bogue trained at Edinburgh University and Divinity Hall for the ministry of the Church of Scotland. But the evil of patronage which placed the presentation of the churches in the hands of gentry blocked his way. He thus came south and commenced preaching in London in 1772. In 1777 he was called to the Independent Church at Gosport, a seaport on the west side of Portsmouth. A powerful preacher and a man of prayer, Bogue's influence soon grew. In 1789 a London Nonconformist banker arranged to meet the expenses of three students who would be trained by Bogue for the ministry. From this insignificant beginning there commenced what was to be one of the most influential theological schools in Nonconformist history.

On March 30, 1792, Bogue had the opportunity of preaching the annual sermon in London of the Society in Scotland for Propagating Christian Knowledge. This Society, like the Society for Promoting Christian Knowledge (S.P.C.K.) and the Society for the Propagation of the Gospel in Foreign Parts (S.P.G.), had been founded at the beginning of the century with an express missionary purpose. Yet, despite royal patronage, the subscriptions of the nobility and the general approval of clergy, these agencies seem to have made comparatively little impression abroad. Their British personnel had indeed only attempted work in the colonies of North America. It was the S.P.G. which had sent John Wesley on a salary of £50 a year to Georgia in 1735 – ignorant though he then was of the gospel. The Scottish Society had the honoured name of David Brainerd on the roll of its early missionaries, but in the near half century which had passed since Brainerd's death it seems to have given little attention to what was involved in that honoured missionary's prayer, 'that God might be known to be God in the whole earth'. Now in 1792, David Bogue stood before the Society as an impassioned advocate of the wider vision. His sermon, based on the text 'Thy kingdom come', was in stark contrast to the parochialism and complacency reflected in earlier annual sermons preached for the same Society:

'We call ourselves the disciples of Christ: but is it owing to the coldness of the zeal of Christians for the glory of God and the salvation of their fellow-creatures, that in so great a part of the world the darkness of paganism envelops the people? . . . Had we employed our most active endeavours for the conversion of the heathens, and had God frowned on the attempt in every place, we might have sat down with some degree of quietness of mind, concluding that the time to favour them was not yet come. But this is far from being the case. We have been slothful, I wish we may not also be found wicked servants. To our coldness and want of zeal it is owing that millions of our fellow-creatures are still sitting in darkness and in the shadow of death. And shall we sit unconcerned under such a charge? God forbid! . . . We pray daily for the conversion of the heathen, and for the glory of the latter days. So far we do well. But if there be a plan proposed by which we may be instrumental in conveying the gospel to them, our prayers, if unaccompanied with exertions to carry the plan into execution, are nothing better than hypocrisy. . . .

'Great good has been done by the Society. . . . In the northern parts of this kingdom it has been peculiarly successful. . . . The Society can likewise boast of many hundreds of converts among the rude tribes of Indians in North America. . . . And ought it not to be our earnest wish that this noble work may be continued, and may increase? I confess to you I am anxious to promote it; and I appear here this day before you as an advocate for the heathen tribes in America, in Africa and in Asia. . . . I ardently wish to see the Society extend its efforts for propagating the gospel in every quarter of the globe.'[11]

The lead which Bogue clearly hoped the Society would give – he specified their commencing work in Africa – was not forthcoming. Two years later in September, 1794, he renewed his appeal, this time to the Christian public in general, in an address on Missions, published in the *Evangelical Magazine*. By that time, however, events had occurred which were already electrifying the interest of Christians and which were to set in motion endeavours, hitherto unparalleled, for the evangelization of the earth.

What had not been achieved by the Christians of London was put in hand by a few churches, poor and unknown to the wider world, in the English Midlands. There, in a back-parlour, twelve feet by ten, in the town of Kettering, twelve ministers, a student and one deacon, formed the Baptist Missionary Society on October 2, 1792. Their combined resources for the enterprise, not in cash but in promised contributions, amounted to a mere £13 2s. 6d. The one possession which secured the anticipated success was the faith given to the five leaders – John Ryland, John Sutcliff, Andrew Fuller (the first secretary), Samuel Pearce and William Carey. This faith was all the stronger for the slowness of its growth. Through the previous eight years the missionary need had been a subject of thought, discussion and prayer among the Strict Baptist pastors of the Northampton Association. Carey had joined the number of these men in 1785 when he commenced the work of the ministry in the country village of Moulton. Here he eked out his small stipend with school-mastering and shoemaking, but his thoughts were never far from the need which pressed upon him. 'His pupils', writes his biographer, 'saw sometimes a strange sight, their master moved to tears over a geography lesson, as, pointing to continents, islands and peoples, he would cry, "And these are pagans, pagans!" '[12] Andrew Fuller, his close friend, writes of this period:

'I knew Carey when he made shoes for the maintenance of his family; yet even then his mind had received an evangelical stamp, and his heart burned incessantly with desire for the salvation of the heathen . . . even then he had drawn out a map of the world, with sheets of paper pasted together, besmeared with shoemaker's wax, and the moral state of every nation depicted with his pen; even then he was constantly talking with his brethren on the practicability of introducing the gospel in all nations.'[13]

Though it is very doubtful if the story is true of the rebuke Carey is supposed to have received from the elder John Ryland when he first broached the missionary issue at the Northampton Association of ministers,[14] there were certainly few encouragements for Carey and his friends in their hope of the speedy establishment of a new work in the Far East. Carey persisted, believing with John Eliot, in whose steps he followed, that 'Prayer and pains, through faith in Jesus Christ, will do anything'. On May 31, 1792, the great turning point came. Preaching before the Northampton Association's meeting at Nottingham, Carey took as his historic text, Isaiah 54.2–3:

'Enlarge the place of thy tent, and let them
Stretch forth the curtains of thine habitations:
Spare not,
Lengthen thy cords, and
Strengthen thy stakes;
For thou shalt break forth on the right hand
  and on the left; and
Thy seed shall inherit the Gentiles, and
Make the desolate cities to be inhabited.
Fear not:'

From these words, in a sermon which has been called 'a

burning bush of missionary revelation', Carey delivered the prophet's great message, which he summarized as: 'Expect great things from God. Attempt great things for God.' The next morning the proposal was passed that a plan be prepared 'for forming a Baptist Society for propagating the Gospel among the heathens'. This was the plan which came to fruition at Kettering the following October.

In June of 1793, from the deck of the Krön Princessa Maria, Carey saw England for the last time, at the commencement of his 15,000-mile voyage to India. With him were his family of six and a colleague, John Thomas. Five months later he began his forty years' work in Bengal. The obstacles were immense. Problems of poverty and illness, overshadowed by the darker burden of a land where in Carey's words, 'ten thousand ministers would find scope for their powers', were constantly with them. Through the first five and a half years they saw not a single Indian convert. Yet though sometimes cast down, Carey's faith did not waver:

'When I left England, my hope of India's conversion was very strong; but amongst so many obstacles, it would die, unless upheld by God. Well, I have God, and His Word is true. Though the superstitions of the heathen were a thousand times stronger than they are, and the example of the Europeans a thousand times worse; though I were deserted by all and persecuted by all, yet my faith, fixed on that sure Word, would rise above all obstructions and overcome every trial. God's cause will triumph.'[15]

And again, he writes to Pearce:

'I would not abandon the Mission for all the fellowships and finest spheres in England. . . . The work, to which God has set His hands, will infallibly prosper. Christ has begun to besiege this ancient and strong fortress, and will assuredly carry it.'[16]

The first evidences of progress – the conversion of Krishna Pal in 1800, and the appearance of Carey's Bengali New Testament in 1801 – were so small as to be unnoticed by the world. But to Carey and his colleagues the Hindu's conversion was momentous; 'He was only one, but a continent was coming behind him. The divine grace which changed one Indian's heart, could obviously change a hundred thousand.'[17] Such was their interpretation of the event. The Bengali New Testament was likewise only the beginning of what they expected could be done; the Scriptures must go out in *all* the languages of India, indeed by 1806 they had conceived the purpose of translations to reach the three hundred millions of the Chinese Empire. In this spirit they wrote home, 'We only want men and money to fill this country with the knowledge of Christ. We are neither working at uncertainty nor afraid for the result.'[18] 'He *must* reign, till Satan has not an inch of territory.'[19]

With these objectives before them the Baptist missionaries regarded their base at Serampore as a 'red-hot centre from which the light and influence of Christianity might radiate throughout a gradually widening circle'.[20] By 1813 more than five hundred had been baptized – some at the cost of their lives* – and the Scriptures were being printed in fifteen languages. In 1818 a College was erected at Serampore to accommodate two hundred men who would be native evangelists or who would generally benefit from Christian education. Carey was already sixty by the time this new venture was completed, and though progress was slow when compared with the enormous need, he worked steadfastly on in hope: 'We are ready to think that our labours may operate effectually. . . . We are certain to take the fortress, if we can but persuade ourselves to sit down long enough before it. We shall reap if we faint not.'[21]

When Carey died, in 1834, he had lived to see twenty-six gospel churches planted in India, with more than forty fellow-labourers engaged in the work. He had himself translated the Scriptures or parts of them into no less than thirty-four languages, including six completed translations of the whole Bible and twenty-three of the New Testament!

Within these same forty years, following Carey's step in

* Carey was slow to accept a profession of Christianity even though the sacrifice involved was often great: 'Let nothing short of a radical change of heart satisfy you in your converts' was one of his sayings.

1792, an immense change had taken place in Britain as the best strength of the Church began to be devoted to the furtherance of the missionary cause. In 1795, the Missionary Society (later renamed the London Missionary Society) was formed, the first public meetings being attended by thousands. This interdenominational society was followed in 1799 by the Church Missionary Society, formed by the evangelical party which had arisen in the Establishment since Whitefield's day. Between 1793 and 1834 no less than thirteen British missionary societies came into being, including the Jews' Society in 1809. Writing of this amazing expansion, which he rightly traces to 'the awakenings of the seventeenth and especially of the eighteenth century',[22] the American Church historian Kenneth Scott Latourette says:

'This Protestantism was characterized by an abounding vitality and a daring unequalled in Christian history. Through it, for the first time, plans were seriously elaborated for bringing the Christian message to all men and to make the life of all mankind conform to Christian ideals. In the first century some Christians had believed it to be their obligation to "preach the Gospel to every creature". . . . Never before, however, had the followers of any faith formulated comprehensive plans covering the entire surface of the earth to make these purposes effective.'[23]

*　　*　　*

We have already stated above the conviction that the theological impetus which lay behind the new missionary era came from the Puritan divinity of the seventeenth century. As this has been so little recognized it deserves further consideration, both in regard to the general beliefs of the missionary leaders which must be classified as Calvinistic, and also in regard to their particular view of unfulfilled prophecy. In both areas, the general and the particular, the best expositions of their faith were those written some hundred or more years before their day.

On the printed page the influence of the Puritans had lived

on and many of the leaders of the eighteenth-century revival were indebted to them for their first understanding of historic Christianity. George Whitefield's debt to Matthew Henry was matched by William Grimshaw's to Thomas Brooks and John Owen; by Augustus Toplady's to Thomas Manton; and so on. Nor was this mid-eighteenth-century return to the Puritans limited to the clergy; it equally affected the common people, the change in whose reading habits is frequently alluded to by those who reported the several revivals. Samuel Blair, writing in 1744, says:

'Those awakened were much given to reading in the Holy Scriptures and other good books. Excellent books that had lain by much neglected, were then much perused and lent from one to another: and it was a peculiar satisfaction to people to find how exactly the doctrines they heard daily preached, harmonized with the doctrines maintained and taught by great and godly men in other parts and former times.'[24]

Of the same period Thomas Prince of Boston, Massachusetts, reported:

'The people seemed to have a renewed taste for those old pious and experimental writers, Mr. Hooker, Shepard, Gurnall, William Guthrie, Joseph Alleine, Isaac Ambrose, Dr. Owen and others. . . . The evangelical writings of these deceased authors, as well as of others alive, both in England, Scotland, and New England, were now read with singular pleasure; some of them reprinted and in great numbers quickly bought and studied.'[25]

In Britain many of the evangelical revival leaders personally recommended Puritan reprints. Daniel Rowland, for instance, wrote a preface to Bunyan's *Holy War*, and James Hervey gave his support to the reissue of *The Works of Robert Traill*. Whitefield, not long before his death in 1770, especially commended the books of Henry, Flavel and Owen, along with Bunyan, and these authors, he noted, 'are enquired after, and bought up, more and more every day'.[26] Of the Puritans in general, he asserted: 'Though dead, by their writings they yet speak: a peculiar unction attends them to this very hour;

and for these thirty years past I have remarked, that the more true and vital religion hath revived either at home or abroad, the more the good old puritanical writings, or the authors of a like stamp who lived and died in communion of the Church of England, have been called for.'[27]

The great popularity of these authors is evidenced by the number of times that they were reprinted. In the case of Matthew Henry, for instance, the British Museum Catalogue lists eleven editions of his Commentary and two American reprints. Of this work, it is said, 'more than two hundred thousand single volumes had been circulated up to 1840'.[28]

The Calvinistic understanding of the gospel embodied in this literature powerfully influenced the whole general thought of the later eighteenth century. Whitefield unashamedly owned his position: 'You know how strongly I assert all the doctrines of grace as contained in the Westminster Confession of Faith, and in the doctrinal Articles of the Church of England.'[29] This outspokenness contrasted markedly with the defensive and accommodating attitudes of the moderate Calvinists who had led Nonconformity in the early eighteenth century. Even more remarkable was the difference between this and the attitude of practically all Anglican clergymen before the revival who dreaded bearing the stigma of anything 'Puritan'. While Whitefield's open avowal of the old theology was not the direct cause why Henry Venn, John Berridge, Augustus Toplady, John Newton and other Churchmen became Calvinists, he was in considerable measure responsible for the general change of climate. Calvinism, far from being a thing to be apologized for, had become a source of inspiration for those engaged in the spread of the gospel.

Much could be said on this in the case of the pioneers of the Baptist Missionary Society. Carey was by upbringing a latitudinarian Anglican who, after his conversion, became a dissenter. Yet it was Thomas Scott, an Anglican of Whitefield's school, who did much to mould his convictions in the early years of his Christian life. In the autumn of 1779, when Carey first met Scott, the curate of Weston Underwood, Bucks, had just come into the public eye by the publication of his testimony *The Force of Truth.* In this he told how since his entrance into the Christian ministry his beliefs had been transformed. In fact, Scott had become an avowed defender of Calvinistic orthodoxy. In later years his Commentary upon the Bible was to be second only to Henry's in popularity. He was the author of several books, including a *History of the Synod of Dort.* This was the international Synod convened in the Netherlands in 1618 to counter the rise of Arminianism, and the five 'heads' of doctrine which it drew up, affirming the effectual redemption and final salvation of all whom God has sovereignly chosen, became known to history as the Canons of Dort. It is significant that it was a writer who wrote to defend the theology of that Synod who should have been used to put mettle into Carey's beliefs, while the latter was still a teenager, a fact which Carey always remembered with gratitude: 'Pray give my thanks to dear Mr. Scott for his history of the Synod of Dort,' he writes from India to John Ryland. 'I would write to him if I could command time. If there be anything of the work of God in my soul, I owe much of it to his preaching, when I first set out in the ways of the Lord.'[30]

Carey plainly found no inconsistency between the theology of Dort and urgent missionary endeavour. He held the same balance as characterized the Puritans. This is well illustrated in his '*Form of Agreement* respecting the *great principles* upon which the Brethren of the Mission of Serampore think it is their duty to act', drawn up in 1805. We read in the first paragraph: 'We are sure that only those who are ordained to eternal life will believe, and that God alone can add to the church such as shall be saved. Nevertheless we cannot but observe wth admiration that Paul, the great champion for the glorious doctrines of free and sovereign grace, was the most conspicuous for his personal zeal in the work of persuading men to be reconciled to God.'[31]

In the case of all the leaders of the Baptist Mission it appears that the evangelical Calvinism or Puritanism which they held was not the traditional outlook of their personal background.

Andrew Fuller, second only to Carey in his influence upon the mission, has written of how he was led to what he calls 'strict Calvinism'.[32] In one of the last letters Fuller dictated before his death in 1815 he responded warmly to the charge that some of the leaders of the Mission would have been more useful if they had paid less attention to Jonathan Edwards: 'If those who talk thus preached Christ half as much as Jonathan Edwards did, and were half as useful as he was, their usefulness would be double what it is. It is very singular that the Mission to the East should have originated with men of these principles; and without pretending to be a prophet, I may say, If ever it falls into the hands of men who talk in this strain, it will soon come to nothing.'[33] The same day as he dictated this letter, says his biographer, 'he lifted up his hands and exclaimed, "If I am saved, it will be by great and sovereign grace", which last words he repeated very emphatically – "by great and sovereign grace".'

John Ryland, another of the original five, went through the same change of outlook. 'Though the pastor of Northampton', writes James Bennett, 'had commenced his ministry on what would be called high principles, he soon joined Mr. Carey and Mr. Fuller in adopting the more just views of the reformers and puritans.'[34] Among the Puritans whom Ryland and his friends studied were Richard Blackerby (1574–1648), who had been converted under Perkins, and John Rogers. From such sources these Baptists of the Midlands strengthened their souls in the years preceding Carey's departure to India. An extract from Ryland's diary reads:

'*January 21, 1788.* – Brethren Fuller, Sutcliffe, Carey and I, kept this day as a private fast, in my study; read the Epistles to Timothy and Titus, Booth's Charge to Hopkins, Blackerby's Life in Gillies [*Historical Collections*] and Rogers of Dedham's Sixty Memorials for a Godly Life, and each prayed twice. Carey, with singular enlargement and pungency. Our chief design was to implore a revival of the power of godliness in our own souls, in the Churches, and in the Church at large.'

[146]

This return to Puritan theology explains a good deal of the abuse with which the Baptist Mission was assailed by the refined and enlightened press of that day. Carey and his brethren were dubbed 'fools, madmen, tinkers, Calvinists and schismatics'. 'Their preaching', said the opponents of Indian missions, 'is puritanical rant of the worst kind.'[35]

Precisely the same general theological convictions were in evidence in the London Missionary Society. Speaking of the new missionary movement of the 1790's, Dr. E. A. Payne writes: 'Throughout it is an evangelicalism with a strong Calvinistic strain. . . . The historian of the L.M.S. states categorically that almost all the first generation of L.M.S. missionaries would have had no difficulty whatever in signing the full Westminster Confession.'[*][36]

Some of the first leaders and pioneer missionaries of this great Society had been nurtured from childhood in the old theology. Robert Morrison, pioneer missionary to China in 1807, for instance, wrote before he commenced training: 'With respect to my principles, it will perhaps be sufficient to observe that, being educated in the doctrines of the Church of Scotland, as contained in the Westminster Confession of Faith; so far as I have been enabled to examine them as yet, I have espoused them from principle.'[37]

Others came to the same position through a revolution in their own beliefs. Such was the experience of John Love, first secretary of the Society. In his *Fathers and Founders of the London Missionary Society*, John Morrison writes of Love: 'From being an Arminian of the lowest school, he was brought, from the study of the great question of his own acceptance with God, to renounce the entire system of theology which had engaged his early speculations, and to rank himself with that section of the Church of Scotland, then a small one, in which the doctrines

* It is remarkable that during the voyage of the missionary ship, *The Duff*, to the Pacific in 1797, two of the company of missionaries were suspended from Church privileges by the majority until they renounced Arminian errors on the extent of Christ's death and on falling from grace. cf. *The History of the London Missionary Society*, Richard Lovett, 1899, vol 1, 48–9.

of the Westminster Confession were not only subscribed, but cordially believed and faithfully proclaimed.'[38]

Thus, though the L.M.S. was intended to be thoroughly inter-denominational in its principles, affirming no one system of church government, it did not disguise for a moment the conviction that the doctrines of grace, generally known as Calvinism, provided a common platform for the best missionary action. Rowland Hill was not embarrassing his colleagues when in one of the sermons which marked the formation of the L.M.S. in September, 1795, he acknowledged the commencement of overseas work by Wesley's followers but wished them a better theology. 'I heartily pray that the Arminian Methodists, so called in their mission, may send a *free grace* Gospel throughout the world.'[39]

The commitment of the Society is also illustrated by its decision to entrust the training of students for the mission field to David Bogue at Gosport. Bogue's Academy had a number of limitations. The only accommodation was that provided by his chapel, a red-brick building able to hold a thousand people, with an adjoining vestry, thirty feet by eighteen, which was used as the classroom. Students lodged in the cottages of members of the church situated nearby. Added to these practical difficulties was the fact that Bogue seems to have carried the tutorial burdens practically alone, despite his many other public commitments. Yet one thing Bogue could do thoroughly, and John Angell James, who went to Gosport at the end of 1802, tells us what it was:

'Dr. Bogue, though possessing a great mind and noble heart, was not a great scholar. His *forte* was theology – that is, the systematic theology of the Puritan school – the theology of Owen, Bates, Charnock, Howe and Baxter, together with the foreign divines, Turretin, Witsius, Pictet and Jonathan Edwards. . . . We certainly acquired a great deal of acquaintance with old divinity, and a relish for the writers and their works of bygone times.'[40]

Listed among the practical matters of ministerial ethics which Bogue dealt with is the question, 'What proportion as

to expense ought a minister's library to bear to his furniture?'
Whether James was following the advice given on this question
when he paid £3 13s. 6d. for Thomas Manton's Works in 1805
we are not told! It was a princely sum in view of the fact that
a student had to live on £30 a year maintenance grant.

The comparatively small group of men trained under Bogue
were to have an influence across the world upon the lives of
nations – Morrison and Milne, fellow-labourers in China,
Richard Knill in Russia; and several more outstanding men,
some of whom, like John Angell James, served the Church at
home.[41] It was a testimony to the far-flung influence of Bogue
that a translation of his publications was even in the possession
of Napoleon I at the time of his death and marked with the
Emperor's pencil. Yet this influence was, as we have sought to
show, nothing more than the force of the revitalized Puritan
divinity which the Gosport pastor represented. The driving
force of the missionary movement came from its theology.

      *   *   *

We have sought above to show that the evangelicalism of
the age of modern missions which began with Carey was in
essence that of Puritan Christianity. It remains to be said, in
conclusion, that the particular view of unfulfilled prophecy
which the leaders of the new missionary era held in common
was also, in its main features, the view which had come down
from the Puritans. This has been little recognized. Some have
traced the global aspirations of the Church in the late eighteenth century simply to a renewed optimism which the mid-
century revivals had brought. It is certainly true that revival
created a wider expectancy. Whitefield, for example, is often
to be found writing, 'O for faith to expect great, and very great
things from God!'[42] Yet this renewed confidence – epitomized
in Carey's Nottingham sermon of 1792 – was bound up with
their understanding of Scripture. So Whitefield, in 1763, after
he had seen thousands on both sides of the Atlantic brought
into the Kingdom of God, asserts that the anticipation of yet
greater revivals is a biblical duty. In his *Observations on some*

Fatal Mistakes in a book by William Warburton, Bishop of Gloucester, he writes:

'The Scriptures are so far from encouraging us to plead for a diminution of divine influence in these last days of the gospel that on the contrary, we are encouraged to expect, hope, long, and pray for larger and more extensive showers of divine influence than any former age hath ever yet experienced. For, are we not therein taught to pray, "That we may be filled with all the fulness of God", and to wait for a glorious epoch, "when the earth shall be filled with the knowledge of the Lord, as the waters cover the seas"?'[43]

This was the very belief which we have noted in an earlier chapter as inspiring missions in America in the mid-seventeenth century. It was the same faith which had been preached in the dark years of the early eighteenth century and which, when there were scarcely any signs of that darkness breaking, had been sung by Nonconformist congregations across England.

> *Jesus shall reign where'er the sun*
> *Doth his successive journeys run;*
> *His kingdom stretch from shore to shore,*
> *Till moons shall wax and wane no more.*

The hymn, published in 1719, was a paraphrase of Psalm 72 by a successor to the pastorate of Joseph Caryl and John Owen, the eminent Isaac Watts.

The remarkable unanimity of prophetic views to be found among the multiplied ranks of evangelicals after the 1740's throughout the English-speaking nations is itself indicative of the formative influence of the Puritan school. Everywhere the belief held sway that through the work of the Holy Spirit* in

---

* The indispensable necessity of the Spirit was much emphasized. Speaking of the men needed, Carey writes, 'The Missionaries must be men of great piety, prudence, courage, forbearance; of undoubted orthodoxy in their sentiments . . . and, above all, must be instant in prayer for the effusion of the Holy Spirit upon the people of their charge.' *An Enquiry into the Obligations of Christians to Use Means for the Conversion of the Heathens*, 1792, 75-6. John Venn, one of the founders of C.M.S., laid down these four

fulfilment of scripture promises, Christ would yet possess the earth. A bright day would come when, in Jonathan Edwards' words, 'the work of conversion will go on in a wonderful manner and spread more and more'. Sometime in that same future period the Jews would be called and the world enjoy a 'latter-day glory' or 'millennium', as the same period now became more commonly called.

This was the view of all the leaders in the Welsh revival. Daniel Rowland's colleague and friend, William Williams, put it to verse in his beautiful hymn of 1772:

> *O'er those gloomy hills of darkness*
> *Look, my soul; be still, and gaze;*
> *All the promises do travail*
> *With a glorious day of grace:*
> *Blessed jubilee!*
> *Let thy glorious morning dawn.*

Thomas Charles held the same hope fervently;[44] as did John Elias who could write, 'All that we have witnessed is but the dawn of a brighter day.'[45] The same is true of Scotland, as we shall subsequently notice.

The importance of this international oneness of belief should not be overlooked as it had vital consequences in terms of the help and corporate endeavour which flowed from it. In 1744, several Scottish ministers determined together to observe the first Tuesday of February, May, August and November (or the first convenient day after these dates) for special prayer. A Memorial to this effect was circulated in America and led Jonathan Edwards to publish a *Call to United Extraordinary Prayer* in 1748. Edwards' book is best known by the first words of its sub-title, the whole of which is worth giving in full, *An Humble Attempt to Promote an Explicit Agreement and Visible Union of God's people through the world, in Extraordinary Prayer, for the*

---

principles: '(1) Follow God's leading. (2) Begin on a small scale. (3) Put money in the second place, not the first; let prayer, study and mutual converse precede its collection. (4) Depend wholly upon the Spirit of God.' *History of the C.M.S.*, Eugene Stock, vol. 1, 67.

Revival of Religion and the Advancement of Christ's Kingdom on Earth, Pursuant to Scripture Promises and Prophecies concerning the Last Time. This work, which underlines the links between prayer, prophecy and the world's evangelization, was warmly received in Scotland, and endorsed by James Robe of Kilsyth in the Preface to a volume of his sermons published in 1750. In a moving plea to others to join in prayer, Robe says:

'Methinks I hear the nation of the Jews (for such is the cry of their case) crying aloud to you from their dispersion, We were once the church of God, beloved, while you were not; we have now been rejected of God more than sixteen hundred years, because of our unbelief, and for this long, very long while, wrath to the uttermost hath been lying upon us! There are many promises and predictions that we shall be grafted in again. . . . Pray therefore, and wrestle with God, that he may, according to his promise, "pour forth upon us the Spirit of grace and supplication, that we may look upon him whom we have pierced, and mourn" . . .

'Methinks, I hear the many populous kingdoms and nations of Mahometans and Pagans, dolefully crying, We are perishing, as aliens from the commonwealth of Israel, and strangers from the covenant of promises, without God, without Christ. . . . Help us with your prayers.'[46]

In April, 1784, John Erskine, Church of Scotland minister in Edinburgh and an earnest circulator of good literature, sent a copy of Edwards' *Humble Attempt* to John Ryland at Northampton. It was the year after Carey's baptism and the book played a part not only in the Northampton Association's decision to establish a prayer meeting 'for the general revival and spread of religion' but also in moulding the thought of the five young men whose crucial action in 1792 was to be a turning point in history. It was one of the 'five', John Sutcliff of Olney, who reprinted the *Humble Attempt* in 1789, and four years later, when Carey left for India, Jonathan Edwards was the treasured author whom he carried with him. Incredulous at the audacity of the Baptist Mission the *Edinburgh Review* wrote, 'We see not the slightest prospect of success; we see much danger in making the attempt.' But Carey and his brethren could see what the world saw not, and they voiced the authentic Puritan hope in their *Form of Agreement* at Serampore:

'He who raised the Scottish and brutalised Britons to sit in heavenly places in Christ Jesus, can raise these slaves of superstition, purify their hearts by faith, and make them worshippers of the one God in spirit and in truth. The promises are fully sufficient to remove our doubts, and make us anticipate that not very distant period when He will famish all the gods of India, and cause these very idolators to cast their idols to the moles and to the bats, and renounce for ever the work of their own hands.'

It would astonish the modern reader to observe just how prominent the driving power of this hope was in all the missionary activities which followed 1792. At the formation of new societies and at the thronged annual sermons it was a constant theme. It was preached at the inauguration of the L.M.S. in 1795,[47] at the meeting of the New York Missionary Society in 1797,[48] at the meeting of the Glasgow Missionary Society in 1802,[49] – these being some of the first of innumerable similar sermons. The leaders of the Church Missionary Society, 1799, held the same view no less certainly. Old Henry Venn, the friend of Whitefield, looked forward to hearing in heaven of the general conversion of the heathen.[50] John Newton, Richard Cecil and Thomas Scott (first Secretary of the C.M.S.) preached the same view of unfulfilled prophecy in London pulpits, while in Cambridge Charles Simeon communicated it, along with a profound missionary concern, to the many students who filled the pews of Trinity Church just as they had done for Richard Sibbes' preaching in the same building over a hundred and fifty years earlier.*

Best known among those who left Cambridge in Simeon's day for overseas was Henry Martyn who sailed for India in 1805.

* Richard Sibbes ministered from Trinity pulpit from 1610 to 1615, and again from 1634 to 1635. Simeon was minister of the parish for fifty-four years, 1782–1836.

His *Journals* illustrate the heroic endurance which this belief served to strengthen. After little apparent success, Martyn died at Tokat in Asia Minor, in 1812, at the age of thirty-one. But in all his labours in India and Persia as a pioneer Bible translator Martyn took the long-term view. Challenged by a Mohammedan why Christianity was so weak in the world 'if the heathen nations have been given to Christ for an inheritance', 'I rejoined', says Martyn, 'that he was not yet come to the end of things.'[51] For that end he longed. While toiling on his Persian translation of the New Testament, aided by natives who had no concept of the significance of their labour, the frail Englishman looked forward in hope: 'They are employed in a work, of the importance of which they are unconscious, and are making provision for future Persian saints, whose time is, I suppose, now near. "Roll back, ye crowded years, your thick array!" Let the long, long period of darkness and sin at last give way to the brighter hours of light and liberty, which wait on the wings of the Sun of Righteousness.'[52]

By this whole evangelical school, from whom we have been quoting in this chapter, the conversion of the Jews was also awaited with keen anticipation. Their interest, as we have seen, was world-wide, and it was indeed for that very reason that their desire for the recall of Israel was quickened, believing as they did that it would gloriously advance the gospel among the Gentiles. 'Though we do not know the time in which this conversion of Israel will come to pass,' writes Edwards, 'yet thus much we may determine by Scripture, that it will be before the glory of the Gentile part of the church shall be fully accomplished, because it is said that their coming in shall be life from the dead to the Gentiles' (Rom. 11.12, 15).[53] So Carey and Martyn, in India, tempted to weariness, thought thankfully of the promise of the Jews' ingathering.[54] So also Andrew Fuller thought it worth while at home to write his *Expository Remarks Relative to the Conversion of the Jews*, even though his primary duties concerned the Mission to India.[55] We read also of Charles Simeon, who gave much of his attention to the extension of Christ's kingdom, that the conversion of the Jews was perhaps the warmest interest of his life.[56] Once at a missionary meeting Simeon had seemed so carried away with the future of the Jews that a friend passed him a slip of paper with the question, 'Six millions of Jews and six hundred millions of Gentiles – which is the most important?' Simeon at once scribbled back, 'If the conversion of the six is to be life from the dead to the six hundred, what then?'[57]

We may say in conclusion that, given beliefs like these, there should be no surprise that the century following the 1740's witnessed the greatest outburst of praise in missionary hymnody that the world has ever heard. Isaac Watts and William Williams were followed by a whole host of writers who breathe the same spirit: Edward Perronet's 'All hail the power of Jesu's Name', William Shrubsole's 'Arm of the Lord, awake! awake!', James Montgomery's 'Hail to the Lord's Anointed', Thomas Kelly's 'Zion's King shall reign victorious', Thomas Hastings' 'Hail to the brightness of Zion's glad morning' – all these, and many more, gave voice to the great hope. The most characteristic of all was perhaps Reginald Heber's 'From Greenland's icy mountains' with its lines:

> *Waft, waft, ye winds, his story*
> *And you, ye waters, roll,*
> *Till, like a sea of glory*
> *It spreads from pole to pole.*

When these hymns ceased to be sung in the faith with which they were written a memorable age had passed away. Why that change in evangelical belief came about will be the subject of a later chapter.

VIII

THE HOPE AND
SCOTLAND'S MISSIONARIES

*The manse of the parish of Kilsyth where
James Robe ministered (1713–1753) and
where W. C. Burns was born in 1815.
When Burns died in Manchuria in 1868
his grave was 'the advanced post of
Christian conquests'*

'The missionary from Livingstonia tells us that Scotland is so diminutive that, were its surface divided into portions like the segments of a dissected map, it could be all packed within the limits of Lake Nyassa. That lake is so small, though 350 miles long, as almost to require to be searched for, as we scan the map of Africa. Yet see what God has already done by Scotland. Scotland, small as she is, has already told on the destinies of the world. Why should she not gird herself for a new enterprise on behalf of the noblest object that can engage the enthusiasm of man – the salvation of millions.'

ALEXANDER N. SOMERVILLE, 1886,
A Modern Apostle, A. N. Somerville, George Smith, 311

'Oh, what promises are ours, if we had only faith to grasp them! What a promise is that in the great commission – Go and do so, and lo I am with you, even to the end of the world! We go forth amongst the hundreds of millions of the nations, we find gigantic systems of idolatry and superstition consolidated for 3,000 years, heaped up and multiplied for ages upon ages, until they tower as high mountains, mightier than the Himalaya. . . . But what does faith say? Believe and it shall be. And if any Church on earth can realize that faith, to that Church will the honour belong of evangelizing the nations, and bringing down the mountains.'

ALEXANDER DUFF
Speech of the Rev. Dr. Duff on Foreign Missions and America,
May 29, 1854, 19

SPEAKING of the movement for the reformation of the Church which issued in the Westminster Confession and Catechisms in the mid-seventeenth century, Samuel Rutherford once wrote, 'Posterity will know to the second coming of Christ from whence came the first stirring of the wheels of Christ's Chariot in Britain'. But if Scotland gave the lead in the 1630's, it is equally true that England, one hundred and sixty years later, was first in preparing the way for the evangelization of the world. In the new era of missionary endeavour which began, as we have seen, in 1792, Scots had indeed played an important part. David Bogue and several of the first leaders of the London Missionary Society were from north of the Border. Yet the Scottish Church itself had taken no initiative, and for a while it seemed that the call to the North was simply for individuals to assist in a supporting role the work begun in England.

In the history of world missions, however, a greater part was in store for Scotland, and though we can only sketch the outline in these pages the story is one which cannot be omitted from a consideration of the effect of 'the hope' upon history. Nowhere does the outlook inherited from the Puritan era come to a more powerful or effective expression than in Scotland's missionaries of the nineteenth century.

The first attempt to move the Church of Scotland to give new attention to foreign missions occurred in 1796 when the

Synods of Moray and of Fife both laid overtures before the General Assembly in Edinburgh. These overtures petitioned the Assembly to consider the methods by which the gospel was to be spread over the world. The debate which resulted on May 27 of that year has been called 'the most extraordinary perhaps, and the richest in character that ever originated in the Courts of a Protestant Church'.[1] Its drama arose from the composition of that Assembly, for its members represented very different and far from homogeneous parties.

On one side there were evangelicals such as William McBean, minister of Alves, and John Erskine, joint minister of Old Greyfriars, Edinburgh, from 1767 until his death in 1803, in his eighty-second year. Erskine's ministerial work had begun in the stirring revival period of the early 1740's and he owed a personal debt to Whitefield's example. We have noted how forty years later, this Edinburgh minister had provided the Baptists of the Northampton Association with Jonathan Edwards' books. McBean was thirty-seven years old at the time of the great debate of 1796. He had been brought up under the ministry of James Calder who served the Inverness-shire parish of Croy from about 1747 until his death in 1775 and whose diaries, which record some of the years of revival in that parish, are among the finest devotional literature.[2]

On the other side were men of a very different school, 'the Moderates', whose cold morality and anti-evangelical policies had long brought a blight which, despite the mid-century awakening, still remained in many parishes. Among their leaders was Dr. Alexander Carlyle of Inveresk. The character of 'Jupiter' Carlyle, as he was nicknamed, may well be judged by an incident which occurred during another General Assembly. The Moderates were just about to carry through some business favourable to their interests when Dr. Jardine, a friend of Carlyle's, suddenly collapsed. Amid commotion he was carried out and it seemed that, in view of the general concern, voting would have to be deferred. Fearing the consequences of a delay, Carlyle made his way out, ascertained that Jardine was dead, and returned forthwith to assure the Assembly that there were hopes of his recovery! The voting then proceeded. 'One hardly knows', comments W. G. Blaikie, 'which was worst; the moral recklessness that could utter such a lie in the house of God, and in the presence of death; or the moral levity that could see his friend hurried into eternity with such awful suddenness, and at the very moment, devise a mean and lying trick to make sure of a party motion.'[3]

In the famous debate of 1796 William McBean spoke earnestly for his Synod's overture. Addressing his ministerial brethren, he reminded them how they prayed every Lord's day 'for the speedy and universal diffusion of the gospel' and that it was therefore incumbent upon them to prove their sincerity 'by shewing an example of active zeal, in bringing about this happy event'. 'Scripture prophecy,' the minister of Alves concluded, 'points our faith to the accomplishment of this promised event, and while we anticipate, it ought also to be our endeavour to hasten the time when the knowledge of the Lord shall cover the earth "as the waters cover the sea".'

This appeal was speedily countered by the Rev. Mr. Hamilton of Gladsmuir who affirmed: 'To spread abroad the knowledge of the gospel among barbarous and heathen nations seems to me highly preposterous . . . The apostle Paul preached, not to naked savages, but to the inhabitants of cultured cities.' Such a claim was too much for the conscience of John Erskine to endure in silence; rising to his feet and stretching his hand to the bookboard before the Moderator, the seventy-five year old evangelical leader exclaimed, 'Rax me that Bible!' He then proceeded to read from Acts 28, a passage which shows Paul preaching in the very kind of situation which Hamilton would have had them regard as impossible.

But Erskine's long-to-be-remembered intervention made no impression upon 'Jupiter' Carlyle, who rose to support Hamilton's motion that the two overtures on missions be dismissed. Dr. Hill, not wishing to put the Assembly in such an entirely negative position, suggested a rider to Hamilton's motion of dismissal committing them to 'resolve that they will embrace with zeal and thankfulness any future opportunity of contributing by their exertions to the propagation of the Gospel of Christ'. This expedient carried the day by a majority of fourteen and so, though apathy and unbelief had been rudely disturbed in the General Assembly of 1796, their reign was not yet broken.

Another twenty-eight years were to pass before the General Assembly in 1824 gave its formal support to foreign missions. Sinful though this delay was, it came within the overruling providence of God, for the means he had chosen to awaken the attention of Scotland to the crying needs of the overseas world had still to be fashioned.

Foremost among these means was the succession of births in Christian homes which marked the first quarter of the new century – John Wilson in 1804, John Anderson in 1805, Alexander Duff in 1806, David Livingstone and Alexander Somerville in 1813, William C. Burns in 1815, and John G. Paton in 1824 – to name but seven of a larger number whose future work was to make districts in far-off India, Africa, China and the New Hebrides household words in Scotland.

Even while these men were infants, missionary work un-attached to the Church was being organized from Scotland. The Edinburgh Missionary Society (later to be called the Scottish Missionary Society) and the Glasgow Missionary Society had both been formed in February, 1796. John Erskine preached the first sermon for the former, while John Love's return from London to Glasgow in 1800 gave added strength to the Glasgow Society. These two agencies, which had close connections with the London Missionary Society, began work in widely diverse fields: Sierra Leone, Karass (between the Caspian and the Black Sea), Jamaica, Kaffraria (South Africa) and finally India, where the first Church of Scotland minister, Donald Mitchell, landed at Bombay in January, 1823. Within eight months of Mitchell's arrival one of the many illnesses of the East had claimed his life: 'His last words,' writes D. MacKichan, 'uttered just as he was passing, breathed the hope which had guided his steps to India as a missionary of the Cross: "The earth shall be full of knowledge of the Lord. Amen and Amen." '[4]

These early beginnings, coupled with the widespread interest which the Baptist and London Missionary Societies had awakened in Scotland, led to a rising tide of zeal for overseas endeavour. Robert Haldane, a wealthy landowner, sold his estate at Airthrey near Stirling and laid aside £25,000 for missionary work: 'The object was of such magnitude,' writes his biographer, 'that, compared with it, the affairs of time appeared to sink into nothing, and no sacrifice seemed too great in order to its attainment.'[5] Robert Findlater, a Ross-shire merchant, was of humbler rank but of the same spirit. In his will, written in 1800, he appointed £100 to the London Missionary Society with this testimony: 'The Lord has much honoured that Society. It was from it that my soul first caught the blessed flame that has so often warmed my cold heart and affections since; and at this present time while I am writing, *the fire is burning* – my heart and eyes are full, viewing with joy the spreading glory of Immanuel's kingdom, when all His people's prayers, and all His Father's promises for the glory of His Kingdom, shall be fulfilled. . . . O Lord, hasten the glory of the cross of Christ among all lands, that He may see of the travail of His soul, and be satisfied!'[6]

Robert Findlater's views of the gospel were such as were being deeply impressed upon many Scottish families at this period when local revivals were common. Findlater's parents, like William McBean mentioned above, had attended the ministry of James Calder at Croy. The fragrance of that ministry was continued in that of his son, Charles Calder, who for thirty-eight years (1774–1812) was minister of Ferintosh, Ross-shire. Charles Calder was popularly known as 'the piper of one tune', for he had but one theme in his preaching, 'all was subordinated by him to the great end of setting only Christ before the eyes of sinners'. It was to Ferintosh that Robert Findlater and his family would journey on the Lord's Day and, as he tells us, Calder's preaching was the means which awakened his longing for the further extension of Christ's kingdom.[7]

[163]

On Charles Calder's death, John MacDonald, 'the Apostle of the North', succeeded him at Ferintosh.[8] His son, also John, was to go as a minister of the gospel to India in 1837. The, same connection between the power of the Spirit witnessed at home and the thrusting out of men overseas appears in many other instances. Wm. H. Burns ministered for fifty-nine years, commencing in 1800, and in his long pastorate at Kilsyth he saw a great spiritual harvest such as James Robe had witnessed in the same place in the 1740's. It was his son, William C. Burns, who died in far-off Nieu-chwang in 1868, one of the most outstanding of all the first missionaries to China's millions.[9] The work done in parishes like Ferintosh and Kilsyth moulded the men who were to be the leaders of Scottish missionary endeavour.

Another parish where the effect of a spiritual awakening was to touch a distant continent was that of Moulin in Perthshire. Until the month of June, 1796, Alexander Stewart, the minister of that parish was, like too many others of his day, a professional cleric with no personal experience of the grace of God. In that month, however, Charles Simeon of Cambridge, while passing through Perthshire, made an unpremeditated stop at Moulin, was invited to preach, and as a result the minister himself became a new man in Christ. The consequent change in his preaching and his adoption of what his critics called 'Puritan principles' was by no means generally welcomed, but God blessed the parish of Moulin with fruit hitherto absent. By the autumn of 1798 the convicting work of the Spirit was clearly manifest in the congregation and particularly in those of about twenty-five or thirty years of age. The following March, Stewart commenced a series of practical sermons on Regeneration which continued until the beginning of July. 'These', he writes, 'were attended with a more general awakening than had yet appeared amongst us. Seldom a week passed in which we did not see or hear of one, two or three persons, brought under deep concern about their souls, accompanied with strong convictions of sin, and earnest inquiry after a Saviour.'[10]

Among the young people thus drawn into the kingdom of God were James Duff and Jean Rattray who married shortly after and began life together on their farm of Auchnahyle, a mile from Pitlochrie, and in the parish of Moulin. There Alexander Duff was born to them on April 25, 1806.

We must enter into Duff's career in some detail for he was to become to nineteenth-century Scotland 'the very embodiment of missions',[11] and turning-points in Duff's life were to affect profoundly the whole missionary cause. The first influence upon the Perthshire boy as he grew up amid the grandeur of the Grampians was that of his own father, whose great interest when the day's toil was done was in the writings of the Puritan school: 'Next to the Bible my father's chief delight was in studying the works of our old divines, of which,'in time-worn editions, he had succeeded in accumulating a goodly number. These, he was wont to say, contained more of the "sap and marrow of the gospel" and had about them more of the "fragrance and flavour of Paradise", than aught more recently produced.'[12] And James Duff found no disharmony between his old books and the reawakening of missionary interest. His son wrote in later years, 'Into a general knowledge of the objects and progress of modern missions I was initiated from my early youth by my late revered father, whose catholic spirit rejoiced in tracing the triumph of the gospel in different lands.'[13]

A second powerful influence upon Duff was that of Thomas Chalmers. Chalmers, minister of Kilmany, Fife, was a brilliant product of the Moderate school, more interested in science than the Bible, until the years 1809–10, when he also experienced a saving change. Among the factors which established him in evangelical Calvinism were the reports of the Baptist missionary work in India. Little did he know at that time that he was to help train the man whom many came to regard as Carey's successor. In 1815, Chalmers was called to the Tron Church, Glasgow, and as he there became a famous preacher there was considerable surprise when in 1823 he left the crowded congregations of that city for the classrooms of St. Andrews. But Scotland, and the world, were to gain from the five years which

Chalmers spent as Professor of Moral Philosophy in the old university city. Among those who watched as the evangelical testimony of the new professor stirred the students as they had not been stirred for two hundred years was Alexander Duff, and his own spiritual life, 'which had been slumbering into formalism', was quickened into a burning enthusiasm. One result was that Duff and several fellow-students, in the session of 1824–25, founded the Students' Missionary Society. The disapproval of the university authorities was registered by the denial of any meeting-place, and so it was, as Duff's biographer tells us, that in a small schoolroom obtained in a dingy lane in St. Andrews, 'this society, noteworthy in the history of Scottish Missions as the fruitful parent of the most apostolic missionaries of the country, met first'.[14] In the following year, forty-seven-year-old Chalmers became President of the Society and the monthly meetings, at which he spoke on missions, had to be moved to the Town Hall on account of the numbers attending.

Without taking account of men who entered the home-ministry under Chalmers' influence, of the three hundred students who passed through his classes at St. Andrews, six, or two out of every hundred students, consecrated their lives to the work of Christ overseas.

Meanwhile, in the very year that the students formed their society at St. Andrews, the General Assembly had reversed its anti-missionary decision of twenty-eight years before. A committee was appointed to consider the evangelization of the heathen world. India was chosen as the first field of labour, and at length, on August 12, 1829, Alexander Duff was ordained in St. George's Church, Edinburgh, as the Church of Scotland's first missionary, 'Dr. Chalmers preaching the subsequent address with his wonted ability and fervour'.

Duff's responsibility was a formidable one. Others had gone out supported by the organization of societies, but his calling involved a new and comparatively untried concept, namely, that the Church *herself* is a missionary society. Arriving in Calcutta in 1830, he was not there long before it was apparent that members of the Church's committee at home little understood what this concept meant. In 1833 they informed their first missionary that they were calculating on a missionary income of £1,200 a year with which they hoped to support three men. From Calcutta came the reply, 'Oh, do not fix on £1,200 a year as your maximum. Put down £10,0000 without fixing any maximum at all.' An astounded committee member wrote in the margin of Duff's letter when it reached Edinburgh, 'What! is the man mad? Has the Indian sun turned his head?'[15]

From the outset Duff had thus a double work to do, the one in India, the other in Scotland. He began the former with a school in Calcutta, later to be a complete college, but at the first the work was done single-handed, including six hours a day teaching Bengali youths the English alphabet! With characteristic independence of judgment (for other missionaries, except the aged Carey, thought differently) he determined that education must come through English: 'The beliefs and habits of the peoples of India are one mass of soul-destroying error: let them perish!'[16] Later, when one Indian convert of this institution was asked what constrained him to Christ, he replied, 'The bigotry of Dr. Duff', and added that the school's founder 'could teach nothing, not even mathematics and logic, without making these an avenue to Christ'.[17]

This, then, was one part of Duff's work – confronting the heathendom of one hundred and fifty million in India. The other part, no less essential, was arousing the Church at home by assailing the general indifference and neglect which had long treated missions as an almost superfluous part of the Church's calling. It was an overruling providence which unexpectedly directed Duff to this second duty and which gave him the opportunities to address the consciences of his fellow-countrymen. Becoming seriously ill in 1834, he was put on board a homeward-bound ship by doctors who feared he might be dying. Returning to India in 1840 he was forced home again in 1850. Once more Duff went back in 1856, but seven years later he was finally obliged to leave the country which was closest to his heart.

These long intervals at home became perhaps the most extraordinary part of Duff's career. Probably never in their recorded history had the General Assembly of the Church of Scotland listened to such an address as the twenty-nine year old missionary delivered to them in 1835: 'Rising from his bed, Mr. Duff made his way to the church in time to speak in connection with the Foreign Mission Report, pushing aside all remonstrances of the friends who feared he would do himself harm. When he sat down, after two or three hours, "drenched in perspiration as if he had been dragged through the Atlantic", all his hearers, moderates and lawyers quite as much as evangelicals, were overwhelmed; all wept. After Dr. Gordon had prayed, it was found that indifference to the great cause was gone like summer snow. Those who had heard Fox and Pitt declared that they had never heard any speech to equal this "in transcendent eloquence and overpowering impressiveness".'[18]

The impression made by Duff's speech, of which 40,000 copies were printed, was immense. The *Scottish Guardian* wrote, 'It has furnished principles and information for guiding our church which will lead to entire new model of missions.'[19] It led also to the calling of another man of Duff's own calibre to do in Madras what was already being done in Calcutta. This was John Anderson, who in later years wrote of Duff's first speech on Indian missions: 'Though not privileged to hear him deliver it, we know that its statements flew like lightning through the length and breadth of Scotland, vibrated through and warmed many hearts hitherto cold to missions, and tended to produce unity among brethren standing aloof from each other. Never will we forget the day, when a few of its living fragments caught our eye in a newspaper in our quiet retreat on the banks of the Nith, near Dumfries, when suffering from great bodily weakness. It kindled a spirit within us that raised us up from our bed, and pointed, as if with the finger, to India as the field of our future labours, should it please God to spare our life and to open up the way.'[20]

By the year 1842 the Indian mission of the Church of Scotland had thirteen ordained missionaries and one unordained in India, though their influence, as one London Missionary Society missionary noted of the four in Calcutta, was equal to more: 'We want', he wrote to his home directors of the L.M.S., 'men of the stamp of our four Scottish brethren . . . the work they go through is amazing.' The mission was based on three central stations – Calcutta, Bombay (where John Wilson was the leader from 1829 until his death in 1875) and Madras, with many branch stations. In the same year, 1842, there were in the schools of the mission some 2,000 scholars and several able converts in training for the ministry, while the missionary income of the Church had reached £5,802:4:2½.[21]

The next year came the historic Disruption of the Church of Scotland when the rising tide of evangelical conviction could endure no longer the interference of patrons over the scriptural right of congregations to elect their own ministers, and 451 ministers seceded to form the Free Church of Scotland, with Thomas Chalmers as the first Moderator. All fourteen of the Indian missionaries joined the Free Church and for the next few decades there can be little question that this body became the most missionary-minded denomination in Britain. Despite the double financial burden in losing all their property both in Scotland and India, the Free Church raised missionary income to £7,282 7s. 9d. in 1845, to £10,023 0s. 11d. in 1848, and thereafter for many years it was above £10,000.[22] At the same time only her very best leaders were appointed to the convenorship of the Foreign Missions Committee.[23] The concept of the Church as a missionary society was thus approaching realization, though in Duff's estimation – as he told the Free Church General Assembly on several occasions – they were still very far short of the ideal. If ministers were supplied to Scotland in the same proportion as to India, he warned his brethren, then their homeland would have but twelve men! Speaking of all the missionaries provided by Britain, perhaps as many as 800, he declared, 'While we need one minister for every thousand of our home population, it is enough to send one for every million of the heathen . . . the

Churches in Britain have abundance and to spare, but they will not spare it; God then, I say, may some day require the blood of these millions at our hands.'[24]

Probably the most moving of all Duff's later speeches came in the Assembly of 1866, when at the age of sixty he had seen India for the last time. In a long, impassioned address he laid down the principle that God must only be served with our best, and that the finest ministers were needed at once in India, yet since his return not one ministerial candidate had applied to him for the work abroad. If, then, no young men are to be found, he told the awed Assembly, he must himself go back to-morrow to die on the banks of the Ganges – 'if this is to be formally acknowledged that we can no longer get men to go forth to work, we must be satisfied to get men to go forth as witnesses or martyrs, ready to die, and in dying to bear testimony to the grandeur of the missionary enterprise'.[25] Already moved by the sensation caused by these words the Assembly had to watch as Duff, prostrated with exhaustion from this supreme effort, left the platform. But his message was not finished; after a pause the ageing missionary resumed again and with almost overwhelming earnestness called upon his Church to greater faith and sacrifice. The voice of past history, of the glorified in heaven, of the Reformers and of those who gave Scotland her Creed and Confession, the voice of the perishing on earth and the tormented in hell, all summoned them to realize 'the great doctrine of Christ's Headship and Kingship over the whole world'. And so Duff, who had first attended a General Assembly thirty-seven years before, concluded a speech which runs to nearly thirty closely printed pages: 'Let us press forward – resolved that we shall not desist or pause in our onward cause and career of victory till it [Christ's crown] be triumphantly planted on the last citadel of the hitherto unconquered realms of heathenism.' He was then 'assisted out of the hall in a state of extreme exhaustion'.

*　　*　　*

What was the state of the missionary cause at that hour in history? In India, though conversions had been slow, the mood of Christians was one of expectation. The Free Church Mission alone had some forty stations and their colleges were now producing able native teachers and Scripture readers. In Bombay and adjoining mission stations, 1,071 converts were admitted to the Church between 1829 and 1877. By 1871 there were some forty-eight educated converts resulting from Duff's institution in Calcutta, including nine ministers. One Parsee convert, who became 'a revered minister and missionary in Western India', wrote: 'I think we may put down the year 1865 as the year in which the conviction prevailed generally among young India that of all the forms of religion Christianity is the best.' Elizabeth Hewat, who reports this, adds: 'Remarks such as, "Our children will adopt your religion", or "In thirty or forty years we shall all be Christians" were often heard.'[26] Duff had such things in mind when he told the General Assembly in 1866: 'While we cannot talk of great multitudes being converted, yet we can talk truly of individuals being everywhere turned unto the Lord; and of a prodigious work in the way of preparation, the relaxation of prejudices, the upsetting of old superstitions and obnoxious usages, and the opening up of the minds and hearts of numbers to hail something better that is coming.'[27]

At the same time matters were no less hopeful in Africa, where Robert Moffat, Scotland's first pioneer missionary in the South, had gone on behalf of the London Missionary Society in 1816. The Glasgow Missionary Society had also begun a mission in South Africa or Kaffraria (so named by Mohammedans from 'Kaffirs' – unbelievers) in the early 1820's. The greater part of the latter work passed into the hands of the Free Church in 1845 and consisted in 1866 of twenty-eight stations, the most influential of which was Lovedale (named after Dr. John Love) where a college trained 6,000 men and women by 1902.

In the 1840's, work on the West Coast of Africa, which had failed in the initial attempt by the Glasgow Missionary

Society, was resumed, this time at Calabar by the United Secession Church. At that date the great interior of Central Africa was still a blank space on the map with vast populations not only unevangelized but virtually unknown. Twenty years later the position had been transformed by the labours of the best known of all Scottish missionaries of the nineteenth century, David Livingstone.

Livingstone went out to South Africa with the L.M.S. in 1841. He was soon persuaded of the necessity to expand the mission northwards into the relatively unexplored interior. Beginning a new venture into regions beyond he discovered Lake Ngami in 1849. The years 1852–1856 were spent on his amazing first expedition when, after discovering the upper Zambesi, he turned east in search of a new route to the coast which would replace the long journey from the Cape into Central Africa. This brought him at last to the Atlantic coast, south of the Congo river, where instead of taking ship to England – a step which would have been more than justified by the state of his health – he returned on the perilous journey back to the Zambesi from whence he proceeded upon a similar journey eastwards to the Mozambique Channel!

There were some Christians who asked why a missionary should thus spend valuable time in 'wanderings', while the British press began to represent him as a great explorer, but neither understood Livingstone's great vision. Exploration was not his goal: 'Viewed in relation to my calling, the end of the geographical feat is only the beginning of the enterprise.'[28] The great object was to 'bring unknown nations into the sympathies of the Christian world'[29] and thus to introduce the gospel. He wrote in his diary in 1852:

'O Jesus, fill me with Thy love now, and I beseech Thee, accept me, and use me a little for Thy glory. I have done nothing for Thee yet, and I would like to do something. . . . I will place no value on anything I have or may possess, except in relation to the kingdom of Christ. If anything will advance the interests of that kingdom, it shall be given away or kept, only as by giving or keeping of it I shall most promote the glory of Him to whom I owe all my hopes in time and eternity.'[30]

This was Livingstone's spirit to the end. On his birthday in 1872, the year before his death, he recorded: 'My Jesus, my King, my Life, my All; I again dedicate my whole self to Thee.'[31] So far was he from civilization at the time of his death that eleven months passed before his body – carried by faithful native hands to the coast – was buried in Westminster Abbey on April 18, 1874.

His books and above all the testimony of his life had drawn the attention of the Protestant world to Africa, and a whole succession of men, including many from Scotland, came forward to lead new missions in the territories which had been discovered. The Free Church, at the initiative of James Stewart, established a new work in the area between Lake Nyasa and Northern Rhodesia – named Livingstonia; the Church of Scotland followed at Blantyre in Nyasaland; and Peter Cameron Scott of Glasgow formed the Africa Inland Mission in 1895. The dawn of a gospel day had come to the 'Dark Continent'.

*   *   *

Before this brief sketch of Scotland's part in world missions is concluded it remains to relate this subject to the theme of the book, and in doing so we shall note three things: first, that the theology of these missionaries was invariably that of the Puritans and of the Westminster Confession; second, that belief in the general conversion of the Jews was prominent in the missionary thinking of Scotland a century ago; and third, that the conviction that the gospel would triumph across the the entire globe was paramount in their missionary endeavour.

On the first, little need be said for the fact is plain. The first generation of Scots missionaries were in the great majority of cases born, like Livingstone at Blantyre, in homes where the atmosphere itself conveyed the attachment of parents to 'the old Scottish theology'. What is written of John MacDonald of India was equally true of many others: 'Trained first in the school of his father . . . and then moulded or largely influenced by the profound and spiritual views of John Owen, John Howe, and Jonathan Edwards, who were his favourite authors, his theology was massive and substantial.'[32]

In Livingstone's first letter to the Directors of the London Missionary Society, W. G. Blaikie records that 'he tells them that he had spent most of his time at sea in the study of theology', and it was through the strength of that knowledge of God that he became, in the words of the same writer, 'a prodigy of patience, faith and courage'. In one letter to his parents from the heart of Africa in 1850, he speaks of his brother Charles who in going to study at C. G. Finney's College at Oberlin had put himself under an influence alien to Puritan theology:

'Charles thinks we are not the descendants of the Puritans. I don't know what you are, but I am . . . Dr. Wardlaw says that the Scotch Independents are the descendants of the Puritans, and I suppose the pedigree is through Rowland Hill and Whitefield. But I was a member of the very church in which John Howe, the chaplain of Oliver Cromwell, preached and exercised the pastorate. I was ordained too by English Independents . . .'[33]

One more illustration of the same doctrinal orientation can be taken from Duff's life. After his final return to Scotland he was appointed, in his closing years, Professor of Evangelistic Theology at the Free Church College, Edinburgh, and in his Inaugural Address, delivered on November 7, 1867, he sought at once to point the students to that rich theological inheritance in which he and all the older generation had found their strength: 'My great anxiety is to enjoy the privilege of doing what I can, however insignificant, towards elevating the sacred cause of Missions.' To that end he exhorted them to see to it that, whether they laboured at home or abroad, they were converted men and men who drew all their teaching from the Word of God: 'Strive for yourselves to dig deep into that unfathomable mine. Or, if human help be resorted to, let it be that of the Reformers and old Puritans rather than, with a few signal exceptions, that of the modern German divines. Bear in mind the earnest counsel of the godly Brainerd – "Strive to penetrate to the bottom of Divine truths, and never be content with a superficial knowledge".'[34]

*   *   *

As this doctrinal outlook was so predominant, it is not surprising that the old conviction that Israel's future is bound up with the evangelization of the earth exerted a powerful influence in Scottish missionary thinking. With the new missionary societies of the early nineteenth century came auxiliaries with a special concern for the Jews. At one such auxiliary at Dundee in 1811, Walter Tait, a minister of Tealing, summarized the traditional belief in a sermon in which he gave three reasons why Christians should have a particular regard for the Jews:

'1. Because their salvation must be peculiarly honouring to God.

'2. Because taking a peculiar interest in the salvation of the Jews is only making a proper return for the spiritual advantages we enjoy by them.

'3. Because their final restoration must have a favourable aspect on the conversion of the whole Gentile world.'

This same belief was to be expounded and preached upon with energy and fervour for many years to come. It is to be found in the influential commentaries of Robert Haldane and Thomas Chalmers on *The Epistle to the Romans*. Sometimes whole volumes were given to it, as in Archibald Mason's *Sixteen Discourses from Romans 11.25–27*, published in 1825, and in the work, *The Conversion of the Jews*, 1839, containing the lectures of Glasgow ministers upon the subject.

By the latter date the attention of the whole country had been directed to Israel by the deputation of four Church of Scotland ministers appointed to visit Palestine in 1839 as a Mission of Inquiry into the state of the Jews.[35] Among the four was R. M. M'Cheyne who, on his return to Dundee, preached on 'To the Jew first'. Converted Israel, he declared, 'Will give life to the dead world. . . . Just as we have found, among the parched hills of Judah, that the evening dew, coming silently down, gave life to every plant, making the grass to spring and the flowers to put forth their sweetest fragrance, so shall converted Israel be when they come as dew upon a dead, dry world. "The remnant of Jacob shall be in the midst of many people as a dew from the Lord, as the showers upon the grass, that tarrieth not for man, nor waiteth for the sons of men" (Micah 5.7).'[36]

One practical result of the Mission of Inquiry was the establishment of a work among the Jews at Budapest with John Duncan and four others appointed as the Church of Scotland's first missionaries to the Jews. The work was abundantly blessed,[37] but at the Disruption Duncan was recalled by the Free Church to take the Oriental Chair in their new theological school, New College. Though disappointed at leaving the Jews, Duncan was persuaded that their interests would now receive yet more attention. Speaking of his return from the Continent in the summer of 1843 he later commented, 'I was cheered by learning from the *Witness* that the first thing our Church had done after its exodus was to take up heartily the mission to the Jews.'[38] Through the following twenty-eight years until his death in 1870, 'Rabbi' Duncan continued his work at New College and on several occasions thrilled the General Assembly of the Free Church as he pleaded the necessity of maintaining hope in the future conversion of Israel by the outpouring of the Spirit.

At the same period the Scottish missionaries to the Gentiles in India also remembered Israel's place in the unfulfilled promises of Scripture. The three outstanding Free Church missionaries in Madras, John Anderson, John Braidwood and Robert Johnston, would meet with converts and other Christians on the first Monday of the month, 'to plead for the world's conversion'. At one of these meetings Robert Johnston addressed the little gathering on *The Conversion of the Jews; and Its Bearing on the Conversion of the Gentiles.* His address was published posthumously in Edinburgh in 1853. In a Preface, Braidwood writes, 'We could not but express our conviction that the circulation of it was fitted to edify the body of Christ generally; while it would prove to all how strongly the missionaries to the Gentiles sympathize in efforts for the conversion of the Jews.' And he closes his Preface with these considerations 'to stir up our hearts to faith and prayer for Israel':

'1. *The national restoration of the Jews, and its blessed effects on the world.* For what have they been preserved, but for some wondrous end? If their lapse is the world's wealth, and their loss the wealth of the Gentiles, how much more shall their replenishment be all this? Rom. 11.12.

'2. *The Jews are the whole world's benefactors.* Through Jewish hands and eyes God has sent his lively oracles of truth to us. They penned, and they preserved the Bible.

'3. *Our Redeemer – the God-man – who has all power in heaven and earth, is their kinsman.* "He took on Him the seed of Abraham."

'4. *Viewed nationally, the Jews are the most miserable of all nations.* The Messiah wept over Jerusalem, their capital, before the curse fell on it: ought not we to weep over the accumulated progressive woe springing from the curse, and drinking up the nation's spirit for eighteen centuries?

'5. *Their covenant prospects are bright beyond all conception.* On the grand day of their realization, will anyone of us all regret that we pitied Israel apostate and outcast?'

Johnston's address closed with a quotation from Samuel Rutherford, and there can be no doubt that in mid-nineteenth-century Scottish missions the beliefs of two centuries earlier had come to their fullest practical expression.

As the century drew to its close it is true that this outlook upon history was already becoming obscured in Scotland, though there were prophetic voices which still spoke with undiminished conviction. One such aged spokesman was Alexander N. Somerville, a Free Church missionary statesman, who in the early years of the century had played as a boy with Robert M'Cheyne in Edinburgh and who later had met Duff on his first return from India. Though most of Somerville's life had been given to the Gentiles, it was of Israel's six and a half millions, and of the day when the Lord would turn again the captivity of Zion, that he spoke to the Free Church Assembly in 1887.[39] Two years later, as the invited guest of the General Assembly of the Church of Scotland, he spoke for the last time upon the same theme with words of earnest warning: 'Let the Churches of the Gentiles beware, at this late hour of the world's history, not perhaps of resisting the re-entrance of the Jews into their own privilege, but of yielding to unbelief in the promises of God, and of betraying apathy on the subject of Israel's conversion. By such neglect we shall commit a perilous mistake and incur the displeasure of the Lord.'[40]

*   *   *

In conclusion, much could be said upon how Scotland's missionaries displayed unwavering commitment to the belief that all their endeavours were towards the realization in history of the kingdom of Christ filling the whole earth. This goal would be reached, not in their day, but before the Second Advent, and it was their privilege to draw constant energy and hope from the assurance which possessed them. 'Never for a moment', Duff charged his fellow missionaries, 'lose sight of the grand ulterior object for which the Church was originally constituted, and spiritual rights and privileges conferred, viz. the conversion of the world.'[41]

There is no need, however, to elaborate on this school of belief for its outlines have already been extensively covered in the preceding chapters. But one thing which does call for emphasis is the manner in which the promises of unfulfilled prophecy affected missionary labour on the most practical level. It prepared men to face a baptism of sufferings, disappointments and set-backs with unwavering confidence in the final outcome. Thus although Sierra Leone and Karass, early fields occupied by the Scottish Societies, had to be abandoned, and four of the first six missionaries lost their health or lives in the cause, this was no deterrent to the continuance of the endeavour. John Love, preaching on 'The Glorious Prospects of the Church of Christ' for the Glasgow Missionary Society in 1802, reminded his fellow-workers that they had more than enough scriptural hope to sustain them. His text was Isaiah 49.18, 'Lift up thine eyes round about, and behold: all these gather themselves together and come to thee,' upon which he declared: 'The Spirit of promise draws the picture of a whole earth, thick set with living converts, like the sky bespangled with stars. It is a crowd, every individual of which appears rich with divine glory . . . The subject has enough in it, if brought home by the Spirit of truth, revelation and power, to form those Missionaries against whom the gates of hell shall not prevail. . . . . Those gloomy, those burning shores shall become, sooner or later, a part of the triumphal ornaments of the Christian Church.'[42]

The truth of Love's words was to be demonstrated by the calibre of the many men who were to go from Scotland. David Livingstone illustrated it when he made his momentous decision to penetrate the interior of Africa. To his faithful wife, the daughter of Robert Moffat, he wrote, '*I will go, no matter who opposes:* I know you wish as ardently as I can that all the world may be filled with the glory of the Lord.' To another he wrote, 'I am trying now to establish the Lord's kingdom in a region wider by far than Scotland. Fever seems to forbid; but I shall work for the glory of Christ's kingdom – fever or no fever.'[43]

Precisely the same persuasion can be seen in John G. Paton, pioneer with his wife to the island of Tanna in the South Pacific in 1858. Two previous missionaries had been compelled to flee from the island, while on nearby Erromanga John Williams had been martyred in 1839. Within months of their landing in this dark place Mary Paton died after childbirth, and, writes her husband, 'To crown my sorrows, and complete my loneliness, the dear baby boy was taken from me after one week's sickness.' Of the burial of these two loved ones, far off from their own land, he thus writes in his *Autobiography*:

'I built the grave round and round with coral blocks, and covered the top with beautiful white coral, broken small as gravel; and that spot became my sacred and much-frequented shrine, during all the following months and years when I laboured on for the salvation of these savage Islanders amidst difficulties, dangers and deaths. Whensoever Tanna turns to the Lord, and is won for Christ, men in after-days will find the memory of that spot still green – where with ceaseless prayers and tears I claimed that land for God in which I had "buried my dead" with faith and hope.'[44]

Such was the effect of Puritan belief upon individual lives: the isles of the sea would one day be Christ's!

Still more important, however, was the effect which the same theology had in the formulation of over-all missionary strategy. Because of their outlook upon the future all the Scottish missionary leaders took the long-term view in evangelization, that is to say, they did not regard the number of individual converts in the present as the first consideration, but rather that energy should be deployed in work which would have the maximum influence upon nations in subsequent generations. Accordingly Alexander Duff, though few could have surpassed him as a popular preacher, gave his best time in India to education because he believed that the schools, if thoroughly based on Scripture, would change the tone of society and be nurseries for the Church of the future. For the same reason he regarded his influence upon the minds of natives who might be expected to become preachers as more important than anything he could personally do by way of direct evangelism. This policy was questioned more than once and was discussed and endorsed, particularly at the Free Church Missionary Conference in Edinburgh in 1861. One powerful argument in its favour was Scotland's own spiritual history where long periods of preparation and patient sowing – in which the tone of the public mind had been gradually changed – had been succeeded by great revivals and far-reaching missionary enterprise.[45] As the Rev. Alexander B. Campbell wrote to the Conference from Madras, this was the object in view in the Indian work:

'Christian education, more than anything else, has *prepared* a large body of the people for a wide rejection of Hinduism, and for a reception of Christ as the Saviour, should it please

God graciously to pour out His Spirit from on high on this land. All history proclaims that this is the way in which God generally works. There are long seasons of preparation; the truth is spread; obstacles are removed out of the way, and then God comes in His power and turns the people to Himself. A nation is then born in a day; a little one becomes a thousand; and a small one a strong nation.'[46]

Alexander Duff put the case with his own characteristic forcefulness:

'We think not of individuals merely; we look to the masses. Spurning the notion of a present day's success and a present year's wonder, we direct our views not merely to the present, but to future generations. While you engage in directly separating as many precious atoms from the mass as the stubborn resistance to ordinary appliances can admit, we shall, with the blessing of God, devote our time and strength to the preparing of a mine and the setting of a train which shall one day explode and tear up the whole from its lowest depths.'[47]

In Africa this same long-term view was equally prominent in all Livingstone's planning. Early in his career he had to choose between concentrated missionary endeavour among the individuals of a small tribe, or the opening up of Africa – surveying the Continent, locating healthy sites for mission stations, paving the way for a civilization which would break the horrors of the slave trade and which would, by commerce, introduce a new social economy, using the products of the country to the best advantage. Livingstone followed the wider policy, not because he overlooked the need for the conversion of the individual – indeed 'probably no missionary in Africa had ever preached to so many blacks',[48] – but rather because conviction compelled him to lay the foundations for broader results in the Africa of the future. Thus as he traversed his twenty-nine-thousand miles we find such entries as this in his Journal: 'At the confluence of the Loangwa and Zambesi. Thank God for His great mercies thus far. . . . On Thy word alone I lean. But wilt Thou permit me to plead for Africa? The cause is Thine . . .'[49] Elsewhere he writes: 'I do not undervalue the importance of the conversion of the most abject creature that breathes; it is of overwhelming worth to him personally, but viewing our work of wide sowing of the good seed relatively to the harvest which will be reaped when all our heads are low, there can, I think, be no comparison.'[50]

How much the vision of the future permeated all his endeavours in the present can be seen from innumerable passages in his Journal:

'A good and attentive audience, but immediately after the service I found the Chief had retired into a hut to drink beer. . . . A minister who had not seen so much pioneer service as I have done would have been shocked to see so little effect produced by an earnest discourse concerning the future judgment, but time must be given to allow the truth to sink into the dark mind, and produce its effect. The earth shall be filled with the knowledge of the glory of the Lord – that is enough. We can afford to work in faith, for Omnipotence is pledged to fulfil the promise. . . .'[51]

'A quiet audience today. The seed being sown, the least of all seeds now, but it will grow a mighty tree. It is as it were a small stone cut out of a mountain, but it will fill the whole earth. He that believeth shall not make haste. . . . The dregs of heathenism still cleave fast to the minds of the majority. They have settled deep down into their souls, and one century will not be sufficient to elevate them to the rank of Christians in Britain. . . . [52]

'Our work and its fruits are cumulative. We work towards another state of things.[53]

'Missionaries in the midst of masses of heathenism seem like voices crying in the wilderness – Reformers before the Reformation; future missionaries will see conversions follow every sermon. We prepare the way for them. May they not forget the pioneers who worked in the thick gloom with few rays to cheer, except such as flow from faith in God's promises! We work for a glorious future which we are not destined to see. We are only morning-stars shining in the dark, but the glorious morn will break. . . .'[54]

When Livingstone was found by his natives, dead upon his knees, on May 4, 1873, it was a fitting end to such a life. He had died in the act of prayer and who can doubt that the last prayer, like so many that preceded it, had borne up to God 'this poor long downtrodden Africa'? Though his death occurred in an area where darkness and ignorance of God were universal, he had passed on with undiminished confidence in his testimony of former years: 'Missionaries do not live before their time. Their great idea of converting the world to Christ is no chimera: it is Divine. Christianity will triumph. It is equal to all it has to perform.'[55]

St. Andrews

IX

THE ECLIPSE OF THE HOPE

The funeral of the late Mr Spurgeon. Removing the coffin from the Metropolitan Tabernacle.

In the nineteenth century British evangelicalism largely lost its old expectation of the coming of greater days of revival and the funeral of C. H. Spurgeon (February, 1892) was regarded by many as the conclusion of Puritan influence

'What we are about to consider will tend to shew that, instead of permitting ourselves to hope for a continued progress of good, we must expect a progress of evil; and that the hope of the earth being filled with the knowledge of the Lord before the exercise of His judgment, and the consummation of this judgment on the earth, is delusive.

'We are to expect evil, until it becomes so flagrant that it will be necessary for the Lord to judge it . . .

'I am afraid that many a cherished feeling, dear to the children of God, has been shocked this evening; I mean, their hope that the gospel will spread by itself over the whole earth during the actual dispensation.'

> J. N. DARBY in a lecture delivered in Geneva in 1840 on 'Progress of Evil on the Earth'. *The Collected Writings of J. N. Darby*, Prophetic, vol 1, 471 and 483

'The spirit of Sandemanianism has infected many who have quitted the Establishment, and has been imparted to the Plymouth brethren in this country. Here Millenarianism, engrafted on the crab stock, is producing strange hybrid fruits. A profession of extraordinary catholicism is combined with the sectarian pride of the old Sandemanian school; and an auspicious study of the Scriptures is neutralized by the fanaticism of Millenarianism, which is nearly allied to Irvingism. . . . The Millenarianism, which is not ostensibly a term of communion, is as restless as it is fanatical, and gives to the body a character which is ominous for the future.'

> JAMES BENNETT
> *The History of Dissenters During the Last Thirty Years, 1839, 376–77*

BELIEF in a pre-millennial advent of Christ, which as
we have earlier noted found some advocates in the mid-
seventeenth century, practically disappeared from the
main-stream of evangelical thought in the century which
followed. Those who maintained it might still be found, particularly in some backwaters of Nonconformity, but the belief
had no place in the creed of the leaders of the eighteenth-
century Revival, nor in that of the men who led the missionary
movement which followed. Consequently, when the nineteenth
century dawned the cause of pre-millennialism was at a very
low ebb. David Bogue, preaching in 1813, could regard it as
one of the oddities of Church history:

'How wise and pious men could ever suppose that the saints,
whose souls are now in heaven, should, after the resurrection
of the body from the grave, descend to live on earth again;
and that Jesus Christ should quit the throne of his glory above,
and descend and reign personally over them here below, in
distinguished splendour, for a thousand years, may justly excite
our astonishment, since it is in direct opposition to the whole
tenor of the doctrinal parts of the sacred volume. Such, however, have been the opinions of some great men. Happy will
it be if we take warning from their aberrations.'[1]

Dr. Bogue, an earnest supporter of missions to the end,
died in 1825. At his last public engagement, a missionary meeting in Brighton, he closed the service with a prayer which

[187]

breathed the whole spirit of the age through which he had lived his seventy-five years and the final petitions were a fitting conclusion to his life: 'Thy kingdom come; thy will be done on earth, as it is in heaven: let all nations call the Saviour blessed, and the whole earth be filled with thy glory. Amen and Amen.' What Bogue did not know was that the year of his death was to prove memorable for the public commencement of a revolution in prophetic thought, a revolution which was to have far-flung influences upon the future of Protestant Christianity.

The leader of this change of direction was Edward Irving. Born at Annan in the south-west of Scotland in 1792, he was licensed to the ministry of the Church of Scotland in 1815 and four years later came into prominence as the assistant of Dr. Chalmers in his Glasgow parish. In 1822 Irving accepted a call to the Church of Scotland congregation at Hatton Garden, London, and within a short time he attained an extraordinary influence in the religious life of the capital. In the opinion of De Quincey, he was 'by many degrees the greatest orator of our times'. This public esteem qualified Irving for preaching the May anniversary sermon of the London Missionary Society in 1824, and a wet and dreary day did not prevent the immense Chapel, built for Whitefield in Tottenham Court Road, from being filled long before the meeting was due to commence. 'So early was the congregation assembled, that to keep so vast a throng occupied, the officials considered it wise to begin the preliminary services a full hour before the time appointed.'[2] When, three and a half hours later, Irvine was through his sermon on 'an ideal missionary' there was general astonishment and a very mixed reaction. To some the Scottish preacher was a prophet, to others a visionary quack. The officers of the Society did not approve and made their mind known in a letter from the Secretary. This was, however, only the beginning. The next year, 1825, Irving was invited to speak for the Continental Society at a similar London gathering, and on this occasion he poured all the eloquence at his command into a statement of the prophetic belief which Bogue had so recently considered an aberration of the past. The address was on 'Babylon and Infidelity Foredoomed', and in it Irving advanced the assertion that the Church, far from being on the threshold of a new era of blessing, was about to enter a 'series of thick-coming judgments and fearful perplexities' preparatory to Christ's advent and reign. This address was later published and dedicated, with a frank acknowledgement of indebtedness, to Hatley Frere, a layman of pre-millennial convictions. The link between the two men is explained by Irving's biographer:

'Several years before, Mr. Hatley Frere, one of the most sedulous of those prophetical students who were beginning to make themselves known here and there over the country, had propounded a new scheme of interpretation, for which, up to this time, he had been unable to secure the ear of the religious public. Not less confident in the truth of his scheme that nobody shared his belief in it, Mr. Frere cherished the conviction that if he could but meet some man of candid and open mind, of popularity sufficient to gain a hearing, to whom he could privately explain and open up his system, its success was certain. When Irving, all ingenuous and ready to be taught, was suddenly brought into contact with him, the student of prophecy identified him by an instant intuition.'[3]

Irving certainly had the very platform which was needed to gain the attention of his age, and at Christmas, 1825, he commenced a series of discourses on prophecy in his crowded church. His popularity was still rising, so much so that by the time his church's splendid new building was opened in Regent Square two years later a thousand sittings had already been taken.

Early in 1826, not long after Irving was launched into the study of prophecy, a work purporting to be by a converted Jew, Ben-Ezra, came into his hands. Finding this to be in general accord with his own convictions, Irving personally translated it and added a preliminary discourse of two hundred pages. The work, entitled *The Coming of Messiah in Glory and Majesty*, was published in 1827 and at once attracted widespread attention. Irving's celebrity ensured this and the fact, revealed in the preliminary discourse, that the real author was

Manuel De Lacunza (1731–1801), a South American Jesuit whose eyes had been opened to the corruption of Rome, stirred further interest.[4] The prefatory material supplied by Irving contends for the premillennial advent with great persuasiveness and also includes a statement of the development of his own convictions. Speaking of the sermons on unfulfilled prophecy which he commenced at Christmas, 1825, he writes:

'These three points of doctrine concerning the Gentile church, the future Jewish and universal church, and the personal advent of the Lord to destroy the one and to build up the other, I opened and defended out of the scriptures from Sabbath to Sabbath, with all boldness, yet with fear and trembling so far as the sweet harmony and communion of saints, in which I delight, was concerned; for at that time I did not know of one brother in the ministry who held with me in these matters, and of those to whom I broke the subject, I could not get the ear, even for preliminaries. So novel and strange a doctrine . . . such uncivil and implacable language, concerning overwhelming judgments upon the very eve of the millennial blessedness . . . such low and derogatory ideas of the risen and exalted Saviour, as that he should ever again come to visit earth, and be visibly present in it for any length of time, could not fail, and certainly did not fail, to call down upon my head all possible forms and degrees of angry and intemperate abuse. . . . But the more I examined, the more I was convinced, and resolved, though alone and single-handed, to maintain these three great heads of doctrine from the holy scriptures, against all who should undertake to uphold the commonly-received notion, that the present Gentile dispensation was about to burst forth with great verdure and fruitfulness, and fill the whole earth with the millennial blessedness, after which, to wind up and consume all, the Lord would come in the latter end.'[5]

The isolation which Irving felt on account of his new beliefs was only temporary, for he soon became the centre of a group of ministers and aristocratic laymen who were eager to crusade for what they regarded as a revived faith in scriptural truth. One of the first to be gained by Irving was Henry Drummond

(1786–1860), a London banker and also at one time High Sheriff of Surrey. After a period in Parliament, Drummond had a religious experience in 1817 which changed the course of his life; thereafter he became a mainstay of the Continental Society and other evangelical agencies. Drummond's new commitment to a pre-millennial advent had wide repercussions. On the first day of Advent, 1826, he opened his beautiful home of Albury Park, close to the main road between Guildford and Dorking, to invited guests who for a full week were to deliberate on prophetic questions. Irving was enraptured by this gathering of some twenty men and spoke afterwards of 'the six days we spent under the holy and hospitable roof of Albury House, within the chime of the church bell, and surrounded by the most picturesque and beautiful forms of nature . . . of which the least I can say is this, that no council, from that first which convened at Jerusalem until this time, seemed more governed, and conducted, and inspired by a spirit of holy communion.'6

These conferences on prophecy, the first of many in the nineteenth century, were apparently held annually at Albury until 1830, and some forty-four individuals attended one or more. Of this number, nineteen were Church of England clergy, one a Moravian, two Nonconformist ministers, four Church of Scotland ministers, eleven English laymen, and half a dozen or more others. For the most part these were persons of position and influence and through their combined efforts Irving rejoiced that 'the truth of his Son's glorious advent maketh winged speed in all the churches'.

In the early summer of 1828, Irving carried the excitement of the new message to Scotland and, while the General Assembly was meeting in Edinburgh, he gathered prodigious crowds for twelve early morning lectures on prophecy. On his first attempt even Dr. Chalmers found it quite impossible to gain admittance to one of these services. Upon the phenomena of these addresses Chalmers commented: 'Certainly there must have been a marvellous power of attraction that could turn a whole population out of their beds so early as five in the morning. The largest church in our metropolis was each time overcrowded. I heard him once; but I must just be honest enough and humble enough to acknowledge that I scarcely understood a single word, nor do I comprehend the ground on which he goes in his violent allegorizations, chiefly of the Old Testament.'[7]

The clamour to hear Irving during this visit to the North had one tragic result when the gallery of a church in Kirkcaldy collapsed shortly before Irving was due to commence a service. Some thirty-five people were killed. Recovering from the shock, Irving continued his Scottish tour and preached shortly afterwards to a full congregation at the East Church, Perth. A hearer recalled that service many years later:

'His text was taken from the 24th chapter of Matthew, regarding the coming of the Son of Man. I remember nothing of the sermon, save its general subject; but one thing I can never forget. While he was engaged in unfolding his subject, from out of a dark cloud, which obscured the church, there came forth a bright blaze of lightning and a crash of thunder. There was deep stillness in the audience. The preacher paused; and from the stillness and the gloom his powerful voice, clothed with increased solemnity, pronounced these words: "For as the lightning cometh out of the east, and shineth even unto the west, so shall the coming of the Son of Man be." You can imagine the effect.'[8]

Later the same year Irving, with characteristic confidence, wrote to Chalmers who, at the age of forty-eight, had just been appointed Professor of Divinity at Edinburgh. After advising his senior on the best type of theological training and mentioning his desire to be examined at Edinburgh for a doctorate in divinity, Irving concludes by turning to the great theme and solicits Chalmers' aid:

'I think there is some possibility of my being in Edinburgh next May. Will any of the brethren permit me the use of their church to preach a series of sermons upon the Kingdom, founded upon passages in the New Testament? . . . The second coming of the Lord is the '*point de vue*', the vantage ground, as one of my friends is wont to word it, from which, and from which alone, the whole purpose of God can be contemplated and understood.'9

Irving travelled to the northern capital again in May, 1829, and once more took a series of meetings 'with an extempore sermon of two hours, every morning at seven o'clock'. But it was without Chalmers' help and Irving could only get the use of the out-of-the-way Hope Park Chapel. This was better than the open-air to which he had expected he would be reduced. The truth is that the evangelical ministers in the North, having given Irving a patient hearing, had reached their conclusions and were acting accordingly. As early as 1827 Chalmers had observed in private correspondence, 'I really fear lest his prophecies, and the excessive length and weariness of his services, may unship him altogether.'10

By the end of 1829 all the factors were present which were to cast such shadows over the closing years of Irving's ministry. His fascination for the curious and the speculative had led him to accept conjectures on Christ's humanity which alarmed those who saw the danger of obscuring the Redeemer's perfect sinlessness; he had also used language subversive to the doctrine of imputed righteousness. To Irving, confident of the guidance of the Spirit and no longer bound by 'received traditions', the opposition he provoked was proof of the decadence he had complained of in the churches since 1825. A further proof of the unspirituality of the religious world was now added. By 1829 he was convinced that the supernatural powers present in the first century should be possessed by the Church 'as surely and richly now as in the days of the Apostles'.11 The absence of miraculous gifts was the fruit of the Church's long unbelief. Within a year the 'gift of tongues' had appeared on Clydesdale and by 1831 it was present in numerous instances in Irving's congregation at Regent Square.

In 1830 Irving was called to account for his beliefs before the London Presbytery of the Church of Scotland, but the die was already cast. Irving separated from the Presbytery. Significantly the Continental Society, the same year, carried a resolution by Henry Drummond, 'That this Meeting, impressed with the thought that the day of labour is far spent, and must soon close . . . do recognise the great duty and privilege of raising the cry throughout apostate Christendom, "Come out of her, my people, that ye be not partakers of her sins, and that ye receive not of her plagues." '[12]

Irving and a number of members adhering to him, who together became founders of the Catholic Apostolic Church, were ejected from the Regent Square building in 1832. The next year he was deposed from the ministry by the presbytery of Annan where he had been first licensed in happier days. Lesser men would have been overwhelmed by the shadows now gathering around his ministry, but the hope of Christ's impending advent and the 'miraculous' gifts which were serving to announce the nearness of the end impelled Irving onwards. It was not for long. His amazing energies were exhausted and on a preaching visit to Scotland in 1834, at the age of forty-two, death overtook him. Robert Murray M'Cheyne, then a theological student at Edinburgh, was one of thousands who thrilled at the news of his sudden death and his diary entry for November 9 is fitting:

'Heard of Edward Irving's death. I look back upon him with awe, as on the saints and martyrs of old. A holy man in spite of all his delusions and errors. He is now with his God and Saviour, whom he wronged so much, yet, I am persuaded, loved so sincerely.'[13]

Today very little remains to speak of Irving. A tomb in the crypt of Glasgow Cathedral, an impressive statue by the roadside at Annan, a desolate Irvingite church, close by Albury Park in the fields of Surrey – these are all sights hardly noticed by a generation which has forgotten his name. We have given considerable space to his ministry, however, because its influence was indeed a great turning point in the history of prophetic study, and the ideas he did so much to set in motion are now to be found all over the English-speaking world. To the fact of Irving's great influence and to its consequences we shall now turn.

The influence was probably least upon his own Scottish countrymen, yet even there some notable exceptions were to be found. Andrew Bonar, speaking in Edinburgh, in 1888, on 'The Hope of the Lord's Return', recalled how he and his brother Horatius had been led to the pre-millennial view half a century before:

'May I tell you the history of some of us in Edinburgh? It is about sixty years since I myself felt the first thrill of interest in this subject – when Edward Irving was preaching in this city. He had lectures at seven in the morning during the time of the General Assembly, and for two or three years in succession, on prophetic subjects. We used to go at six in the morning to get a good seat. But I remember what led me to decision was the calm reading of Matthew 24. That chapter decided me on this subject. I could not see a foot-breadth of room for the Millennium before Christ comes in the clouds. It is wave upon wave of tribulation till the Son of Man appears.'[14]

After their student days, Andrew and Horatius Bonar became the most eminent and saintly expositors of the pre-millennial view in Scotland. The prophetic volumes of Horatius, his years as editor of *The Quarterly Journal of Prophecy*, and his many hymns bearing on the advent theme, detached some of the younger evangelical ministers from the traditional view and gained them the nickname of 'The Evangelical Light Infantry'.[15] Little did the majority of evangelicals think that a day would come when the powerful beliefs of the old brigade in Scotland would pass almost completely away.

In England the stir produced by Irving's ministry, the Albury Conferences, and *The Morning Watch* (a prophetic journal which, under Irving's guidance, commenced in 1829), was profound and many clergy and laity of the Established Church were influenced. John Ellerton who as a child was in the midst of Anglican evangelical circles in London in the 1830's – when Irving's personal popularity was waning – records this of the Scottish preacher:

'I thought of him chiefly as an open-air preacher, for more than once on Sunday mornings, on my way to St. John's, Bedford Row, with my father, had I had a vision of that marvellous face and form, in his little movable wooden pulpit, sometimes in pouring rain, holding an umbrella over his head with one hand, as he poured forth his fervid oratory to a scanty group of hearers outside the walls of the great prison. But the favourite, the inexhaustible subject of talk among serious people was unfulfilled prophecy. The Irvingite movement (as people would call it) had popularized Millenarian speculations among many who resisted steadily all belief in the new 'Miracles' and 'Tongues'. Names now utterly forgotten of writers on prophecy formed the staple reading, I am afraid, for a good many of the religious folk among whom I lived; and their speculations turned chiefly on the chronology of the future – in what year the Jews were to be restored, Popery to be destroyed, and the Millennium to begin.'[16]

A belief in Christ's personal advent to introduce a millennium was certainly taken up by many clergy who had no sympathy with the 'miraculous gifts' and separation of Irving's Catholic Apostolic Church. While the Irvingite excesses ended the inter-denominational fellowship at first characteristic of the Albury meetings, the clergy who had been there, among them Lewis Way and Hugh McNeile, continued to spread the new prophetic belief, and the number professing it increased rapidly in the Church of England. Edward Bickersteth, eminent for his work as Secretary of the Church Missionary Society, changed his view and came to believe 'that our Lord would return to an unconverted world . . . and that after His return there would be further great events upon earth'.[17] Until his death in 1850 Bickersteth was a fluent propagator of the premillennial position. His biographer, T. R. Birks, was also a prolific writer on the same theme. Scholars, including Edward Greswell and E. B. Elliott, added the weight of learning to the cause and succeeded in winning the commitment of a number who were to become Anglican evangelical leaders in the next generation. Among the latter was J. C. Ryle.[18]

Elliott (1793–1875), in his later days incumbent of St. Mark's, Brighton, is an example of the remarkable energy devoted to advocating the pre-millennial view. It is hard to say which is more extraordinary, the massive size of his four-volume *Horae Apocalypticae* (Hours with the Apocalypse), which runs to 2,500 pages, or the fact that in eighteen years it went through five editions! Yet even by the time the first edition of this work appeared, as he tells us, a great change in thought had taken place:

'In the year 1844, the date of the first publication of my own Work on the Apocalypse, so rapid had been the progress of these views in England, that instead of its appearing a thing strange and half-heretical to hold them, as when Irving published his translation of Ben Ezra, the leaven had evidently now deeply penetrated the religious mind; and from the ineffectiveness of the opposition hitherto formally made to them, they seemed gradually advancing onward to triumph.'[19]

According to another Anglican clergyman, Mourant Brock, some seven hundred ministers of the Establishment were said to believe that Christ's coming must precede His kingdom upon earth. This was in 1845.[20] The number almost certainly increased in the latter half of the century and it is noticeable that a Prophetical Conference of pre-millennial persuasion, held in London in 1873, had the backing of such notable evangelical churchmen as the Earl of Shaftesbury, the Earl of Cavan and Lord Radstock.[21]

*   *   *

The group which was to be most closely identified with the prophetic ideas of the 1820's has still to be mentioned and this group, more than any other, was to be responsible for replacing the old Puritan outlook on the future with a new 'orthodoxy'. I refer to the Brethren whose outstanding leader on prophetic subjects was J. N. Darby. Born in London in the year 1800, Darby, at his death eighty-two years later, left forty volumes of writings and some fifteen hundred assemblies across the world, 'who looked to him as their founder or guide'.[22] The movement which these assemblies represented was distinguished from the first by its attention to unfulfilled prophecy, or perhaps 'it would be more correct to say that it was one of the main foundations of the whole system'. Through Darby's writings, which include four volumes on prophecy and five giving a *Synopsis of the Books of the Bible*, his pre-millennial prophetic system was carried to all parts of the English-speaking world. Among the many who absorbed Darby's teaching was Henry Moorhouse, an evangelist among the Brethren, who, in turn, influenced D. L. Moody.[23] Before the end of the nineteenth century Moody was probably the most esteemed evangelical figure on both sides of the Atlantic, and the Bible College named after him at Chicago became a seminary of ardent pre-millennial belief. The impact of Darby on another American, C. I. Scofield, was still more momentous, for Scofield's notes made his master's teaching on prophecy an integral part of the Reference Bible first published in 1909 and thereafter wedded to Scofield's name. Within fifty years approximately three million copies of the *Scofield Reference Bible* were printed in America, a proportionate number were issued by the Oxford University Press in Britain, and the volume had vast influence in making Darby's prophetical beliefs the norm for evangelicals in the English-speaking world.[24]

There can be no doubt that one reason for the influence of Darby's writings was their constant appeal to Scripture, and his claim, so repeatedly made, that 'express revelation' alone weighed with him. Thus at the outset of his *Brief Remarks on the Work of the Rev. David Brown, entitled, 'Christ's Second Coming, Is It Pre-Millennial?'*, Darby tells us, 'I have not thought it necessary to follow Dr. B. in all his comments on men's views. It sufficed to take up those of scripture.'[25] Brown, we are told, 'borrowed enormously' from other sources;[26] 'his reasoning is the effect of judging new truths by old traditions;'[27] confusion on prophecy is due to the fact that men 'mix up traditional theology with the word of God'.[28] Darby, on the other hand, considered it enough to connect his interpretation with particular texts of Scripture plus comments such as, 'the smallest attention to the passage makes this clear',[29] or, 'Nothing can be simpler or clearer'.[30] Again, 'There are those who must have scripture testimony for what they believe.'[31] Someone who had never read David Brown might be pardoned in supposing that if this was the state of the case, the controversy for or against pre-millennialism was just a question of being for or against Scripture.

The historical links between the origins of the Brethren and excitement created by Edward Irving puts this matter in quite a different light. David Brown, who was Irving's assistant at Regent Square before the congregation was broken up, could have pointed this out well had he chosen to answer Darby.

The first groups of Brethren in Dublin, London and Plymouth, dissatisfied with the unspirituality of the Church of England – to which in most cases they belonged – began to meet together for fellowship, additional to that of their Church connection, in the second half of the 1820's. Darby, who was in touch with the Dublin group, resigned his curacy in County Wicklow in 1828, though he did not sever all connection with the Church of England until some six years later. At the same time several other young men, including a number of university graduates, were moving in the same direction as Darby. This was just the period when Irving's influence through his preaching and writing, through the Albury Conferences and through *The Morning Watch*, was at its height. Amongst these Brethren, all earnestly exercised about spiritual things, Irving's warnings on the worldliness of organized religion and his re-iteration of the biblical teaching that the Bridegroom's advent is the blessed hope received a ready hearing.[32]

In Ireland, in particular, those influenced by Irving were in touch with future leaders of the Brethren. Lady Powers-court, whose estate of Powerscourt House was situated at Enniskerry, Co. Wicklow, attended at least one of the Albury Conferences and in 1830 she was an enthusiastic hostess to Irving when he preached in the south of Ireland.[33] This led in 1831, and two successive years, to a prophetic conference at Powerscourt House. Among the four hundred who were present from different parts of Britain at the 1831 Powerscourt Con-

ference, described by one participant as 'the élite of Evangelicals', was J. N. Darby.[34]

All the salient features of Darby's scheme are to be found in
Irving: the expectation of impending judgments upon Christendom, the imminence of Christ's advent, his consequent millennial reign upon earth – these beliefs, as we have already seen,
were those of the Scottish preacher. There were, however,
elaborations of detail. At Albury and in Irving's London
congregation a curious belief, practically unknown in earlier
Church history, had arisen, namely, that Christ's appearing
before the millennium is to be in two stages, the first, a secret
'rapture' removing the Church before a 'Great Tribulation'
smites the earth, the second his coming with his saints to set
up his kingdom.[35] This idea comes into full prominence in
Darby. He held that 'the Church' is a mystery of which only
Paul speaks. She is Christ's mystic body and will be complete
at the 'rapture'. The Jews and other Gentiles converted thereafter will never be Christ's bride: 'I deny that saints before
Christ's first coming, or after his second, are part of the Church.'
With breath-taking dogmatism Darby swept away what had
previously been axiomatic in Christian theology:

'The assertion that His mystical body is the universal family
of the redeemed, is unscriptural; all the declaration is founded
on this gross and unscriptural error, that all the saved belong
to the Church.'[36]

Such was the 'dispensational' branch of pre-millennialism,
to be held, with few exceptions, by all the Brethren and later
to be so widely popularized in the *Scofield Reference Bible*.

Another development from Irving was Darby's doctrine of
separation from ecclesiastical connections. If the Churches were
languishing in unbelief and worldliness, and if the Advent was
at hand, then the reformation of these bodies could not be the
intention of God. Darby's charge that the 'Church is in ruins'
was not made so that believers, by reassembling on a New
Testament pattern, should recover the Church to her true
position; rather it was separation to escape apostasy and to
await a speedy translation to heaven. 'I believe from Scripture

that the ruin is without remedy, that the professing church will be cut off.'[37] Darby believed his scriptural justification to be his prophetic scheme. The Church belonged to a 'dispensation' – a favourite word with Irving – which failed; God's method is not to restore a dispensation but to usher in a new one, hence the next great event would not be a reformation – to attempt it would be to fail – but the advent of Christ. Thus to expect such promised blessings as the conversion of the Jews in this dispensation was for Darby a positive delusion.

These ideas were in the process of formulation in Darby's mind in the early 1830's when, as he tells us, one of the subjects considered at Powerscourt was: 'What light does scripture throw on present events, and their moral character? What is next to be looked for and expected? Is there a prospect of a revival of Apostolic churches before the coming of Christ?'[38] By the time Darby delivered his eleven prophetical lectures on *The Hopes of the Church of God* at Geneva in 1840, these questions were firmly settled in his mind. In his fifth lecture, on the 'Progress of Evil on the Earth', he spoke thus to the inhabitants of John Calvin's old city:

'What we are about to consider will tend to shew that, instead of permitting ourselves to hope for a continued progress of good, we must expect a progress of evil; and that the hope of the earth being filled with the knowledge of the Lord before the exercise of His judgment, and the consummation of this judgment on the earth, is delusive. . . . Truly Christendom has become completely corrupted; the dispensation of the Gentiles has been found unfaithful: can it be restored? No! impossible.'[39]

The reader is now in a position to see what we mean by 'the eclipse of the hope'. Under the new teaching the expectation that the Church would yet advance to claim vast numbers of the inhabitants of the earth as Christ's inheritance was nothing less than presumption and error. The petition 'Thy kingdom come, thy will be done on earth as it is in heaven', took on an entirely different meaning as men ceased to look for its progressive fulfilment through revivals and the gospel ministry and viewed the kingdom as something to be established only by Christ's advent. And yet the constant claim of pre-millennialism was that it was restoring 'hope' to the Church. Darby and his movement, says Alexander Reese, 'filled Evangelical Christendom with the new hope'.[40] This statement proceeds on the assumption that only by belief in the immediate return of Christ can we be possessed of a true hope in that event – if his coming lies distant in time, hope must be excluded. We shall deal with this false assumption in the following chapter, but it should be noted that if this teaching was scriptural when it was first preached it is very hard to account for the passing of another one hundred and forty years. In William Blair Neatby's *History of the Plymouth Brethren*, published in 1901, Darby's charge comes full circle when the author closes his fascinating volume with these words:

'If any one had told the first Brethren that three quarters of a century might elapse and the Church be still on earth, the answer would probably have been a smile, partly of pity, partly of disapproval, wholly of incredulity. Yet so it has proved. It is impossible not to respect hopes so congenial to an ardent devotion; yet it is clear now that Brethrenism took shape under the influence of a delusion, and that that delusion was a decisive element in all its distinctive features.'[41]

The old Puritan teaching allowed both for hope in a mighty spread of the gospel in the earth and for a yearning for Christ's glorious appearing. The new teaching, by reversing the order of these two things, nullified the first hope as far as the experience of the Church on this side of the Advent is concerned, and by making the imminence of the Advent an essential part of what Paul calls 'the blessed hope', it introduced practical effects into the present life of Christians which were far from beneficial. Foremost among these effects was that a thorough pessimism about the world, and a refusal to take a long-term view of the prospects of the Church in history, came to be regarded as attitudes which were the hall-marks of orthodoxy.

There is evidence enough to support this criticism. Neatby says:

'Everybody that has a practical acquaintance with the Brethren must have noticed how strong a tendency there is amongst them to substitute for St. James's formula – "If the Lord will", – a formula of their own – "If the Lord tarry". And more and more the persuasion gained ground that the "tarrying" would not last long, and a suggestion that several years might yet intervene would be disapproved, not indeed as theoretically inadmissible, but as indicating an unworthy attitude of mind towards the Great Hope.'[42]

The same author gives us these striking words from F. W. Newman, who was with the Brethren in the early days:

'My study of the New Testament at this time had made it impossible for me to overlook that the apostles held it to be a duty of all disciples to expect a near and sudden destruction of the earth by fire, and constantly to be expecting the *return of the Lord from heaven* . . .

'The importance of this doctrine is, that it *totally forbids all working for earthly objects distant in time*; and here the Irish clergyman [Darby] threw into the same scale the entire weight of his character. For instance, if a youth had a natural aptitude for mathematics, and he asked, ought he to give himself to the study, in hope that he might diffuse a serviceable knowledge of it, or possibly even enlarge the boundaries of the science? my friend would have replied, that such a purpose was very proper, if entertained by a worldly man. Let the dead bury their dead; and let the world study the things of the world. . . . But such studies cannot be eagerly followed by the Christian, except when he yields to unbelief.'[43]

Practically no area of life remained unaffected by this eclipse of the old hope. Political and social endeavour, such as marked the lives of a number of prominent Christians in the Reformation and Puritan periods, and, in more recent times, in William Wilberforce* and the 'Clapham sect', was no longer

---

* It is interesting to note that in the Dedication of his *Evening Exercises* to William Wilberforce, William Jay, writing in the year 1831, takes up this subject and says: 'I rejoice, my dear Sir, that a person of your consideration is in the healthful number of those who, notwithstanding the contemptuous denial of some, and the gloomy forebodings of others,

regarded as legitimate evangelical activity. To engage in such pursuits savoured of the error that the world could be made better and it involved participation in a 'human' order of things. Thus we find Calvin criticized by one of the pre-millennial writers: 'Instead of animating his fellow-christians by preaching and instruction to await patiently and in faith the establishment of the kingly rule that Jesus had promised in connexion with his Parousia, he considered it his task to make the secular authorities submissive to his interpretation of the Divine commandments.'[44] To the Reformer these two things were not mutually exclusive; according to the new teaching they were.

But the teaching went further than encouraging a withdrawal from the secular. It fostered a new attitude towards foreign missions. According to the general pre-millennial view, the predictions of the prophets concerning the blessing of the whole world are not to be realized through the Church or the means of grace now at her disposal; a new order of things – a personal reign – will have to come into being before the day of salvation for humanity in general dawns. Only then will it be that 'all nations shall call him blessed' (Psa. 72.17). By this standpoint the old beliefs of Christ receiving all nations for his inheritance through the preaching of the gospel, and of the Church's working to fulfil the promises of prophecy were errors; nineteenth-century pre-millennialism had no hesitation in so describing them. In the words of B. W. Newton they were beliefs 'hastily indeed and erroneously formed'.[45]

A. A. Hodge of Princeton, who was himself a missionary in India in his early years, correctly saw the major change in missionary strategy which the new prophetic viewpoint had brought:

---

believe that real religion *has* been advancing, and *is* spreading, and *will* continue to spread, till, without any disruption of the presnt system, "the earth shall be filled with the knowledge of the Lord as the waters cover the sea: for the mouth of the Lord hath spoken it. . . ." If we are not to be weary in well-doing, we need not only exhortation, but hope, which is at once the most active as well as the most cheerful principle. Nothing so unnerves energy and slackens diligence as despondency.'

[204]

'Millenarian missionaries have a style of their own. Their theory affects their work in the way of making them seek exclusively, or chiefly, the conversion of individual souls. The true and efficient missionary method is, to aim directly, indeed, at soul winning, but at the same time to plant Christian institutions in heathen lands, which will, in time, develop according to the genius of the nationalities. English missionaries can never hope to convert the world directly by units.'[46]

Perhaps of all the tendencies of the new teaching none was worse than the effect which it had in belittling the importance of the visible Church. In the minds of the generations of evangelicals who lived before the eclipse of the hope, the conversion of the nations was related to the Church of history. Through the centuries God had been building that Church, enriching her with understanding, giving her teachers and preachers, and spreading her bounds through revivals. All this looked forward, in their view, to an era when the Church, garnering the lessons of the past and refreshed by new supplies of grace from heaven, would be more faithful to Scripture, more united in government and discipline, and more able to proclaim to all the earth the salvation of God.

The new teaching almost totally reversed this outlook. Now the Church was regarded as an institution without a future, and disparagement of church ties and duties affected the thinking of many evangelicals, even though they did not go as far as Irving and Darby in separating from all 'ecclesiastical connections'. Whatever Christian work remained to be done before the Advent belonged to new groups, or simply to earnest individuals, who often professed no connection with the Church in her historic past. Even the pastoral office was viewed as no longer necessary and the trained ministry was accordingly set aside. The study of the Church's teachers in former ages was discountenanced as turning 'to human traditions' and each Christian was not only supposed to grasp all scriptural truth without such aids but also to be able to fulfil the role hitherto expected of those appointed to the preacher's office.

This revolution in thought was, as we have seen, constantly

represented by its leaders as an advance in spiritual light. Yet, in truth, it was a repetition of what had occurred before in Church history. On a large scale it had been seen in the Montanist movement in the third century A.D., when Christians, dismayed at the laxity of the Church and at the corruption of the world, proclaimed the end of the world to be at hand. In the words of Gerhard Uhlhorn:

'The coming of the Lord was then believed to be quite near, and this hope dominated the whole life. No provision was made for a long continuance of the Church on earth, and all efforts were exclusively directed towards remaining in the world without spot, till the day of Christ's coming. The mission of Christianity to conquer the world, to permeate it with the Christian spirit, and thereby to shape it anew, had scarcely received any attention. . . . '[47]

Similarly in the eighteenth century, at the time of the Great Awakening in New England, James Davenport had withdrawn himself and his followers from all Church connections and announced that 'in a very short Time all these Things would be involv'd in devouring Flames'.[48]

From the errors of the Montanists the Church had recovered and, purged of despair, gone forward with growing might. And the deviations of a Davenport had not turned the evangelical leaders of the eighteenth century from their confidence in the victories which were yet to be given by the ascended Christ. Yet the mood of pessimism, shaken off before, had come to settle heavily upon many evangelical Christians at the dawning of the twentieth century. The growing defection from the Bible to liberalism within the Churches was, without doubt, one major cause, but the courage needed to face this defection had been sapped by the notion that pessimism over the future is Christian orthodoxy. Indeed so prevalent by then was the new prophetic teaching that the outlook of the Puritans, the eighteenth-century leaders, and the pioneers of world missions, was temporarily almost to disappear from the English-speaking churches.

X

CHRIST'S SECOND COMING:
THE BEST HOPE

*Six martyrs dying in one fire at Canterbury,
August 1555, being part of the number whom
John Knox described as those 'within the realm of
England that love the Coming of our Lord Jesus'.
Thereafter the nearness of eternity and the hope of
Christ's Advent remained themes of the Puritan
movement*

'What manner of holiness should we use, – *looking for and hastening unto the coming of the day of the Lord*, that is, dispatching and doing all for our lives against that day. Our lives should, as it were, be in a hurry after the day of judgment, as those that are to remove at quarter day, they hasten to do all against the time.'

THOMAS GOODWIN

Quoted by J. B. Williams in his Life of the Rev. Philip Henry,
1825, 140

'Hope holds up a period, even within the limits of time, a heaven compared with the present state of things, when "holiness to the Lord shall be written as upon the bells of the horses, and Zion shall become a quiet habitation!" But this, say you, is a period that *we* have but little hope of living to see. Perhaps so: still you live in prospect of a better. Blessed society, where purity and amity for ever reign! Yes, brethren, immediately on entering members of the church triumphant, you will "enter into peace", and *each one* of you "walk" for ever "in his uprightness!" '

ANDREW FULLER

'The Excellency and Utility of the Grace of Hope', 1782

> 'O hope all hope surpassing
>   For evermore to be,
> O Christ, the Church's Bridegroom,
> In Paradise with thee:
>   For soon shall break the day,
>   And shadows flee away.'

HORATIUS BONAR

'The Mountain of Myrrh'

PROBABLY the most common contemporary prejudice among orthodox Christians against the view of prophecy advocated in the preceding pages arises from the belief that it misdirects the true hope of the Church. That hope, it is said, is nothing less than the Second Advent of Christ, together with the ushering in of an eternal kingdom – it is not a temporal hope relative to the prospects of this world.

There is an understandable reason for the fear that an expectation of the extensive triumph of Christianity in history must lead to the displacement of the hope of Christ's advent. In the last hundred years much has been said of progress, of the forward march of mankind and of the establishment of the kingdom of God. On this subject both the Church and the world sometimes appeared to be saying the same thing, yet evangelicals noted that the agreement was marked by its silence in respect to Christ's return in glory and judgment to come. It was too often no more than pagan hopefulness veneered with Christianity – a false anticipation of what could be achieved by human effort and science. Kuenen, a nineteenth-century leader of Higher-Critical religious thought, spoke for this whole outlook when he said, 'Our chiliasm can be no other than a fervent and active faith in moral and social progress'.[1] There can be no doubt that the anti-supernaturalism implied in such words led many Christians to view with deep suspicion all talk of progressive victories for the gospel within history.

Except, however, for its seeming resemblance to Puritan belief on the matter of unfulfilled prophecy, the naturalistic optimism of the nineteenth century stood opposed to the old theology all along the line. Its willingness to use some of the language of the old school, and particularly its hymns, only disguised the great contradiction that existed between the Puritan hope and this outlook. Instead of dependence on divine grace and upon the powerful operations of the Holy Spirit, the new idea of progress substituted concepts of a universal fatherhood of God and of a human race basically good and therefore capable of unlimited improvement. In the same way emphasis was moved from the promises of God as the only basis for the expectation of success to the philosophy of evolution. It is not therefore surprising that when the new teaching which thus reduced the gospel to the human and temporal became prevalent, evangelical Christians came to suspect all teaching which viewed future world history as hopeful. They assumed that any belief in the world-wide success of the gospel must rest on the same errors upon which liberalism relied, and that, just as this naturalistic optimism destroyed faith in eternal salvation by giving Protestantism the false goal of an earthly Utopia, so any outlook which offers an assurance that the victories of the Church will yet be far more extensive in the world must similarly cease to represent Christ's coming as the glorious hope. But these assumptions rested upon a failure to distinguish between two different and indeed inimical schools of thought. The liberal view of progress current in the nineteenth century prevailed, not because it had Puritan belief to build upon but just because the hold of the old theology upon the Churches had grown so weak.

In view, however, of the persisting tendency to treat Puritan beliefs on unfulfilled prophecy as akin to liberalism, we must take up in this chapter the place which the Puritans certainly gave to the Second Advent. The possibility that their prophetic views may have misdirected attention away from the end of time can be dispelled at once, for there was a never-absent note in Puritan preaching on 'the last things'. They viewed every hearer as bound shortly for another world, and it may be questioned whether any other school of evangelical preachers have so brought the implications of eternity home to men's consciences as they were enabled to do. Probably the finest devotional volumes on the Second Advent in the English language belong to the Puritan era. For spiritual power what books have superseded Theophilus Gale's *A Discourse of Christ's Coming*, Isaac Ambrose's *Looking unto Jesus in his Second Coming*, Thomas Vincent's *Christ's Certain and Sudden Appearance to Judgment*, or Christopher Love's *Heaven's Glory*? Yet these were not the works of pre-millennial writers. They expressed beliefs which could be found in any number of Puritan sermons, and these beliefs were in no way inconsistent, in their judgment, with the view of unfulfilled prophecy that we have outlined earlier. They held their hope in respect to Christ's work in history in conjunction with the anticipation of his coming when history ends.

It may be replied that, though the Puritans may have seen no inconsistency, there is surely an impossibility involved in holding their prophetic outlook and at the same time maintaining the scriptural duty of a daily watchfulness for Christ's appearing; for if we believe that prophecies remain to be fulfilled – the Jews to be converted, and widespread revival to occur among the Gentiles – *before* Christ comes, how can we watch for an event which cannot be at hand? If, in John Howe's words, there is to be 'a state of very great prosperity for a considerable tract of time, appointed for the church of God on earth',[2] how can this teaching do other than cause Christians to forget what the Scriptures say on the nearness of the Lord's Second Coming?

In answer to this several things must be observed:

First, the same apparent problem exists in the New Testament itself. There the Lord's return is presented as the goal of all moral endeavour and as the supreme comfort of the Church. The Christians of the apostolic age were taught to live in the light of that day and they were to keep themselves in constant expectation of its coming. How could such watchfulness be required of them when, as history has since shown, many centuries lay between them and the Second Advent?

Those who do not believe in the inspiration of all apostolic testimony have met this difficulty by asserting that, 'The Apostles shared, and contributed to produce, the belief that the Lord would come again soon, within the lifetime of some who were then alive . . . Only by the force of experience was the mind of the Church cleared . . .'[3] If we reject this solution, as we must, the conclusion remains that the nearness of Christ's return spoken of in the New Testament is compatible with the passing of what is from the human viewpoint a long period of time. Nineteen centuries have gone by since Christians were first told, 'Surely I come quickly'. Moveover, we may note that it is our Lord himself who both instructs his first disciples to be constantly ready for his coming, and also gives them a commission which in the very nature of the case could not have been realized in their lifetime: all the world is to be discipled, the kingdom is to grow as a mustard seed into a great tree and as leaven 'hid in three measures of meal, till the whole was leavened'. Here is an extensiveness promised which could not belong to the first century A.D., yet Christ is conscious of no inconsistency. Though the Second Advent was not to occur in the immediate future the apostles were not relieved of the duty of watchfulness.

It can thus be seen that living in expectation of the advent of Christ is *not* the same as believing the advent to be just at hand in point of time. If the latter belief were required of Christians, then all the generations of the Church except the last would be required to believe a deception. The 'nearness' of Christ's return, properly understood, is plainly consistent with the passage of many centuries. If a further prolonged period in our calendar should elapse before he comes – a period in which the world-wide preaching of the gospel will witness far greater success – how would this be any more incompatible with the New Testament? Supposing such a lengthy period to be still before the Church the duty of watchfulness would be just as great in our case as it was for the first-century Christians.

Second, Christian biography shows that the practical influence of the doctrine of the Second Coming is not nullified when Christians do not believe that event to be close to them in time. Simon Peter is a biblical illustration. He was distinctly told before Christ's ascension that a lengthened period of service reaching into old-age would be crowned with a martyr's death (John 21.18), yet that awareness did not hinder in his case an earnest desire for the approaching Advent, 'Looking for and hasting unto the coming of the day of God' (2 Pet. 3.12). Paul, too, knew that death must come to him (2 Tim. 4.6), yet though martyrdom was nearer to him in point of time, this did not exclude, in his case also, the love of Christ's appearing.

So was it with the Puritans and their successors. John Elias, for instance, in contrast with those who expected to see Christ come within their lifetime, wrote in 1841, 'I do not expect to see Christ with my bodily eyes till the last day';[4] between him and that day death must interpose and yet waiting for Christ's coming was a reality in his experience. George Whitefield exemplifies the same outlook. In a sermon on the text, 'Go ye into all the world, and preach the gospel to every creature', he says, 'We do not live up to our dignity till every day we are waiting for the coming of our Lord from heaven'.[5] He could preach this even though he expected future great revivals and the conversion of the Jews to occur before the Advent.

Biographies in the Puritan tradition similarly show that the expectation of a brighter period in history was not incompatible in the case of many others with the inspiration drawn from looking for Christ's glorious appearing. It was Rutherford who wrote so longingly of the Advent: 'O if he would fold the heavens together like an old cloak, and shovel time and days out of the way, and make ready in haste the Lamb's wife for her husband. . . . O heavens, move fast. O time, run, run, and hasten the marriage day; for love is tormented with delays! . . . Look to the east: the day-sky is breaking. Think not that Christ

loseth time, or lingereth unsuitably . . .'[6] The same attitude is
to be seen in the lives of John Eliot, Henry Martyn and Robert
Moffat – to name but three of the pioneer missionaries.
Whatever theoretical considerations may be alleged to the
contrary, Christian experience thus shows that an expectation
of the return of Christ in the immediate future is not a prere-
quisite to the possession of earnest desires for his Advent.

Third, the New Testament reveals why the Second Advent
has a direct relevance for Christians of every generation.
What is of ultimate significance is not whether Christ will come
in our lifetime or later, not whether or not our death must intervene, but the truth that whether he come 'sooner' or 'later' we
shall all share alike in the full redemption which that day will
bring.* It is by not appreciating this truth sufficiently that
Christians have sometimes entertained an unbalanced view of
Christ's Coming. They have observed in Scripture that the
Advent and not death is the believer's hope; for the one we are
urged to long but not for the other. This scriptural emphasis
is misread, however, when it is understood to mean that in
point of chronology our duty is to anticipate the Advent
without our dying, as though death were a calamity not to
be contemplated. In sharp contrast to the words of John Elias,
quoted above, this has been the attitude which pre-millennialism
has tended to engender. The son of the pious Philip Henry
Gosse, for instance, tells us this of his father's death in 1888:
'When it become evident that he could not long survive, he
said, turning to his wife in her distress, "Oh, darling, do not
trouble. It's not too late; even now the Blessed Lord may come
and take us both up together." '[7]

These words suggest a considerable misunderstanding. The
reason why the scriptural emphasis does not fall upon death is
not because death is a step *away* from the Advent, it is because

* 'Warning is given us by the course of nature, and by the word, that in a
few years more we may be all turned out of this world: and our dying is
of equal importance, as to our eternal state, with Christ's coming; what
difference is there if thou shouldest die this week, or if Christ should
come to judge the world this week? Thy eternal state is equally concerned
in both.' Robert Traill, *Works*, reprint 1810, vol. 4, 206.

death does not usher the believer into the final state of glory. Death is gain and paradise for the individual believer, yet the bliss is incomplete. As long as the soul is separate from the body the believer is only in an intermediate state; he must await resurrection, glorification and full redemption. And that, he knows, will come publicly and simultaneously for the whole Church at Christ's appearing! With this understanding, the Christian can both love Christ's appearing and also know that, though he meets death first, that in no wise reduces his hope nor sets it further from him. 'To fall asleep will not be to miss the glory of the Advent'[8] (1 Thess. 4.5).

This underlines again the truth that a strong desire for Christ's coming does not depend upon our regarding it as imminent in our individual lifetime. The sanctifying power of the Advent upon our present conduct has indeed nothing to do with our being able to fix its time; it has to do rather with a true scriptural appreciation of what that event means.

On this subject the summary given by the Westminster divines in *The Shorter Catechism* has not been surpassed in its comprehensive brevity:

'Q. 37. *What benefits do believers receive from Christ at death?*

'A. The souls of believers are at their death made perfect in holiness, and do immediately pass into glory; and their bodies, being still united to Christ, do rest in their graves till the resurrection.

'Q. 38. *What benefits do believers receive from Christ at the resurrection?*

'A. At the resurrection, believers being raised up in glory, shall be openly acknowledged and acquitted in the day of judgment, and made perfectly blessed in the full enjoying of God to all eternity.'

These two statements on the privileges brought by Christ to the believer at death and at his Coming rightly represent the latter as the culminating glory. It is incomparably the blessed hope. Made strong by this sound theology Christians of the seventeenth century could both face death with confidence and

Q [215]

yet long for the Advent. Samuel Rutherford's dying testimony, versified by Anne Ross Cousin, brings both things together and treats death rightly as a step in the way to resurrection:

> *I shall sleep sound in Jesus,*
> *Fill'd with His likeness rise*
> *To live and to adore Him,*
> *To see Him with these eyes.*
> *'Tween me and resurrection*
> *But Paradise doth stand;*
> *Then – then for glory dwelling*
> *In Immanuel's land!*

In the fourth and last place, in reference to the question how watching for Christ's coming is consistent with the passage of long periods of time, it needs to be observed that faith has a peculiar power at precisely this point. The exercise of faith can bring very near events which, chronologically considered, may lie a long way from us. Faith annihilates distance and faith finds a *present* reality and substance in things hoped for and yet not seen (Heb. 11.1). To faith it is but 'a little while' until 'he that shall come will come' (Heb. 10.37). By faith the apostles in the upper room, and the believers at Thessalonica, were intended to draw present comfort from the promise of Christ's coming – just as Abraham, long before, had, by faith, obtained joy over Christ's first advent even when it was more than a thousand years distant in time. In the words of David Brown: 'Faith lays hold, not on chronological dates or arithmetical calculations but on "the Strength of Israel, who will not lie", as he speaks in the promises of his blessed Word. What faith believes, hope brings near. To the hope of the believer, even as to the Lord himself, *"a thousand years are as one day"*. Though chronologically far off, if so it should be found – no matter. Faith sees him coming "leaping upon the mountains and skipping upon the hills".'[9]

Robert Candlish, in a sermon entitled *Christ Coming Quickly*, expands on this principle of faith. He writes:

'To a believer, the mere possibility, or even absolute certainty, of ages being yet to elapse before the Lord come again, ought no more to diminish the influence of that event upon his mind, and heart, and conscience, than the fact of ages having elapsed since the Lord came at first lessens the moral weight of his constant vivid sight of Christ and him crucified. . . . I know no chronology and no chronological computation of long eras, in dealing with that Saviour, who eighteen hundred years ago trod with his blessed feet the soil of Judea, and expired on the cross of Calvary. Then why should there be any real difficulty in applying this principle in the prospect, more than in the retrospect? Does faith mounting up in the ascending series of years to the opening up of the fountain, long centuries ago, lose all sense of distance and remoteness, in the bright and vivid apprehension of the cross? And will not the same faith in its keen glance downwards and onwards along the stream of time, seize the one great and only object of its hope, and bring it near, even to the very door, ay, though ages may seem to come in between?

'. . . These are the two events, the death of shame, the coming in glory, which faith, when rightly exercised, grasps; which I, believing, grasp. I grasp them as equally real, equally nigh. Christ dying, near and present, Christ coming, near and present. What though ages have run since that death and ages more are perhaps to run before that coming! It is nothing to me. The world's history, past and future; the Church's history, past and future; all is to me for the present as if it never had been and never were to be. . . . Wherever I am, whatever I am about, ought I not to be alive to my position between these two manifestations of Christ, and these alone? Behind me Christ dying; before me Christ coming. Is it not thus, and only thus, that I live by the faith of him who loved me and gave himself for me; that I live also by the power of the world to come; enduring as seeing him who is invisible?'[10]

*   *   *

In conclusion two things may be added.

First, however bright, comparatively, the world may become

when the Church reaches her fullest development in history, the Advent of Christ will ever remain the pole-star of faith and hope. For earth, however blessed, will never begin to equal heaven. As Bengel points out, even in that future time when there shall be 'an overflowing fulness of the Spirit', Christians will still be in conflict with indwelling sin, they will still face temptation and meet with death.[11] Watchfulness will thus never be laid down this side of eternity. The Christian life will remain a life of faith, and the higher degree of influence attending the preaching of the law and the gospel will only make believers look more earnestly to the Saviour whose death they will continue to show forth till he come. The thankful words with which the Puritan Thomas Hall died in 1665 will always in this world be suitable for every dying Christian: 'I am now going where I shall have rest from sin and Satan, from all fear, weariness, and watching; and from all the evils and errors of a wicked world; even so come, Lord Jesus, for I long for thy coming.'[12] This world will never be the Church's rest.

Second, in recognizing all the imperfection of the present world and the trials which it has for a Christian, it needs also to be seen that there is an 'other-worldliness', an excessive preoccupation with the future state, which militates against the Christian's true calling. The wonders of the world to come are not revealed to us in order that we may live our present lives in sadness, asking how much longer it must last. The Puritan viewpoint, despite all that critics have sometimes said to the contrary, was entirely against that attitude. It was a minister of the Puritan school, William Tennent, Jr., who once gently reproved George Whitefield in a way which illustrates this point well. Among a group of ministers, in his younger days, Whitefield spoke of the burden of labouring in the ministry and of his great consolation that in a short time his work would be done and he be with Christ.

'He then appealed to the ministers around him, if it were not their great comfort that they should soon go to rest. They generally assented, excepting Mr. Tennent, who sat next to Mr. Whitefield in silence; and by his countenance discovered but little pleasure in the conversation. On which Mr. White-field, turning to him and tapping him on the knee, said, "Well! brother Tennent, you are the oldest man amongst us, do you not rejoice to think that your time is so near at hand, when you will be called home and freed from all the difficulties attending this chequered scene?" Mr. T. bluntly answered, "I have no wish about it." Mr. W. pressed him again; and Mr. T. again answered, "No, sir, it is no pleasure to me at all, and if you knew your duty it would be none to you. I have nothing to do with death; my business is to live as long as I can – as well as I can – and to serve my Lord and Master as faithfully as I can, until he shall think proper to call me home." '13

Perhaps another story illustrates even better the Puritan insistence that Christ is to be glorified in this world by the service of his people. A minister in the period of persecution in Scotland in the time of Charles II, who was less earnest than the Covenanters' leaders, accepted the Indulgence offered by the government. In contrast to the resolute Donald Cargill he defended his action with the question, 'What needs all this ado? We will get to heaven and they will get no more.' 'Yes,' said Cargill, 'we will get more. We will get God glorified on earth, which is more than heaven.'

The opportunity of honouring Christ by fulfilling our present duties is a priceless privilege and those who thus serve him will not be found wanting at his Coming. 'Blessed is that servant, whom his Lord when he cometh shall find so doing.'

XI

THE PROSPECT IN HISTORY:
CHRIST OUR HOPE

*Matthew Henry's Chapel at Chester. The doctrines
once preached in these old buildings are destined
to be heard again across the world: 'Jesus Christ
the same yesterday, and today, and for ever'*

'By a generation such as ours, all talk of the triumph of Christianity is heard with impatient incredulity. This is especially the case in Western Europe and the British Isles, for here the full weight of the tragedies of our day has been felt. In the Americas traces of pre-1914 optimism linger. In some respects, in its attitudes and conditions, the New World is now the Old World and the Old World of Europe has become the New World, a feared foretaste of what is to come universally.'

KENNETH SCOTT LATOURETTE

The Prospect for Christianity, 1949, 185

WE have in these pages sketched in broad outline what may be called the Puritan attitude toward history; in doing so we have noted how their perspective developed from faith in the promises of Scripture respecting Christ's kingdom and how it was part of a theology which proclaimed the controlling plan of God behind all events. It was no accident that hope gained this ascendency when Pauline and Calvinistic orthodoxy possessed the thinking of the Church. John Barlow was a spokesman of characteristic Puritan thought when he told his people at Plymouth:

'Whom he chooseth, shall be created, called, justified, sanctified, glorified; because his purpose cannot be altered, his promise revoked. Let Manasseh repair the high places, rear altars for Baal; the Prodigal run from his Father, drink and swill, consume his portion; Saul make havoc of the saints, put them in prison, do many things against Jesus of Nazareth: yet shall they come to themselves, mourn for their sins, and be saved. For they are elected, beloved of him who is the same for ever. Were it not thus, what hope could the faithful have to see Babel ruinated, the Roman whore burned, the Jew called, the Devil's kingdom destroyed and Christ's perfected?'[1]

For the Puritans there was immense optimism in such doctrine. It was the same optimism which appeared in the prayers of Christian people in the age of decline between the Puritans and the eighteenth-century revival, which came to renewed public expression in that great awakening and led on, as though irresistible, to the world-wide missionary enterprise of English-speaking Protestantism.

While we have sought to comment upon these themes we have had little opportunity to trace the resulting influence of this outlook upon the general thinking of those nations where the hope held sway, though this was of momentous historical significance. There was a connection between this belief and the sense of purpose and destiny established in the common consciousness of Britain and America,[2] which sense of purpose, in turn, instilled a discipline and vigour in national life such as was never witnessed in civilizations where philosophies of fate or chance have prevailed. This consciousness found eloquent expression, for example, in Lord Macaulay's *History of England*, the first two volumes of which were published in 1848. Macaulay was linked by family background to the Church of Scotland and to Wilberforce's 'Clapham Sect'. His 'great work', writes Winston Churchill, 'provided the historical background for the sense of progress which was now inspiring Victorian Britain. Macaulay set out to show that the story of England since the Whig Revolution of 1688 was one of perpetual and limitless advance. In his opening chapter he wrote: "The history of our own country in the last hundred and sixty years is eminently the history of physical, moral and intellectual improvement." This was a heartening note, much appreciated by contemporary readers. Optimism reigned throughout the land. . . .'[3]

From the standpoint of Scripture, Macaulay's thought was certainly mixed, yet it is plain that his was a view of history strongly affected by the perspective which came from the seventeenth century. Nor was Macaulay the last great historian to hold that view. In the darkest days of 1940, Churchill, whose outlook had been early influenced by Macaulay, saw history as directed by the hand of God and believed that the world would not go under. Perhaps the saddest feature of Churchill's closing years, after the Second World War, was that his hold upon this truth seemed to become increasingly tenuous. The appearances of the post-war world – the 'Iron Curtain', the hydrogen bomb, the four hundred million shut within China – all seemed to make the old belief in providence impossible. 'I am bewildered by the world,' Churchill said in 1953, 'the confusion is terrible',[4] and two years later as his great Parliamentary career came to its end, he spoke with pathos of his fears for those who should live in the future 'if God wearied of mankind'.

'What ought we to do if God wearied of mankind? That,' comments Lord Moran, 'was the question that tormented him as he came towards the end of his journey.'[5]

Though this is comparatively recent history, the wider effects of the 'great decay in belief' which Churchill observed,[6] and the truth of his words, 'It is bad for a nation when it is without faith',[7] have been widely evidenced. The loss of national purpose, the loss of will to advance, the indiscipline and futility of permissiveness, all these are the symptoms of an age in which the dominating mood is one of cynicism and pessimism. To the modern mind, history is not under any control.

*   *   *

If the rise of a sense of destiny in Protestant Britain and America stemmed in the first place from Christian thought, it is equally true to say that the collapse of that outlook must be associated with the failure of the Church to maintain the truths committed to her. Today the Church no longer appears before men as a world-transforming power; gone are the anticipations of non-Christians in India that the whole system of pagan thought is soon to collapse about them; gone, too, at home, is that sacrificial enthusiasm for the conversion of the world which was once so common among Christians.

The run-down of missionary endeavour is one of the clearest pointers to this change. When all has been said on such things as the end of the 'pax Britannica' – which facilitated missions as the 'pax Romana' had done in the first century – and the rise of strong nationalism in Africa and Asia, the fact remains that the Church herself has largely lost confidence in her

[225]

mission to the world. S. Pearce Carey tells of a visit to the site of his famous ancestor's work in India and of the shock it brought to him: 'I first saw Serampore College in 1906. The day that should have been most gladsome was disappointment and distress. The scope of the work there had so shrunken. It seemed the sepulchre of an abandoned ideal.'[8] Not only at Serampore were there traces of the 'sepulchre' in 1906. By that date the Church at home and overseas was in general retreat from Puritan Christianity, though it did not yet see that this would radically change the endeavour which that form of Christianity had been responsible for starting. John R. Mott was not lacking in hope when in August, 1900, he published his book, *The Evangelization of the World in This Generation*, nor was the famous Edinburgh Missionary Conference which took place ten years later, but it was not a well-grounded hope, as time subsequently proved.

For many years before the First World War the traditional Christian view of history had in large sectors of Protestantism merged with a worldly philosophy of the certainty of progress. It was a disastrous change for it obscured the fact that the Church cannot advance without the favour of her God. The authentic Puritan hope had regarded confidence in the progress of the gospel as mere presumption where there is not an earnest regard to the rule of God's Word. The Puritans knew that lack of faithfulness to Scripture would grieve the Spirit and bring barrenness upon the Church or even that same judicial blindness in which Israel had been cut off. Nor did they forget that Israel's desolation is held up in Romans 11 as a warning to Gentile churches lest they fall into the same unbelief; their convictions about the bright future of Christ's kingdom thus provided no cushion upon which complacent Gentile churches can rest.

In contrast to this attitude the Christian Church, by and large, entered the twentieth century with a large measure of false hope and little sense of her danger. Even by the mid-nineteenth century commitment to the doctrinal Confessions of the Reformation was on the wane, though it was represented as the growth of a healthier outlook. Disbelief in 'Calvinism', however, was soon followed by the rise of unbelief in the inerrancy of Scripture, and then the gospel itself – the incarnation of the Son of God to bear vicariously in his death the wrath sin deserves – was made a subject for legitimate doubt within the Church. Intellect replaced faith and 'scholarship' gave her support to the spreading delusion. Thus Dr. John Duncan, speaking on the Christian future of the Jews in the Free Church General Assembly in 1867, warned his hearers: 'Do not both indications of Scripture and the signs of the times lead us to think that a new epoch is approaching, when a great Gentile apostasy shall be accompanied or followed by the recall of Israel to Jehovah their God, and David their king? Wondrous, without doubt, will be the results of that event. . . . Dark days, I fear, are to intervene.'[9] It may be considered remarkable that this erosion of faith should have gained ground rapidly in the very Church which had so singularly served the world with the pure gospel of Christ, yet so it was with the Free Church of Scotland. When that Church realigned herself with the United Presbyterian Church in 1900 to become the United Free Church, only twenty-seven ministers remained in the continuing Free Church which, like a relic from antiquity, stood fully pledged to the Westminster Confession of Faith. This phenomenon, however, was not new. The eminent Danish-Halle Mission had been a powerful influence abroad until the last quarter of the eighteenth century when 'rationalism at home dug up its roots'.[10]

Alexander Duff had warned his fellow-countrymen of the danger: 'Let not the day dawn upon old Scotland that shall see the school separated from the Bible and from Christianity' he had said in 1854.[11] And in 1866 he spoke of the new Chair of Missions at New College as the answer of the Free Church to modern error – 'We believe in the Bible – the whole Bible, as Divine; we believe in its plenary inspiration as an absolute revelation from God; and we are determined to establish this Professorship for the express purpose of rearing up young men, who at home and abroad shall authoritatively proclaim these great and vital truths, in the face of all the heresy-mongers on earth.'[12] But Duff's expectation was not realized and within twenty years some professors in the Free Church were encouraging rationalism without any effective discipline being exerted against them. The Rev. M. Macaskill of Dingwall, in the early 1890's, charged Henry Drummond, Professor of Natural Science at the Free Church College, Glasgow, with upholding teaching which is 'throughout, the purest naturalism – of the earth, earthy, and hence Christ-dishonouring and soul-destroying'. The Christ Drummond wrote about, said Macaskill, 'is not the Christ of God, but a social, semi-political Christ, wholly the creation of the writer's own imagination'.[13]

These opinions, as Macaskill well saw, would revolutionize the whole concept of foreign missions. According to the new view, Christ had not come as the only way for sinners to approach God. 'Religion was in the world before Christ came, and it lives today in a million souls who have never heard His name'. So Drummond believed and the current of opinion was increasingly upon his side.

When the World Missionary Conference met at Edinburgh in 1910 the influence of theological liberalism was clear enough. Eight commissions prepared the way for the Conference, the chairman of one of them being Charles Gore, at that time Bishop of Birmingham, of whom W. H. T. Gairdner in his commemorative volume *Edinburgh 1910* tells us that he was 'a Platonist to the core in intellectual attitude . . . a man whose enthusiasm for religious education at home, and abroad also, was simply the Christianisation of his Platonism'.[14] The chairman of another commission was Professor D. S. Cairns, and Gairdner speaks of the report which Cairns laid before the Conference on 'The Missionary Message in Relation to the Non-Christian Religions' as 'one of the most remarkable, perhaps the most remarkable, of a great series'. It certainly struck notes unknown to the former leaders of British missionary endeavour:

'While of course theories as to the origin and significance of the non-Christian religions still vary, there is a general consensus that representing as they do many attempted solutions of life's problems, they must be approached with very real sympathy and respect. . . . More than that, the conviction has grown that their "confused cloud-world" will be found to be "shot through and through with broken lights of a hidden sun". And, these things being true, another conviction has dawned: Christianity, the religion of the Light of the World, can ignore no lights however "broken" – it must take them all into account, absorb them all into its central glow. Nay, since the Church of Christ itself is partially involved in mists of unbelief, failing aspiration, imperfect realisation, this quest of hers among the non-Christian religions, this discovering of their "broken lights" may be to her the discovery of facets of her own truth. . . . Christ's church may recover all the light that is in Christ.'[15]

That such words could be supposed to give new inspiration to missionary endeavour was indeed proof that a new outlook upon the world was being formed; no longer the stress upon repentance and conversion, no longer the assurance that historic Christianity has the only true claim to become the universal religion, instead, a growing belief that if there is to be one world religion it must be in some measure syncretistic in form, Christian perhaps in name and 'spirit', but with little of its doctrine. Herein lay the tragedy of the Church's approach to the world in the twentieth century. Hesitant now to proclaim authoritative truth, she solaced herself in the face of men's unwillingness to receive Christianity with the idea that the old 'dogmatic' approach to evangelizing the earth was no longer legitimate. The run-down of missionary endeavour thus proceeded apace without any profound humiliation and self-examination on the part of the Protestant Churches. Disbelief in Scripture lay hidden beneath professed charity and tolerance.

The most notable attempt to unmask that unbelief occurred in the testimony of J. Gresham Machen in America in the 1930's, by which time the initiative in foreign missions had passed from Britain to the United States. But there, also, as a result of spiritual decline and the financial burdens of the great depression, retrenchment on the mission field was the order of the day. In 1932 there appeared a volume compiled by a distinguished committee from many denominations and chaired by a Harvard professor, entitled *Re-Thinking Missions: a Layman's Inquiry After One Hundred Years*. This was an apologia for the new approach to missions, asserting that 'the relation between religions must take increasingly hereafter the form of a common search for truth'. Liberal missionaries applauded it. Pearl Buck foresaw 'possibly the greatest missionary impetus that we have known for centuries',[16] though what missionary work was to consist in now that Christianity and other religions must co-exist in concord was far from clear.

On the other hand, Machen's reply to the book included these charges: 'It deprecates the distinction between Christians and non-Christians; it belittles the Bible and inveighs against Christian doctrine; it dismisses the doctrine of eternal punishment as a doctrine antiquated even in Christendom; it presents Jesus as a great religious Teacher and Example, as Christianity's "highest expression of religious life", but certainly not as very God of very God. . . .'[17]

When a true spiritual history of the twentieth century is written, Machen's stand against *Re-Thinking Missions*, and the controversy in which it involved him with the Presbyterian Board of Foreign Missions, will be seen as one of the last attempts to stop historic missionary agencies falling under the control of unbelief. The fact that he was not able to do so and that he was even suspended by the Presbyterian Church, U.S.A., in 1935, two years before his death, shows how strongly the tide was running.

We have considered the above comments necessary by way of an explanation as to how the vision which inspired the leaders of the modern missionary era, beginning in the 1790's, came to be abandoned. It was not that the outlook of Carey, Duff and Livingstone was maintained and found wanting; nor that in discipling the nations in faithfulness to Scripture the Churches found their resources unequal to the task, nor that populations increased too fast to allow the Church to maintain her progress in non-Christian lands. The truth is that faith in Christ had waned and without Him the advance of Christianity was found – as had often been found before – impossible with man. 'Without me ye can do nothing.' As Spurgeon said in a sermon preached on July 6, 1890, 'Our want of faith has done more mischief to us than all the devils in hell, and all the heretics on earth. Some cry out against the Pope, and others against agnostics; but it is our own unbelief which is our worst enemy.'

This is not to overlook the burden of missionary endeavour that has been carried on by inter-denominational evangelical missionary societies in the twentieth century, without whom the earth would have been dark indeed and whose spirit of sacrifice and urgency has borne excellent fruit. The chief source of weakness in these societies has generally been their unfamiliarity with those reservoirs of spiritual strength which had meant so much to the pioneers of an earlier age. The lessons of church history, particularly of the revivals of the sixteenth, seventeenth and eighteenth centuries, were not studied; the creeds of the Calvinistic churches were viewed as inimical to the missionary spirit and the idea that the gospel was intended to have dominion in the world before Christ's Return was treated as a tenet of liberalism. Nineteenth-century pre-millennialism, which from Brethren influence tended to despise all church history as mere human traditions, prevailed generally in the evangelical societies and the spreading unbelief in the historic denominations seemed conclusive confirmation of the conviction that the final apostasy before the Advent had commenced. Pessimism over the future of the Church's work in the world was now accepted as orthodoxy.

* * *

If hope is to be regained today, upon what grounds can it be built? It will hardly do to say that we must simply 'hope' for a revival. Until the last century, revivals occurred with a regularity which made some speak as though their recurring cycle was axiomatic; but more than a hundred years have passed since the last general awakening in Britain and America in 1859. Hope needs something more than this at which to look. Some have encouraged themselves with the assumption that as the Second Advent is close at hand there must soon be a widespread repetition of miraculous pentecostal gifts – tongues, prophecy and healing – in a revival which will signal the approaching end. We see no more warrant for this belief than there was in the days of Edward Irving's delusion, and it may not be without significance that in the most powerful revivals in Britain and America these gifts had no place at all.

We only reach sure ground when we remember that revivals are the work of the Spirit of truth bringing home to the mind and conscience of large numbers the teaching of the Word of God with efficacious power. If through the unfaithfulness or ignorance of men that teaching has its cutting edge smoothed down; if such truths as Christ's finished work at Calvary, together with the entire dependence of sinners upon him for salvation are not preached, and the reliability of God's word not fully declared, then hope that the Holy Spirit will do his work is a terrible mistake. If there is any lesson which ought to be beyond doubt it is that revivals come through the preaching of scriptural truth.

For this reason the whole Puritan school of Christianity placed primary importance upon the need for its preachers and missionaries to be men thoroughly grounded in the doctrines of Scripture. In this they were absolutely right. It was the authority of true doctrine which shook the whole structure of the Papacy in the sixteenth century and emptied the Roman Church of multitudes of its adherents; it was from the prayerful study of such doctrine at the Colleges of Edinburgh, Glasgow and Cambridge that the men who preached in the revivals of the seventeenth century came; it was doctrinal preaching again which resulted in the conversion of thousands in the early days of Methodism; and it was the same heart-acquaintance with theology which characterized all the leaders of the modern missionary movement. When the English-speaking churches gained their greatest influence in the world, and when evangelistic endeavour proceeded everywhere with vigour, the inspiration came in the first place from the believing apprehension of biblical truths. As Donald MacLean says of those who initiated the commencement of missions from Scotland, they 'grasped the fact that Paul's declarations of profound mysteries in his Epistle to the Romans were not the cold intellectual conclusions of an exclusive dogmatist, but flames from the soul of a Christian missionary consumed with zeal for the salvation of men.'[18]

This needs particular emphasis in connection with missionary endeavour, for the modern tendency has been to suppose that missionaries need little theological preparation and that the latter might even militate against a zeal for souls. This was not Carey's attitude, nor Bogue's at Gosport. For them sound divinity was fundamental. We likewise find Thomas Scott, to whom was committed the care of prospective missionaries for the Church Missionary Society, regretting in a letter to a friend that, 'The missionaries as they have hitherto come to me, have been pious men, but superficial theologians'.[19] In the same vein Alexander Duff deplored the comparatively small instruction often given to missionaries and the allowance of a difference standard in them from that of home ministers: 'If any difference at all were to be tolerated, I have no hesitation in saying that it ought to be in favour of the enhanced standard of attainment indispensable for the foreign missionary – and especially for the missionary to India or China, or the dominions of the False Prophet.'[20]

Hope, then, respecting the future of the world must not be an expectation that God will work regardless of the failure of his Church, but rather that God will recall the Church and especially her ministry to that standard of full commitment to the gospel of Christ which Scripture commands. Such commitment was the characteristic of the most widely used preachers in the era we have considered. David Bogue believed he was drawing the right lesson when he declared that it will be this same pattern of preaching which, renewed on a wider scale, will bring to pass the world-wide kingdom of Christ:

'One means, and indeed the greatest and most effectual for introducing the glory of the latter days, is the preaching of the gospel. This is the method which the Saviour of sinners appointed for the propagation of his religion: "Go ye", says he to his apostles, Mark 16.15, "into all the world and preach the gospel to every creature." And why was this method appointed, but because it appeared the fittest and the best? and this appointment by so high authority, guided in all its acts by infinite wisdom, gives it an unquestionable superiority to every other. Were we unable to perceive any reason for this preference, that ought not to create a shadow of doubt in our mind: God has said it; and this surely is sufficient to make us receive it as an absolute truth. . . . For general utility and extensive efficacy, what other method can be compared to this? The history of the Christian Church, for nearly eighteen hundred years, can be adduced to display in the most luminous manner, from page to page, its superiority to every other. Let it also be remembered, that whenever the sacred Scripture speaks of the conversion of the world to Christ, and specifies the means by which it is to be accomplished – that means is always the preaching of the gospel. . . .

'To communicate to the preaching of the gospel all the light and power necessary for the accomplishment of this amazing work, God will raise up in great abundance eminent ministers, full of truth, piety and zeal. What can be done by an individual of this class, in promoting the interests of Christ's kingdom, may be seen in the exertions of Knox in Scotland, and Whitefield in England. A hundred such men – if not restrained by the ten horns which gave their power to the beast – would change the face of the Christian Church. In order to introduce the Millennium, many thousands of ministers like them will God raise up, and send forth into the harvest, and he will crown their labours with extraordinary success. From a multitude of such labourers in every country, what may not be expected!'[21]

In these words, and many more that could be quoted, Bogue was reiterating the Puritan belief, and the conviction so thoroughly stated by Jonathan Edwards, that ages when there is outpouring of the Spirit of God are ages marked by faithful use of the Word of God. This does not of course mean that they supposed that all scriptural preaching immediately results in revival. They knew that times and seasons are ordered by God and observed that every era of great advance has generally been preceded by the establishment of firm doctrinal foundations through years of patient sowing, accompanied not infrequently by suffering. Before the fruits of the Reformation were reaped in Britain there was first a great doctrinal struggle, and if this was not so marked in the revival of the eighteenth century, it needs to be remembered that the men of that century were possessors of a heritage which others had bequeathed to them. Christians in their successive generations are but one agency in the hands of God, and for the Puritan, with his long-term view, it concerned him little whether he was called to sow or to reap; what mattered was that the final outcome is certain. So persecution could be faced, as the Scottish Covenanters faced it; or the appalling darkness of entirely non-Christian nations where, as Livingstone said, people hated and feared the gospel 'as a revolutionary spirit is disliked by the old Tories'. For the men of this noble school neither promising circumstances nor immediate success were necessary to uphold their morale in the day of battle.

One final word: if hope is to be regained today it can only be as faith is restored in the scriptural revelation of the Person of Christ. As we saw earlier, the whole Puritan conviction respecting the future success of the gospel rested upon the foundation of his work – his work of substitution, in his state of humiliation, resulting in the ransom of an innumerable multitude, and his continuing work as he is now enthroned in glory, yet present by the Spirit in the Church unto the end of the world. When one compares the extent of his promised dominion – 'all the kindreds of the nations' (Psa. 22.27), 'the whole earth filled with his glory' (Psa. 72.19) – with the unlimited power and authority now given to him as Mediator by the Father, when one remembers how it has already pleased him to reveal his gospel to vast numbers in revival periods, then, at the least, there is cause to consider the words which Charles Hodge, one of the last great expounders of the Puritan hope, wrote in trembling characters a little while before he died: 'I am fully persuaded that the vast majority of the human race will share in the beatitudes and glories of our Lord's redemption.'[22] Whether that be so or not, certain it is that all the conversions which take place in the vast world populations of the future will be through the divine power of Christ. 'When the Lord shall build up Zion, he shall appear in his glory' (Psa. 102.16). And when, with the plenitude of his Spirit, 'the Deliverer shall come out of Zion and shall turn away ungodliness from Jacob' (Rom. 11.26), we are told the extent of that amazing work, 'All Israel shall be saved'. As we ponder such texts, as Carey did the great promises of Isaiah 54 in the momentous year 1792, who can deny that we may have limited sinfully in our thoughts the scope of the victory which Calvary has obtained? While the word 'all' in Scripture in most instances does not mean 'everyone, without exception', it does often point to an immense number. The children of Christ are to be 'like the sand of the sea-shore' and 'like the stars of heaven for multitude.' The sufferings of the cross and Christ's present power guarantee that these millions will all be gathered: 'And I, if I be lifted up from the earth, will draw all men unto me' (John 12.32).

The glory of Christ has indeed been declared in the earth in past ages. In the apostolic age, 'His lightnings enlightened the world: the earth saw, and trembled.' Psa. 97.4 The Reformers and Puritans beheld him as the conquering King and it made them strong. The eighteenth-century Church knew his power and longed with Charles Wesley that

> . . . *the world might taste and see*
> *The riches of His grace.*

The same was true in revivals of the last century. 'It were worth living ten thousand ages in obscurity and reproach,' declared one minister in Ulster, 'to be permitted to creep forth at the expiration of that time and engage in the glorious work of the last six months of 1859.'[23] But this world, according to the word of prophecy, has not seen the last such wonders of salvation; there are reserved for the future such evidences of the efficacy of the blood of Christ that the Apostle, as he anticipated them and contemplated the grandeur of the whole plan of God, exclaimed, 'O the depth of the riches both of the wisdom and knowledge of God!' There is no hope for the world apart from revivals, but it is not in revivals that the faith of the Church is to be rooted. Christ himself is the object of faith. The same faith which looks for his final appearing must also trust in his promised presence as the nations are evangelized. The Church, being united to him in whom the Spirit dwells without measure, will be built; she can no more be deprived of the Spirit's aid than can the finished work of Christ – upon which the mission of the Spirit proceeds – be undone. When, therefore, the people of God find themselves with little evidence of spiritual prosperity, they are not to conclude that henceforth the Church can only be a dwindling minority in a pagan world, nor are they to suppose that they may suspend working until there be some new outpouring of the Spirit: rather their present duty is to exercise a fuller confidence in the word and person of the Son of God. In so doing they will not find the Spirit who glorifies Christ to be absent. 'Christians', says Luther, 'must have the vision which enables them to disregard the terrible spectacle and outward appearance, the devil and the guns of the whole world, and to see Him who sits on high and says: "I am the One who spoke to you." '[24]

When Christ is thus the object of faith, then will his promise always be fulfilled, 'Nothing shall be impossible unto you' (Matt. 17.20).

We close with the words of C. H. Spurgeon:

'The fulness of Jesus is not changed, then why are our works so feebly done? Pentecost, is that to be a tradition? The reforming days, are these to be memories only? I see no reason why we should not have a greater Pentecost than Peter saw, and a Reformation deeper in its foundations, and truer in its

[237]

upbuildings than all the reforms which Luther or Calvin achieved. We have the same Christ, remember that. The times are altered, but Jesus is the Eternal, and time touches him not. . . . Our laziness puts off the work of conquest, our self-indulgence procrastinates, our cowardice and want of faith make us dote upon the millennium instead of hearing the Spirit's voice today. Happy days would begin from this hour if the Church would but awake and put on her strength, for in her Lord all fulness dwells.[25]

'Oh! Spirit of God, bring back thy Church to a belief in the gospel! Bring back her ministers to preach it once again with the Holy Ghost, and not striving after wit and learning. Then shall we see thine arm made bare, O God, in the eyes of all the people, and the myriads shall be brought to rally round the throne of God and the Lamb. The Gospel must succeed; it shall succeed; it cannot be prevented from succeeding; a multitude that no man can number must be saved.'[26]

APPENDICES

One

THE OUTPOURING OF
THE HOLY SPIRIT

Or,

The Prosperous State of the Christian Interest Before the End
of Time, by a Plentiful Effusion of the Holy Spirit.

JOHN HOWE

John Howe (1630–1705), a graduate of Cambridge and Oxford, rose to
prominence as a preacher in the 1650's despite his youth and, though of
the presbyterial way in church polity, he became a domestic chaplain to
Oliver Cromwell. Ejected from Torrington, Devon, in 1662, Howe was
one of the central figures in the troublous period for nonconformity which
began at that date. He was settled in London from 1678. A hearer who
listened to Howe in 1695 says that he 'preached incomparably'. The
following material is extracted from his fifteen sermons on Ezekiel 39.29
preached in 1678 and first published in 1725. They are contained in the
large one-volume edition of Howe's Works, reprinted in 1837 but not,
curiously, in the three-volume edition of 1848. About the same period
they were also reprinted separately by the Religious Tract Society under
the title *The Outpouring of the Holy Spirit*. The sub-title, given above, was
the original title.

'*Neither will I hide my face any more from them: for I have poured
out my Spirit upon the house of Israel, saith the Lord God.*'

Ezekiel 32.29

That which is reasonable to be designed and expected in
discourses of this nature, and concerning such a subject as we
have here before us, should be comprised within such particu-
lars as these:

1. To establish the belief of this thing in the substance of it,
being a thing so very plain in the scripture, that there shall be
a permanent state of tranquillity and prosperity unto the
church of Christ on earth.

2. To settle the apprehension fully on the connexion
between an external prosperity and this internal flourishing
of religion in the church by the communication of the Holy

[241]

Ghost in larger and fuller measure; the connexion of these with one another reciprocally, so as that there can never be an externally happy state unto the church without that communication of the Spirit, and that with it there cannot but be prosperity.

Take the former part of this connexion, that is, that without such a communication of the Spirit an external state of tranquillity and prosperity to the church can never be, we should design the fixing of this apprehension well; for certainly they are but vain expectations, fond wishes, to look for such prosperity without reference unto that large and general communication of the Spirit. Experience hath done very much in several parts of the world, if we had no prospect nearer us, to discover and refute the folly of any such hope, that any external good state of things can make the church happy. How apparent is it that if there should be never so much a favourable aspect of time, yet if men are left to their own spirits, all the business will presently be for one person to endeavour to lurch* another and to grasp and get power in their hands! And then they will presently run into sensuality, or make it their business to serve carnal and secular interests, grasping at this world, mingling with the spirit of it. Thus it cannot but be, it must be, if an effusion of the Spirit be not conjunct in time with any such external smiles of time. There can be no good time unto the church of God without the giving of another Spirit, his own Spirit; that, or nothing, must make the church happy.

And that cannot but do it; which is the other side of the connexion. For, let us but recount with ourselves, what it must needs be, when such a Spirit shall be poured forth, as by which all shall be disposed and inclined to love God, and to devote themselves to him, and to serve his interest, and to love one another as themselves, and each one to rejoice in another's welfare, so as that the good and advantage of one shall be the joy and delight of all! When men shall have no designs one upon another, no endeavours of tripping up one another's heels, nor of raising themselves upon one another's ruins! This cannot but

* Defeat, pilfer.

[242]

infer a good state of things, excepting what may be from external enemies. It is true, indeed, that when there was the largest communication of the Spirit that ever was in the church, yet it was molested by pagans; but then it was not troublesome in itself, it did not contend part by part with itself. And if the communication of the Spirit, as we have reason to expect in the latter days, be very general, so as not only to improve and heighten the church in respect of internal liveliness and vigour, but also to increase it in extent as no doubt it will, then less of trouble is to be feared from without. . . .

There is a very great aptness to distrust the efficacy of such an effusion of the Spirit unto this purpose and to entertain very cold thoughts about it. The Spirit! How should this Spirit do such a thing as this; bring about a universal tranquillity and peace, and in all respects a more prosperous and flourishing state for the church of God in the world? That same expression of the prophet, 'Is the Spirit of the Lord straitened?' Micah 2.7, imports a very great aptitude even in a professing people, to have a great deal of distrust about the Spirit, and the effects to be accomplished and brought about by him. It is a keen and pungent way of speaking to speak expostulatorily, as here. 'What! have you learned no better, you house of Jacob, than to think that the Spirit of the Lord can be straitened? that there can be any limits and bounds set unto his power and influence?'

There is as great an aptness to trust in other means and let out our hearts to them. An arm of flesh signifies a great deal, when the power of an almighty Spirit is reckoned as nothing. And persons are apt to be very contriving, and prone to forecast, how such and such external forms would do our business and make the church and the christian interest hugely prosperous. As great an extravagancy as if we would suppose that fine sights would fill a hungry stomach, or that gay clothes would cure an ulcerous body. It is a very vain thing to think that anything that is merely external can reach this end, or do this business. For it cannot be done by any other way, by any might or power, but by the Spirit of the living God.

[243]

There is nothing that is so genuine and natural a product of the effusion of the Spirit as the life of religion in the world. And it may be shown how the Spirit may have an influence to this purpose, both *mediately* and *immediately*.

I. Mediately: He may have an influence to the promoting of the life, and vigour, and power of religion, by the intervention of some other things: as,

(1) By means of the kings and potentates of the earth. We have had experience how, in all times and ages, our own nation hath felt the different influences of the princes under which we have been. But we are not now to be confined within such narrow bounds; for we are speaking of the state of the church of God in general. And think how it will be if such scriptures ever come to have a fuller accomplishment than they have yet had; when in all the parts of the christian world kings shall be nursing fathers, queens nursing mothers, when the church shall suck the breasts of kings, when the glory of the Gentiles shall, by them, be brought into it! How much will it make for the prosperity of religion everywhere in the world when these shall become, in all places, the proper characteristics of princes, that they scatter the wicked with their eyes, that they are just, ruling in the fear of the Lord, and are upon the people, as showers upon the mown grass and as clear shinings after rain; are men of courage, men fearing God and hating covetousness! Think whether this will not do much to the making of a happy state as to the interest of religion in the world, when they shall universally concur, or very generally, in the practical acknowledgment that Christ is King of kings, and Lord of lords, willingly resign, as it were, their sceptres, or hold them only in a direct and designed subordination and subserviency to him and his sceptre!

(2) By and through them, upon whom the work of the gospel is incumbent in the church, the ministers of it. In such a time, when the Spirit shall be poured forth plentifully, surely they shall have their proportionable share. And when such a time as that shall once come, I believe you will hear much other kind of sermons, or they will who shall live to such a time, than you

[244]

are wont to do now-a-days. Souls will surely be dealt with at another kind of rate. It is plain, too sadly plain, there is a great retraction of the Spirit of God even from us. We know not how to speak living sense unto souls, how to get within you: our words die in our mouths, or drop and die between you and us. We even faint, when we speak; long experienced unsuccessfulness makes us despond. We speak not as persons that hope to prevail, that expect to make you serious, heavenly, mindful of God, and to walk more like christians. The methods of alluring and convincing souls, even that some of us have known, are lost from amongst us in a great part. There have been other ways taken, than we can tell how now to fall upon, for the mollifying of the obdurate, and the awakening of the secure, and the convincing and the persuading of the obstinate, and the winning of the disaffected. Sure there will be a larger share that will come even to the part of ministers when such an effusion of the Spirit shall be as is here signified. They shall know how to speak to better purpose, with more compassion and sense, with more seriousness, with more authority and allurement, than we now find we can.

We go on to speak,

II. Of the Holy Spirit's more *immediate* and direct influence upon the souls themselves to be wrought upon; which was the second head propounded to be spoken to. And so we are to reckon that his greater influence (when there shall be such an effusion of the Spirit as we have been speaking of) will show itself in these two great and noble effects. (1) In numerous conversions; and (2) In the high improvement and growth of those who sincerely embrace religion, their eminent holiness: which, when we consider, will make the matter we were last speaking of more apprehensible to us, what example may do to the spreading of it yet further and further; as things once growing, grow apace, especially such things as are themselves of a very growing and diffusive nature. The scripture speaks very much in many places to both these purposes.

(1) There are many passages of scripture that respect the matter of the church's increase by numerous conversions;

which is an increase as to its extent, as the other will be as to its glory. To instance in some few of the passages that speak of the enlargement of the church by numerous conversions:

We are told in Isa. 2.2 etc. what shall come to pass in the last days. You have these two forms of expression, 'The latter days', and, 'The last days'. The expression of the latter days doth more generally, according to the language of the Jews, intend the times of the Messiah. They divided time into these three great parts, the time or age before the law, the age under the law, and the age (as they called it) of the Messiah. The expression is here 'The last days', which seems rather to import the latter part of the latter time, as there is still later and later, till it come to the very last. Now 'in the last days, the mountain of the Lord's house', which is spoken by way of allusion to Sion, and the temple that stood upon that mountain, 'shall be established in the top of the mountains, and shall be exalted above the hills, and all nations shall flow unto it. And many people shall go and say, Come ye, and let us go up to the mountain of the Lord, to the house of the God of Jacob, and he will teach us of his ways, and we will walk in his paths; for out of Zion shall go forth the law, and the word of the Lord from Jerusalem. And he shall judge among the nations, and shall rebuke many people, and they shall beat their swords into ploughshares, and their spears into pruning-hooks: nation shall not lift up sword against nation, neither shall they learn war any more,' Isa. 2.2–4. Such a time as that the world hath not yet known, so as that it should be said generally concerning it, that this great effusion of the Spirit, and such a cessation from hostilities and wars in the world, should be concomitant and conjunct with one another: we have not had hitherto opportunity to observe a coincidency of these two things.

To the same purpose is that in the prophecy of Micah, which I mention as being of so near affinity with the very letter of this text. 'In the last days it shall come to pass, that the mountain of the house of the Lord shall be established in the top of the mountains, and it shall be exalted above the hills, and people shall flow unto it. And many nations shall come,

and say, Come and let us go up to the mountain of the Lord,
and to the house of the God of Jacob,' Mic. 4.1, 2. The same
words as before, with very little variation. And that passage of a
great prince's dream, of the stone cut out of the mountain
without hands, which became a great mountain, and filled the
earth, Dan. 2.34, 35. I can, for my part, neither understand it in
so carnal a sense as some do, nor in so limited a sense as others.
Certainly it must signify some greater thing than we have yet
seen. And such numerous accessions to the church by the power of the Holy Ghost in converting work, seem plainly intended
and pointed out, Isa. 54.1. 'Sing, O barren, thou that didst not
bear; break forth into singing and cry aloud, thou that didst
not travail with child: for more are the children of the desolate
(of her that was so) than the children of the married wife, saith
the Lord.' There should be a far greater fruitfulness than in
the time of their more formed, stable church state, when they
appeared a people in covenant-relation, married to God. This,
though spoken directly and immediately of the Jewish church,
means in and by them the universal gospel church, whom that
church did in some sort typically represent. 'Enlarge the place
of thy tent, (so it follows, ver. 2, 3.) and let them stretch forth
the curtains of thy habitations; spare not, lengthen thy cords,
and strengthen thy stakes: for thou shalt break forth on the
right hand, and on the left, and thy seed shall inherit the Gentiles, and make the desolate cities to be inhabited.' The like
is in Isa. 66.6, etc. 'A voice of noise from the city, a voice from
the temple, a voice of the Lord that rendereth recompense
to his enemies. Before she travailed, she brought forth; before
her pain came, she was delivered of a man child. Who hath
heard such a thing? Who hath seen such things? shall the earth
be made to bring forth in one day? or shall a nation be born at
once?' What can this intend but some such mighty effusion
of the Spirit by which there shall be great collections and
gatherings in of souls as it were on a sudden? To the same purpose in Isa. 60.5. 'Thou shalt see and flow together, and thine
heart shall fear and be enlarged, because the abundance of the
sea shall be converted unto thee, (the islanders, or those that

S

inhabit the more maritime places,) and the forces of the Gentiles shall come unto thee.' This is introduced in ver. 4, 'Lift up thine eyes round about and see: all they gather themselves together, they come to thee, thy sons shall come from far, and thy daughters shall be nursed at thy side.' And ver. 8, 'Who are these that fly as a cloud, and as the doves to their windows?' Gathering in like great flocks of doves, that, like a dense, opaquous cloud, darken the air as they fly! Which numerous increase is most emphatically signified by the apt and elegant metaphor used, Psa. 110.3, where it is said the subjects of Christ's kingdom should be multiplied as dew from the 'womb of the morning'. That is a vast and spacious womb; imagine how innumerable drops of dew distil out from thence; such shall the multitude of the converts be in the christian church.

That such scriptures have been fulfilling ever since the first dawnings of christianity, there is no doubt; but the magnificence of the expressions of many of these prophecies seems yet to be very far from being answered by correspondent effects. The passage in Joel 2.28 where it is said that the Spirit shall be poured forth upon all flesh, we are told, it is true, in Acts 2.16, that it had its accomplishment: 'This is that which was spoken by the prophet,' said Peter, when the people began to wonder at what they saw, upon that strange pouring forth of the Spirit on the day of Pentecost. But it is plain that he did not intend that the completion of that prophecy was confined to that point of time: for afterwards, in ver. 38, 39 he tells them that were now awakened, and cried, 'Men and brethren, what shall we do?' that they must 'repent and be baptized, and they should receive the gift of the Holy Ghost. For', saith he, 'the promise (that promise, most apparently, that he had reference to before) is unto you, and to your children, and to all that are afar off, even as many as the Lord our God shall call.' So that all that was intended in that prophecy is not fulfilled, till God hath done calling. And may other scriptures seem to intimate that there shall be a time of far more general calling than there hath been hitherto; when the receiving and gathering in of the Jews shall be as life from the dead, as a

[248]

resurrection from the dead, Rom. 11.15. And when 'The fulness of the Gentiles shall come in', ver. 25. The way of speaking implies that that fulness or plenitude was yet behind, to succeed after the apostle's time; and no such time hath succeeded yet.

(2) There are many scriptures also that speak of the great improvement and growth of christians by the immediate work of the Spirit of God. When I say immediate, I do not mean as if the Spirit works without means; but that by the means he doth himself immediately reach his subject; and therefore that all the operations of the Spirit, whether in converting or in building up of souls, lie not in the instruments, but strike through all, so as to reach their subject. But that only by the by. Many scriptures speak of the great improvement of the church in point of holiness; so that it shall increase not only in extent, but in glory, and in respect of the lustre, loveliness, and splendour of religion in it; that it shall become a much more beautiful and attractive thing, according to the representation which it shall have in the profession and conversation of them that sincerely embrace it. Which I suppose to be more especially pointed at in such passages as these: 'Arise, shine, for thy light is come, and the glory of the Lord is risen upon thee. For behold, the darkness shall cover the earth, and gross darkness the people; but the Lord shall arise upon thee, and his glory shall be seen upon thee. And the Gentiles shall come to thy light, and kings to the brightness of thy rising,' Isa. 60.1–3. This speaks that religion should be so glorious a thing in its own subject, as by that means to be inviting and attractive to those who were without the church; and so doth directly and immediately speak of such an effect as should be wrought by the Spirit of God upon persons seriously religious themselves, to make them far to excel and outshine the glory of former times and ages. This also is the more peculiar aspect and reference of that prophecy in Mal. 4.2. 'But unto you that fear my name, shall the Sun of righteousness arise with healing his wings.' That is, in the day of the Lord spoken of in ver. 1. 'Behold, the day cometh that shall burn as an oven; and all the proud, yea,

and all that do wickedly shall be stubble, and the day that cometh shall burn them up, saith the Lord of hosts, that it shall leave them neither root nor branch.' Here is a prediction of such an operation of the Spirit as hath the actual fearers of God already for the subject of it; upon them the Sun of righteousness shall arise with reviving, cherishing beams, and make them spring, and prosper, and flourish, even as calves of the stall, as it is there expressed. Religion will not then be such a faint, languid, impotent thing, as now it is, that makes men differ very little from other men; makes them but to look, and walk, and converse as others do.

(3) Other scriptures speak of both these effects together; and so of the increase of the church both ways at once, both in extent and glory. As I reckon all those may be understood to have that import that speak of the new heavens and the new earth that should be in the latter times: which are only metaphorical expressions; the heaven and the earth being the universe, making up the frame and compages* of nature. These expressions are only borrowed, and denote how universal and glorious a change should be in the world; for these new heavens and that new earth are specified by the same adjunct, 'wherein dwelleth righteousness', in one of those texts. We have it mentioned twice in the prophecy of Isaiah, that he would 'create new heavens, and a new earth', chap. 65.17, 66.22. and in 2 Pet. 3.13 that in these there should dwell righteousness. The renovation should consist in this; and both the universality and the intensive perfection of it are signified. The heavens and the earth, that is, the whole frame of things, should be the subject of the alteration; and this alteration should be a renovation, the making of them new, that is, better; as the newness of things is an ordinary scripture expression of the excellency of them. Now the creation of these must refer to this time of the great restitution: as John speaks, 'I saw a new heaven and a new earth; for the first heaven and the first earth were passed away', Rev. 21.1. The former frame of things was all vanished and gone; nothing was like its former self but 'all things were

* A system of many parts united.

[250]

made new', as is added, ver 5. A day wherein there should be, as it were, a new making of the world.

The following texts also speak of that double increase of the church jointly, Isa. 32.14, 15. A time and state of great desolation is spoken of as preceding and to be continued. Till when? 'Until the Spirit be poured upon us from on high;' and what then? 'The wilderness shall be a fruitful field.' There is the taking in of more from the world, extending the territories of the church further, the inclosing of much more of the wilderness than hath hitherto been. 'And the fruitful field be counted for a forest:' that which was before reckoned a fruitful field, be counted to have been but as a forest, in comparison of what it shall be improved to: there is the increase of the church in respect of the liveliness and power of religion among converts. So in chap. 35.1, 2. 'The wilderness and the solitary place shall be glad for them, and the desert shall rejoice, and blossom as the rose. It shall blossom abundantly, and rejoice even with joy and singing; the glory of Lebanon shall be given unto it, the excellency of Carmel and Sharon; they shall see the glory of the Lord, and the excellency of our God.'

And both these effects, numerous conversions and the high improvements of converts, are so connatural, so of the same kind, do so very well agree with one another, that we may very well suppose them to go together, that the former will be accompanied with the latter. For this great effusion of the Spirit we must understand to be sanative, intended for the healing of a diseased world, and to repair the corrupted forlorn state of things; and therefore must be proportionable to the state of the case, in reference whereto it is to be a means of cure. It is very apparent, that wickedness as it is the more diffusive is always the more malignant. The diffusion and the malignity are wont to accompany one another; just as it is with diseases – the plague and other distempers that are noisome and dangerous, they are always more mortal as they are more contagious and spreading; and so are extensively and intensively worse at the same time. And it must be proportionably so in the means of cure; there must be such a pouring forth of the Spirit that will answer the exigency

of the case in both respects, that there be very numerous conversions, and a great improvement of converts unto higher and
more excellent pitches of religion than have been usually known
in former times.

Objection. But here it may be said that it is very difficult to
conceive how all this should be, considering what the present
state and posture of the world is. As if we cast our eyes about
us and consider how it is in vast parts of it yet overrun with
paganism, in others with mohammedanism, in others with
antichristian pollutions and abominations. When we consider
how the world is generally sunk in atheism and oblivion of
God, drenched in wickedness; and even that part of it that is
called christian, how little it is better than the rest. The great
doctrines of the christian religion – the incarnation, the death,
the resurrection of our Lord Jesus Christ, the future judgment,
and the eternal states of men – all become even as antiquated
things, professedly believed for fashion's sake, because it is
not convenient to pretend to be of no religion. But yet all these
things lie with the most as ineffectual, insipid, unoperative
notions in their minds that do nothing; and notwithstanding
which they practise just as they would do if they believed no
such things. When we consider this to be the present state and
posture of the world, it is hard to conceive how such a change
as this is should come. And many may be apt to say in reference to this renovation or regeneration of the church – the
restitution of religion – as Nicodemus said concerning the regeneration of a particular person, 'How can these things be?'

Answer. Indeed the long-continued restraints of the acts of
absolute omnipotency make omnipotency even to seem but
equal to impotency, and men expect as little from the one as
from the other. When great and extraordinary things have
not been done through a long tract of time, they are no more
expected or looked for from the most potent cause, than they
are from the most impotent. And therefore, when any great
thing is done for the church and interest of God in the world,
it comes under this character, 'things that we looked not for',
Isa. 64.3. Things that do even surprise and transcend expecta-

tion, and which no man would have thought of! Men are very unapt to entertain the belief and expectation of things that are so much above the verge and sphere of ordinary observation. We expect to see what we have been wont to see; and men are apt to measure their faith by their eyes for the most part in reference to such things. Only that can be done which they have seen done, and men are hardly brought to raise their faith and expectation to higher pitches than this.

I shall shut up the present discourse with desiring you to remind and reflect upon the tendency of all this; that our souls may be possessed with a serious apprehension, and thence have a lively hope begotten in them, of such a time and state of things to come, wherein religion shall prosper and flourish in the world, though it now be at so low an ebb. I may say to you as Paul did to Agrippa, 'Why should it be thought a thing incredible with you, that God should raise the dead?' Acts 26.8. Why should it be thought an incredible thing that there should be a resurrection of religion? 'Thy dead men shall live, and together with my dead body shall they arise.' He hath said it who knows how to make it good; he who is the resurrection and the life, Isa. 26.19.

And really it would signify much to us, to have our hearts filled with present hope; though we have no hope (as was formerly supposed, admitting that supposition) of seeing it with our own eyes in our own days. Such a hope would however not be unaccompanied with a vital joy. 'Abraham rejoiced to see my day, and he saw it, and was glad;' though it was above two thousand years before. Plain it is, there is not a more stupifying, benumbing thing in all the world than mere despair. To look upon such a sad face and aspect of things through the world as we have before our eyes; to look upon it despairingly and with the apprehension that it never will, never can be better; nothing can more stupify and bind up the powers of our souls and sink us into a desponding meanness of spirit. But hope is a kind of anticipated enjoyment and gives a present participation in the expected pleasantness of those days, how long soever they may yet be off from us. By such a lively hope we have a presentation, a feeling in our own spirits of what is to come, that should even make our hearts rejoice and our bones to flourish as a herb. Religion shall not be an inglorious thing in the world always; it will not always be ignominious to be serious, to be a fearer of the Lord, to be a designer for heaven and for a blessed eternity. When these things which common and prevailing custom hath made ridiculous, with their own high reasonableness, shall have custom itself and a common reputation concurring, how will religion at that time lift up its head, when there is such a blessed conjunction! It is strange to think that such very absurd things as the neglecting of God and the forgetting of eternity, the disregarding of men's souls and everlasting concernments, should even be justified by custom, so that nobody is ashamed of them because they do but as other men do in these things.

To be immersed all their lifetime in the world – to mind nothing else but earthly business, as if they were made all of earth and only for earth – such most absurd things even seem to be justified by common practice. Men are not ashamed of them because they are but like their neighbours. But when persons shall agree with one another in being serious, heavenly, avowing the fear of God, in express devotedness and subjection to him; when the concurrence of common practice shall be taken in with the high reasonableness of the things themselves; how magnificently will religion look in that day! If we would but labour so to represent the matter to ourselves beforehand, by a lively hope of such a state of things we should have the anticipated enjoyment of the felicity of those times; and have a great deal of reason, though it may be we are to suffer hard and grievous things in the mean while, to compose ourselves, and to enter upon that state of suffering very cheerfully; to wait patiently and pray earnestly that of so great a harvest of spiritual blessings to come upon the world in future time, we may have some first-fruits in the mean time; as it is not unusual, when some very great and general shower is ready to fall, that some previous scattering drops light here and there as forerunners.

And we should encourage ourselves in the expectation of a

present portion, sufficient for our present turn and the exigency of our own case: for we have this comfortable consideration before us that there is always so much of the Spirit to be had that will serve the necessities of every christian who seriously seeks it. He will give his Spirit to his children who ask him, as readily, surely, as they that are evil will good gifts to theirs. At all times there is so much of the Spirit to be had, as, though it will not mend the world, it will mend us; if it will not better the external state of things, it will better our spirits; and so if not keep off suffering, yet will prepare and qualify us for it. That surely is a greater thing than to have suffering kept off, for suffering is but an external and natural evil, this internal and spiritual. It would be a great thing if persons would admit the conviction of this (and there is not a plainer thing in all the world), that patience is better than immunity from suffering: that great and noble effect of the Spirit of God upon the soul whereby it is brought into an entire possession of himself! Is that to be compared with a little advantage that only my flesh and outward man is capable of? Good things are to be estimated by the greatness and nobleness of their subjects. Surely the good of the mind, of the soul, must needs be far better than that which is only for the good of the body, of this perishing, external frame. And therefore for us, it is as great a thing as we can reasonably wish, that we may have such a portion of the Spirit imparted to us that will qualify us to pass well and comfortably through any time. And have not we reason to expect this, even on the grounds of what is foretold concerning what shall be done in the world hereafter? May I not look up with a great deal of hope and encouragement and say, 'Lord, that Spirit of thine that shall one day so flow down upon the world, may not I have some portion of it to answer my present necessities? And that Spirit that can make the world new, that can create new heavens and a new earth, cannot that make new one poor soul? cannot it better one poor heart?' To have a new heart and a right spirit created and renewed in us is better to us than all the world. And we have no reason to look up diffidently and with despondency, but with hearts full of expectation. He will give his Spirit to them that ask him.

Two

C. H. SPURGEON'S
VIEWS ON PROPHECY

It is well known how openly Spurgeon owned his debt to the literature of the Puritans and how, because of his attachment to their theology at a time when it was again being put aside, he was dubbed 'the last of the Puritans'. In his thought on prophecy, Spurgeon certainly continued several of the emphases prominent in the Puritan outlook, particularly belief in the national conversion of the Jews and in the future conversion of the world. In the first volume of his Sermons, for the year 1855, he says, 'I think we do not attach sufficient importance to the restoration of the Jews. We do not think enough of it. But certainly, if there is anything promised in the Bible it is this' (p. 214). He did not place the conversion of the Jews at the consummation of history but rather at the beginning of a period of general revival: 'The day shall yet come when the Jews, who were the first apostles to the Gentiles, the first missionaries to us who were afar off, shall be gathered in again. Until that shall be, the fulness of the church's glory can never come. Matchless benefits to the world are bound up with the restoration of Israel; their gathering in shall be as life from the dead.' (Vol. 17, 703–4).

On this point Spurgeon spoke with certainty throughout his thirty-eight years' ministry in London. Yet on some of the cardinal points which have usually divided interpreters of prophecy, Spurgeon was far from clear, and cannot be said to have followed any previous school of thought consistently. On the crucial issue as to *how* the Jews would be converted and the gospel triumph, whether by Christ's personal advent or by the outpouring of the Spirit, Spurgeon from the outset of his ministry in London appears to have held unequivocally that it would be by Christ's personal appearing, that is, he taught a pre-millennial advent: 'He who understands the prophets, believes not in the immediate conversion of the world, nor in universal peace; he believes in "Jesus only"; he expects that Jesus will first come; and to him, the great hope of the future is the coming of the Son of Man' ('Jesus Only', a Sermon preached in 1857, Vol. 45, 374). Two years later in a sermon 'A Vision of the Latter-Day Glories', he says, 'When Christ shall come he will make short work of that which is so long a labour to his church. His appearance will immediately convert the Jews' (Vol. 5, 198). This pre-millennial belief remained with Spurgeon throughout his ministry, it is expressed in some of the closing sermons of his life, and in a brief confessional statement drawn up in 1891, he subscribed to the tenet, 'Our hope is the Personal Pre-millennial Return of the Lord Jesus in glory' (*The Sword and Trowel*, 1891, 446). In a sermon on 2 Timothy 3.5, preached in 1889, he says: 'Apart from the second Advent of our Lord, the world is more likely to sink into a pandemonium than to rise into a millennium. A divine interposition seems to me the hope set before us in Scripture, and, indeed, to be the only hope adequate to the occasion' (Vol. 35, 301).

There is, however, another strand running through his sermons – what may be called the main strand of Puritan prophetic thought – and this cannot be harmonized with the statements just quoted. In two sermons on the calling of the Jews, and in so far as we are aware they contain his fullest treatment of the subject, one preached in 1864 and the other in 1877, there is no reference whatever to their conversion being through the sight of Christ's person; on the contrary, their salvation is spoken of as the work of the Spirit producing faith. It is 'the unseen but omnipotent Jehovah' who 'is to be worshipped in spirit and in truth by his ancient people' and the means used by the Spirit for their ingathering are preaching and praying: 'Preaching is the blast of the ram's horn ordained to level Jericho, and the sound of the silver trumpet appointed to usher in the jubilee. . . . O for greater faith, to believe that nations may be born in a day, that multitudes may be turned unto God at once, and we shall yet see it – see what our fathers never saw' ('Mourning for Christ', vol. 23, and 'The Restoration and Conversion of the Jews', vol. 10, the quotation being from the latter sermon, pp. 429, 434 and 436).

The theme of the universal spread of the gospel through preaching which will be in demonstration of the Spirit and with power is by no means infrequent, and on some occasions, as for example in a sermon on Psalm 22.27 entitled 'The Triumph of Christianity', it receives extensive exposition. In this sermon Spurgeon attacks the idea that we are not to hope for a glorious future on earth brought about by the preaching of the gospel and opposes those who 'foretell that we are nearing the period of decay, when something better will supplant the gospel'. The heads of this sermon are: '1. The Conversion of the Nations to God May be Expected. 2. The Conversion of the Nations will Occur in the Usual Manner of Other Conversions. 3. The Means to Accomplish this Result Are to be Found At Calvary.' To the same purpose, he spoke as follows at a Missionary Meeting in May, 1867 while dealing with the need for more missionaries: 'It would be easy to show that at our present rate of progress the kingdoms of this world never could become the kingdom of our Lord and of His Christ. Indeed, many in the Church are giving up the idea of it except on the occasion of the advent of Christ, which, as it chimes in with our own idleness, is likely to be a popular doctrine. I myself believe that King Jesus will reign, and the idols be utterly abolished; but I expect the same power which turned the world upside down once will still continue to do it. The Holy Ghost would never suffer the imputation to rest upon His holy name that He was not able to convert the world' (quoted by G. H. Pike, *Life and Work of Charles Haddon Spurgeon*, vol. 4, 210).

This harmonizes with the school of John Owen, John Howe and Jonathan Edwards, while it is foreign to the pre-millennial outlook.

It needs also to be said that on such distinctive points of pre-millennialism as the refusal to apply much Old Testament

[258]

prophecy to the New Testament Church, the emphasis on terrestial Jerusalem as the centre of future hope, the idea of two future Comings of Christ – one to establish his kingdom upon earth and another to conclude it at the day of judgment – on all these Spurgeon is, as far as the present writer is aware, entirely silent. On one occasion he does speak of two future resurrections separated by an interval of time, the duration of which he does not determine (Vol. 7, 346), but this is far from common in his Sermons, where his general practice is to treat Christ's Return and the Day of Judgment as one event. In an article, 'Jerusalem which is above', he makes a pungent attack on the general prophetic outlook of the Brethren though professing, in a sentence, his own attachment to the pre-millennial school of interpretation. Belief in 'two advents of Christ, one before and the other after the Millennium', he characterizes as one of 'the strange vagaries of seducers' (*The Sword and Trowel*, August 1866). One is not surprised, therefore, to find Spurgeon representing the coming of Christ as the means whereby believers will enter upon perfect blessedness and *eternal* blessedness, 'They can say good-bye to sin, and good-bye to sorrow; they can say to all discouragements, to all bafflings, to all defeats, "Farewell" ' (Vol. 45, 597).

Of the alleged difference between 'the Church' and God's people in other 'dispensations', maintained by J. N. Darby, Spurgeon declared: 'We have even heard it asserted that those who lived before the coming of Christ do not belong to the church of God! We never know what we shall hear next, and perhaps it is a mercy that these absurdities are revealed one at a time, in order that we may be able to endure their stupidity without dying of amazement (Vol. 15, 8). Little did he think that within twenty years of his death a dispensationalist, A. C. Dixon, would succeed to his pulpit at the Metropolitan Tabernacle!

While there is much longing for the day of Christ observable in Spurgeon – perhaps particularly so as he grew as a saint and his life approached its end – he never accepted the most common feature of nineteenth-century pre-millennialism, namely, that in point of time the Advent and millennium were at hand. 'You want the millennium to come tomorrow, do you?' he said on one occasion. 'May you get it, but I think it is probable you will not. I do not know how history appears to you who profess to understand it, but it does not read to me like a thing which is going to end yet' (Vol. 11, 273). In accordance with this Spurgeon often spoke and thought of the continuing work of the Church after his death and urged upon believers the duty of so living that posterity would be blessed.

*　　*　　*

We know of no ready solution to the apparently contradictory features in Spurgeon's thought on prophecy. His biographer, G. H. Pike, has suggested that he moved from one position to another and believes he sees a difference between the thought in Spurgeon's first book, published in 1857, and the outlook of his later days: *The Saint and his Saviour* reveals 'what Spurgeon was in those sanguine days of his early prime when the wide world stretched before him as a domain to be won by the Church for her Lord. When he had received a few scars in the conflict, and had sobered down somewhat, he looked more to the Second Coming of Christ to bring about the final conquest which was so ardently desired (*The Life and Work of C. H. Spurgeon*, vol. 5, 96).

It does not seem to us that this solution fits the facts already given above. There are explicit pre-millennial statements in some of the early volumes of his sermons, while some of his stronger words on the other side occur twenty years later.

While we make no attempt here to offer an adequate solution there are, it would appear, at least three facts which any explanation of Spurgeon on prophecy must take into account.

First, it is likely that after his first few years in London, when conversions took place in large numbers, and particularly after what may be called the national spiritual awakening in Ulster in 1859, Spurgeon was more inclined to emphasize and preach the traditional Puritan hope which he had imbibed during his upbringing and youth. Returning from a short

visit to Ireland in January, 1860, he told his congregation at
the Exeter Hall: 'It has been my lot these last six years to preach
to crowded congregations, and to see many, many souls brought
to Christ; but this week I have seen what mine eyes have never
before beheld, used as I am to extraordinary things. . . .'
In the course of the same sermon he declared: 'God is about
to send times of surprising fertility to his Church. When a
sermon has been preached in these modern times, if one sinner
has been converted by it, we have rejoiced with a suspicious
joy; for we have thought it something amazing. But, brethren,
where we have seen one converted, we may yet see hundreds;
where the word of God has been powerful to scores, it shall be
blessed to thousands; and where hundreds in past years have
seen it, nations shall be converted to Christ. God, the Holy
Ghost is not stinted in his power' (A Revival Sermon', vol. 6,
81–8).

Second, Spurgeon possessed a profound distrust of many
pre-millennial dealers in prophecy who, working upon the excitement caused in Victorian evangelicalism by the new ideas of
the Plymouth Brethren, set themselves up as the expounders
of all mysteries and treated the subject of prophecy as though it
were *the* key to Christianity. There are many warnings in
Spurgeon against that sort of interest in prophecy. A biblical
preacher, he told his congregation, 'wants to have souls saved
and Christians quickened and therefore he does not for ever
pour out the vials, and blow the trumpets of prophecy. Some
hearers are crazy after the mysteries of the future. Well, there
are two or three brethren in London who are always trumpet-
ing and vialing. Go and hear them if you want it, I have something else to do' (Vol. 21, 91). Again, addressing the students
at his college, he says:

'I am greedy after witnesses for the glorious gospel of the
blessed God. O that Christ crucified were the universal burden
of men of God. Your guess at the number of the beast, your
Napoleonic speculations, your conjectures concerning a personal Antichrist – forgive me, I count them but mere bones for
dogs; while men are dying and hell is filling, it seems to me

the veriest drivel to be muttering about an Armageddon at Sebastopol, or Sadowa or Sedan, and peeping between the folded leaves of destiny to discover the fate of Germany. Blessed are they who read and hear the words of the prophecy of the Revelation, but the like blessing has evidently not fallen on those who pretend to expound it, for generation after generation of them have been proved to be in error by the mere lapse of time, and the present race will follow to the same inglorious sepulchre' (*Lectures to my Students*, First Series, 1887, 83).

In the same volume he tells his students that, 'A prophetical preacher enlarged so much upon "the little horn" of Daniel, that one Sabbath morning he had but seven hearers remaining' (p. 100). There is much more in Spurgeon in the same vein; he ridiculed the novelties of interpretation which were being hawked about as new insights into Scripture and did not underestimate the spiritual evil which was resulting from the disproportionate attention which a number were giving to prophecy. This, in part, explains why in the long course of his ministry he preached very few sermons indeed in which unfulfilled prophecy receives any major treatment.

Third, in strong contrast with the dogmatism and system-building of the prophetic interpreters who were his contemporaries, Spurgeon was deliberately open in acknowledging the limitations of his understanding. 'There is a whole Book of Revelation which I do not understand, but which I fully believe' (Vol. 45, 402), 'I scarcely consider myself qualified to explain any part of the Book of Revelation, and none of the expositions I have ever seen entice me to attempt the task, (Vol. 21, 313). In a review of a book by B. C. Young entitled, *Short Arguments about the Millennium; or, plain proofs for plain Christians that the coming of Christ will not be pre-millennial; that his reign will not be personal*, Spurgeon makes this interesting comment:

'Those who wish to see the arguments upon the unpopular side of the great question at issue, will find them here; this is probably one of the ablest of the accessible treatises from that point of view. We cannot agree with Mr. Young, neither can we refute him . . . the perusal of this work might be very useful to those dogmatical prophets who think that they are masters of the whole matter, when in fact there are great mysteries surrounding it on every hand. Only fools and madmen are positive in their interpretations of the Apocalypse' (*The Sword and Trowel*, 1867, p. 470).

G. H. Pike says, 'Much interest was felt in Mr. Spurgeon's views on prophecy, and perhaps this interest was the more keen on account of his not preaching so often on prophetical themes as some of his brethren in the ministry.' Pike goes on to give this quotation from a letter from Spurgeon to the editor of *Messiah's Herald*, written in 1874:

'The more I read the Scriptures as to the future, the less I am able to dogmatise. I see conversion of the world, and the personal pre-millennial reign, and the sudden coming, and the judgment, and several other grand points; but I cannot put them into order, nor has anyone else done so yet. I believe every prophetical work I have ever seen (and I have read very many) to be wrong in some points. I feel more at home in preaching Christ crucified than upon any other theme, and I do believe He will draw all men unto Him' (Pike, vol. 5, 133).

This certainly throws light upon why Spurgeon was prepared to allow major ambiguities, and indeed inconsistencies, to co-exist in his thinking on prophecy. There was, as he admits, a fundamental uncertainty in his mind which showed itself in various ways. Sometimes he would by-pass the question of the future with such words as 'I am not now going into millennial theories' (vol. 10, 429) or 'I shall not go into any details about when he will come: I will not espouse the cause of the pre-millennial or the post-millennial advent' (vol. 27, 391). On other occasions he would speak so strongly of the progress and triumph of the gospel through the power of the Holy Ghost that no room is left for a personal advent prior to the conversion of the world. And yet, again, he would proclaim a pre-millennial appearing in such terms that one might assume he had repudiated all his many statements on the other side.

All this means that there are excellent statements in Spurgeon of varied viewpoints and I have made use in this book of some of these which follow in the Puritan tradition. But as Spurgeon would himself have been the first to say, no one should go to him to clarify their thinking on unfulfilled prophecy. He was a preacher like Knox and Whitefield, moulded by God to make history rather than to interpret its future course.

That the pre-millennial hope came more to the fore in Spurgeon's closing years is not surprising. For it was then that he fought the cruel battle of the Down-Grade, when disbelief in any personal advent of Christ began to be heard in the Church and when the idea of 'progress' became a hallmark of liberalism. Even so, despite ill-health and the prevalent and growing unbelief in the churches, he still looked to the Holy Spirit to turn the tide once more:

'At the present moment, it seems as if parts of the church had almost forgotten the gospel of the grace of God. We hear on all hands "another gospel, which is not another; but there be some that trouble you, and would pervert the gospel of Christ". Worldliness is growing over the church, she is mossed with it. The visible church is honeycombed through and through with a baptized infidelity. Unholy living is following upon unbelieving thinking. They boast that they have nearly extirpated Puritanism: some of us are described as the last of the race. Have they quenched our coal? Far from it. The light of the doctrines of grace shall yet again shine forth as the sun. Elijah was wont to say "As the Lord liveth, before whom I stand"; and this also is my confidence: truth lives because God lives. Though truth were dead and buried, it would rise again. The day is not far distant when the old, old gospel shall again command the scholarship of the age, and shall direct the thoughts of men. The fight is not over yet; the brunt of the battle is yet to come. They dreamed that the old gospel was dead more than a hundred years ago, but they digged its grave too soon. Conformists and Nonconformists had alike gone over to a cold Socinianism, and in the old sanctuaries, where holy men once preached with power, modern dreamers droned out their wretched philosophies. All was decorous and dead; but God would not have it so. On a sudden, a voice was heard from Oxford, where the Wesleys and their compeers had found a living Saviour, and were bound to tell of his love. From an inn in Gloucester there came a youth, who began to preach the everlasting gospel with trumpet tongue. A new era dawned. Two schools of Methodists with fiery energy proclaimed the living word. All England was aroused. A new springtide arrived: the time of the singing of birds had come; life rejoiced where once death withered all things. It will be so again. The Lord liveth, and the gospel liveth too' ('Confidence and Concern', a sermon preached in August, 1886, vol. 32, 429-31).

Note: All the quotations from Spurgeon's sermons given above are from the sixty-three volume series *The New Park Street Pulpit* and *The Metropolitan Tabernacle Pulpit*, a number of which are currently being reprinted by the Banner of Truth Trust.

NOTES

I Revival Christianity: England

1. John Knox, *History of the Reformation in Scotland*, edited by William Croft Dickinson, 1949, vol. 1, 62.
2. Quoted by Jasper Ridley, *John Knox*, 1968, 326.
3. Ibid., 327.
4. James Kirkton, *The Secret and True History of the Church of Scotland*, 1817, 21–22.
5. *The Lives of the Puritans*, Benjamin Brook, 1813, vol. 1, 383.
6. *The Works of Thomas Goodwin*, 1861, vol. 2, xiii.
7. Samuel Clarke, in his *Lives of Thirty-two English Divines*, 1652, is one of the few primary sources of information on the Puritan leaders of this period. His biographical accounts are well used and supplemented in William Haller, *The Rise of Puritanism*, 1938, reprinted 1957.
8. Goodwin, *Works*, vol. 2, lvi.
9. Goodwin, *Works*, vol. 4, 252–3.
10. Haller, op. cit., 68.
11. Samuel Clarke, quoted by H. C. Porter, *Reformation and Reaction in Tudor Cambridge*, 1958, 227.
12. Quoted in Goodwin, *Works*, vol. 2, xvii.
13. Life of the Rev. J. Angier, in *The Whole Works of the Rev. Oliver Heywood*, vol. 1, 521.
14. *Reliquiae Baxterianae: Or, Mr. Richard Baxter's Narrative of his Life and Times*, 1696, part 1, 84–97.
15. *Spectator* No. 494 (26.9.1712), quoted in Goodwin, *Works*, vol. 2, xxxiii.
16. Matthew Henry, *The Life of the Rev. Philip Henry*, corrected and enlarged by J. B. Williams, 1825, 19–20.
17. Ibid., 89.

II Revival Christianity: Scotland

1. See the life of Rollock in *The Scots Worthies*, John Howie, revised by W. H. Carslaw, 1902, 74.
2. *Expository Thoughts on the Gospels*, St. John, 1877, vol. 1, xiii. Some of his works were reprinted in the last century by the Wodrow Society, *Select Works of Robert Rollock*, edited by W. M. Gunn, 1859.

3. *Sermons by the Rev. Robert Bruce, with Collections for his Life by Robert Wodrow*, edited by William Cunningham, 1853, 145. A fine full-length biography of *Robert Bruce, Minister in the Kirk of Edinburgh*, was written by D. C. MacNicol in 1907, reprinted 1961.

4. *The Fulfilling of the Scripture*, 1801 reprint, vol. 1, 365, 378.

5. MacNicol, op. cit., 85.

6. From his 'brotherly and free Epistle' in his *Survey of the Spiritual Antichrist*, 1648. It is singularly sad that so little information has survived on Welch's ministerial labours in Scotland. What knowledge there is will be found in James Young's *Life of John Welch*, 1866. David Dickson's words on Welch are very suggestive. When any used to speak to him of the marvellous success of his own ministry, he would say that 'the grape gleanings of Ayr in Mr. Welch's time were far above the vintage of Irvine in his own'.

7. A rich but little known literature exists on the subsequent revivals in this area. It includes Dr. John Kennedy's *The Days of the Fathers in Ross-shire*, 1861, and John Noble's *Religious Life in Ross*, 1909.

8. For Boyd's work at Glasgow see H. M. B. Reid, *The Divinity Principals in the University of Glasgow, 1545–1654*, 1917.

9. *The Life of Mr. Robert Blair, Containing His Autobiography*, edited for the Wodrow Society by Thomas M'Crie, 1858, 10.

10. Life of Mr. John Livingstone in *Select Biographies*, edited for the Wodrow Society by W. K. Tweedie, 1855, vol. 1, 309 and 134. Speaking of the reading which shaped his future life, Livingstone says, 'Those whereby I profited most were the preachings of four men, Mr. Robert Rollock, Mr. John Welch, Mr. Robert Bruce, and Mr. David Dickson, whom I thought of all that I had read breathed most of the Spirit of God, least affected, most clear and plain, and most powerful. . . . Mr. Robert Bruce I severall times heard, and in my opinion never man spake with greater power since the apostles' dayes.' Ibid., 140.

11. H. M. B. Reid, op. cit., 153.

12. *The Theology and Theologians of Scotland*, 1872, 5. An article by George Christie, 'Scripture Exposition in Scotland in the Seventeenth Century' in *Records of The Scottish Church History Society*, vol. 1, part iii, gives a good account of the popular series envisaged by Dickson.

13. *Select Biographies*, vol. 1, 317.

14. *The Fulfilling of the Scripture*, vol. 1, 355. It would appear that the awakening at Stewarton began before May, 1623, for Robert Blair engaged in it and by that date he had crossed to Ireland, *Life of Blair*, 19.

15. Op. cit., 355. It is characteristic of the Puritan age that Livingstone himself, in recalling the day at Shotts, in his *Life* says nothing of the numbers. That five hundred were *converted* under Livingstone's sermon was not stated by Fleming though it has been carelessly asserted by later writers.

16. From a manuscript narrative by Andrew Stewart, whose father, another Scot, apparently crossed to Ireland in 1627. It was evidently the father, Andrew Stewart, senior, who reported what he saw at Oldstone. The best consecutive account of this awakening in Ireland will be found in

History of the Presbyterian Church in Ireland, James S. Reid, new edition 1867, vol. 1. The quote from Stewart is given on p. 110.

17. Reid says, on the authority of Stewart, that the monthly meeting at Antrim commenced in 1626. Wodrow's dating of the awakening as 1636 is undoubtedly wrong and may well be a copying error for 1626. Fleming is not far out in dating the revival 'about the year 1628 and some years thereafter'.

18. John Gillies' abridgement of Blair's words which can be found in full in his *Life*, op. cit., 71–86.

19. *Select Biographies*, vol. 1, 143–4.

20. Op. cit., 356.

21. Wodrow, *Sermons of Robert Bruce*, 151.

22. *History of the Presbyterian Church in Ireland*, vol. 1, 208. Of Robert Cunningham, Livingstone says: 'To my discerning he was the one man who most resembled the meekness of Jesus Christ, in all his carriage, that ever I saw.' At his death, 'besides many other gracious expressions, he said, "I see Christ standing over Death's head, and saying, Deal warily with my servant, loose now this pin, then that pin, for this tabernacle must be set up again".'

23. Kirkton, op. cit., 64–5. Kirkton, born about 1620, was ordained before the Restoration and ejected from his church at Mertoun, in the Merse, in 1662. His history was edited by an episcopalian minister, Charles K. Sharpe, who published it in 1817 with numerous slanderous and inaccurate notes aimed against the cause which Kirkton loved.

III *Unfulfilled Prophecy – the Development of the Hope*

1. *The Institutes of the Christian Religion*, book iii, ch. xxv, 5.

2. Theodore Zahn, quoted in *The Approaching Advent of Christ*, Alexander Reese, 1937, 314.

3. *Sermons on the Epistles of St. Paul to Timothy and Titus*, 1579, 740–1.

4. An interesting biographical account of Broughton is given in *The British and Foreign Evangelical Review*, vol. 18, 678.

5. *A Commentarie upon the first five chapters of the Epistle to the Galatians*, 1617, 159. And elsewhere in his writings, e.g., 'A Fruitful Dialogue Concerning The End Of The World', *The Works of W. Perkins*, 1618, vol. 3, 470.

6. *The Complete Works of Richard Sibbes*, edited by A. B. Grosart, 1862, vol. 1, 99.

7. Ibid., vol. 2, 498. Other references in Sibbes are given by Sidney H. Rooy in *The Theology of Missions in the Puritan Tradition*, 1965, to which I am indebted.

8. William Strong, *Thirty-one Select Sermons Preached on Special Occasions*, 1656, particularly sermons 12 and 20.

9. See a sermon before the House of Commons in *The Works of William Bridge*, 1845, vol. 4, 404.

10. Sermon preached on March 27, 1644, *Works of George Gillespie*, 1846, vol. 1.

11. See the Epistle Dedicatory to his sermon 'Satan the Leader in chief of all who resist the Reparation of Sion', 1643.

12. Published along with a secular piece, *The Hope of Israel*, by Manasseh Ben Israel. Wall's discourses consist mainly of eight reasons 'why we ought to mind their Conversion'.

13. *Epistle to the Romans*, 1568, 349.

14. *A Revelation of the Apocalypse*, Works of Thomas Brightman, 1644, 544-5.

15. Ibid., 847. Brightman had a novel interpretation of Revelation 20. He considered that the chapter predicted not one thousand-year period but two, the first from A.D. 300 to 1300, when the power of heathen Emperors would be bound, to be followed at its close by the 'first resurrection' which he interpreted as the glorious return of the truth to the world in the days of Wycliffe and other early Reformers. The second millennium would run from the conclusion of the first and see the full calling of the Jews; the latter, he believed, was the event predicted in Revelation 20.12 – not the general resurrection of the dead. Chapters 21 and 22 deal with the glorious state of the Church upon earth during this period when the saints will await Christ's personal advent.

There is a good deal that is fanciful in Brightman – earning him Dr. Cooper's rebuke, 'pretending to give us a Revelation of the Revelation he hath set forth an obscuration thereof' – but his work no doubt served to draw closer attention to many areas of Scripture connected with unfulfilled prophecy. Unhappily he led some away with a scheme which fixed the dates of future events. The practice of settling the times when prophetic events would be fulfilled was carefully avoided by most Puritans, including Owen, who warned his congregation in 1680, 'Take heed of *computations*. How wofully and wretchedly have we been mistaken by this!' *Works*, vol. 9, 510. Goodwin gives some of the current 'conjectures' on the time when the Jews would be called (*Works*, vol. 3, 195 f.), soon to be disproved, as usual, by the passage of time.

16. *The Works of Elnathan Parr*, 3rd ed., 1633, 175.

17. *The Beloved City or, the Saints' Reign on Earth a Thousand Years*, translated by W. Burton, 1642. The title is misleading and does not convey the burden of Alsted's thought.

18. John Owen attributes the rise of belief in 'the *personal reign* of Christ on the earth for a thousand years with his saints' to Mede's influence, *Works*, vol. 20, 152, and he rejects it *Works* 8, 259. Mede's views are discussed further by James A. de Jong in *As the Waters Cover the Sea*, Millennial Expectations in the Rise of Anglo-American Missions, 1640–1810, 1970, 16–27.

19. Quoted by P. G. Rogers in his *The Fifth Monarchy Men*, 1966.

20. Among those holding this view were John Cotton (in *The Churches Resurrection or The Opening of the 5th and 6th verses of the 20th Chapter of the Revelation*, 1642), James Durham and Robert Fleming.

21. I suggest this as the explanation of an oft-quoted comment by Robert Baillie, one of the Scottish delegates at the Westminster Assembly. He wrote from London on September 5, 1645, 'the most of the chief divines here, not only Independents, but others, such as Twiss, Marshall, Palmer, and many more, are express chiliasts'. Baillie, *Letters and Journals*, vol. 2, 156.

Andrew Bonar, assuming that Baillie employed the term 'chiliast' with the same fixed meaning which we now give to it, used this quotation to claim that 'the belief of Christ's Pre-millennial Coming prevailed in England among the members of the Westminster Assembly of Divines'. *Redemption Drawing Nigh*, 25. This is certainly a mistake, for pre-millennial Puritan divines were never more than a minority and they never claimed to hold the generally accepted view – rather the reverse. See John Durant, *The Salvation of the Saints by the Appearance of Christ*, 1653, preface to Second Part, and Increase Mather, *The Mystery of Israel's Salvation*, preface to the Reader. I can only conclude that in the sentence referred to in his Letters, Baillie was classing as 'chiliasts' all who took the millennium as still to be realized in history. When, in his book *A Dissuasive from the Errours of the Time*, published in the autumn of 1645, he opposes the distinctly pre-millennial view, he refers to only a few Puritans who held it.

22. Op. cit., 176. Speaking of the general calling of the Jews and the consequent enrichment of the world, he says: 'Some learned men apply hither, Isa. 24.21, Ezek. 38.8 and Rev. 21. I confess I can bring no plain place to back this: But Paul's own authority is sufficient, because we know he wrote by the Spirit.' Brightman was one of these 'learned men'.

23. *Works*, Goold edition, vol. 20, 154. John Howe shows the same caution and declines to build his expectation of the Church's larger future blessing upon the thousand years of Revelation 20, *Works of John Howe*, 1837, 568. B. B. Warfield would have endorsed this approach. He writes: 'We are forced, indeed, to add our assent to Kliefoth's conclusion, that "the doctrine of a thousand-year kingdom has no foundation in the prophecies of the New Testament, and is therefore not a dogma but merely a hypothesis lacking all biblical ground" . . . But this conclusion obviously does not carry with it the denial that a "golden age" yet lies before the Church, if we may use this designation in a purely spiritual sense.' *Biblical Doctrines*, 1929, 662. The view, held by the authors mentioned in note 20 above, became, however, the dominant one in the eighteenth century and became known as postmillennialism.

24. The circulation of the *Geneva Bible* after 1560, with its notes on Romans 11, was itself enough to ensure this.

25. *A Dissuasive from the Errours of the Time*, 1645, ch. 11, 'The Thousand Years of Christ his visible reign upon earth is against Scripture'.

26. *A Confutation of the Millenarian Opinion*, 1657, 73.

27. See his work, *The Glorious Kingdom of Christ, Described and Clearly Vindicated*. Against the bold Asserters of a Future Calling and Reign of the

Jews, and 1,000 years before the Conflagration, 1691. Also his *Auto-biography*, Everyman's Library, 1931, 121. Among non-Puritan divines of the Church of England there appears to have been a more general opposition to a future conversion of the Jews; John Prideaux, Regius Professor at Oxford, delivered a Latin Lecture against the belief in 1621, and Joseph Hall, Bishop of Norwich, published a counter to the millennialism encouraged by Mede and Alsted, *The Revelation Un-revealed*, in the 1640's. Hall writes on this theme with his characteristic eloquence – reprinted in his *Works*, 1837, vol. 8.

28. Christopher Love, in his sermons on *Christ's Glorious Appearing*, preached at Lawrence Jury, London, in the 1640's, says: 'When the Lord shall bring in the Jews with an eminent and general conversion, then you may conclude the day is not far off; for so all the interpreters say, that the Jews' conversion, and Christ's coming to judgment, will not be far distant.' *The Works of Christopher Love*, 1805, vol. 1, 59.

29. It appears that the pre-millennialism of some of the leading Inde-pendents has sometimes been overstated. Speaking of what had led him to adopt the 'more controverted' view, Goodwin commences with this caution: 'It is not that Christ himself shall come down – that is the old error of some – to reign at Jerusalem; which error indeed the fathers spake against and which hath brought a blemish and absurdity upon that opinion.' Sermon 34 on Ephesians 1, *Works of Thomas Goodwin*, 1861, vol. 1, 521. Burroughs expresses himself similarly: 'It shall be the glorious presence of Christ that shall be amongst them. I say, the Glorious Presence of Christ; I do not say, the Personal presence of Christ in his Body . . .' *Jerusalem's Glory*, 60–61. Goodwin's words are hard to reconcile with the sermon attributed to him in volume 12 of his *Works*, 'A Glimpse of Zion's Glory'; the authorship of the latter is, however, a matter of dispute. William Haller attributes it not to Goodwin but to Hanserd Knollys, *The Rise of Puritanism*, 1957, 270 and 396. John F. Wilson, in 'A Glimpse of Syon's Glory', *Church History*, vol. 31, 1962, 223–41, argues against the theory of Knollys' authorship. There is a positiveness in 'A Glimpse' which does not harmonize with the tone of Goodwin's Ephesian sermon, and, further, in the former the personal descent and reign of Christ is asserted (*Works*, 12, 71), while in the latter it is denied. Now as 'A Glimpse' was published in 1641 and the Ephesians series preached later this alone is strong evidence against 'A Glimpse' being Goodwin's work. One extant copy of 'A Glimpse' gives the author as 'T.G.' (on account of which it came to be included in the twelfth volume of the last-century edition of Goodwin) but other copies give no author's name or initials.

Geoffrey F. Nuttall gives some further information on Millenarians in the 1640–1660 period, most of them far less sober than Goodwin and Burroughs and more on the fringe of orthodox Puritanism, *Visible Saints*, The Congregational Way, 1957, 144 ff.

30. *The Complete Works of Thomas Manton*, 1870, vol. 1, 109.

31. *A Commentary on The Psalms*, see Psalm 67.

32. *Letters of Samuel Rutherford*, edited by Andrew Bonar, 1905, 599.

33. 'Mr Rutherford's Testimony to the Covenanted Work of Reformation', appended to *Religious Letters of Samuel Rutherford*, 1796, 524.
34. *Sermons Delivered in Times of Persecution in Scotland*, edited by John Howie, 1880, 457.

IV *Apostolic Testimony: the Basis of the Hope*

1. *The Great Mystery of Godliness Opened, Being an Exposition upon Romans 9*, 1653, 36.
2. *Christ and Israel*, F. J. M. Potgieter, 1961, 33.
3. Mather, op. cit., 14.
4. From his 'Compendium Theologiae Christianae' as reprinted in *Reformed Dogmatics*, 1965, edit. John W. Beardslee III, 180. This volume is made up of extracts from the writings of J. Wollebius, G. Voetius and F. Turretin.
5. Mather, op. cit., 2.
6. *A Commentary upon the Book of Revelation*, 1680, 532.
7. *Works*, 1834, vol. 1, 607.
8. Quoted by William Hendriksen in *Israel and the Bible*, 1968, 41.
9. Parr, op. cit., 197-8.
10. Hendriksen, op. cit., 47.
11. *A Logical Analysis of the Epistle to the Romans*, 1850 reprint (Wodrow Society), 233.
12. Parr, op. cit., 176.
13. *Exposition of Romans*, with Large Practical Observations, 1666, 441-6. It is a pity this valuable commentary is so rare. No less than three Scottish Browns have written on Romans, the others being the better known John Brown (1784-1858) and David Brown (1803-1897); they all take the same view of Romans 11.
14. *Exposition on the Old and New Testaments*, 1848 (3 vol. edit.), vol. 3, 717.
15. Potgieter, op. cit., 29. This was apparently Abraham Kuyper's view and he is quoted on the same page.
16. *Annotations upon the Holy Bible*, 1962 reprint, vol. 3, 519.
17. *The Epistle to the Romans*, John Murray, vol. 2, 1965, 95-6, where the author gives an extended treatment of the phrase 'fulness'.
18. Parr, op. cit., 176.
19. F. Godet gives the following summary of reasons against 'life from the dead' being referred to the resurrection of the body: 1st. Why use the expression *a life*, instead of saying as usual ἀνάστασις, the *resurrection?* 2d. Why omit the article before the word *life*, and not say as usual *the* life, life eternal, instead of *a* life? And more than all, 3d. What so close relation could there be between the fact of the conversion of the Jews and that of the bodily resurrection? Again, if Paul confined himself to saying that the second event will closely follow the first, this temporal relation would be intelligible, though according to him the signal for the resurrection is the return of the Lord (1 Cor. 15. 23), and not at all the conversion of Israel. But he goes the length

of *identifying* the two facts of which he speaks: 'What shall their return be but a life?' It is evident, therefore, for all these reasons, that the expression: *a life from the dead*, must be applied to a powerful spiritual revolution which will be wrought in the heart of Gentile Christendom by the fact of the conversion of the Jews. *Commentary on Romans*, vol. 2, 1895, 243.

20. To the Christian Reader, *Strength Out of Weakness. Or, a Glorious Manifestation Of the further Progresse of the Gospel Amongst the Indians in New England* . . . set forth by Mr. Henry Whitfield, 1652. Reissued for Savin's Reprints, New York, 1865.

21. J. A. Alexander, the nineteenth-century Princeton commentator, follows Calvin in not finding references to Israel's conversion in the Old Testament; thus on Isaiah 59.20 he argues that Paul is not *interpreting* Isaiah but 'employing the familiar language of an ancient prophecy as the vehicle of a new one'. Patrick Fairbairn calls this 'a manifestly untenable view, for how could we, in that case, have vindicated the apostle from the want of godly simplicity, using, as he must then have done, his accustomed formula for prophetical quotations ("as it is written") only to disguise and recommend an announcement properly his own?' *The Interpretation of Prophecy*, 1964 reprint, 284. Alexander appears inconsistent in not accepting that Paul is giving us light on the *meaning* of Isaiah 59 and 60, for in expounding Isaiah 11 he grants that there is unfulfilled prophecy respecting Israel and refers the reader to Romans 11. It appears that he was overmuch influenced by the need to confute those commentators who spoke of 'the future glory of the Jewish people' in a way that is inconsistent with the spiritual and universal emphases of the New Testament. See his *Commentary on the Prophecies of Isaiah*, vol. 1, 257, vol. 2, 377, 381. David Brown endorses Fairbairn's criticism of Alexander's view of Isaiah 59.20, 21 in his book, *The Restoration of the Jews*, 1861, 121.

22. *Sermons by Robert Leighton*, edited by William West, 1869, 17.

23. Hendriksen, op. cit. 49.

24. Murray, op. cit., vol. 2, 77.

25. *Matthew Twenty-Four*, 17-18.

26. The arguments for this belief are given by Durham, *op. cit.*, 531-2; they were not accepted by John Owen, *Works*, vol. 24, 63. William Greenhill wrote in 1654: 'The Jews' return to their own land is denied by some, questioned by many, and doubted by most' *Exposition of Ezekial*, 1863 reprint, 828.

27. An unsigned article in *The British and Foreign Evangelical Review*, vol. 6, 1857, 'Will the Jews, as a Nation, be Restored to their own Land?' The same writer observes: 'It is our impression that we do a great injury to the simple and natural interpretation of Scripture when, because Millenarians incorporate upon this question of the restoration of the Jews, certain Judaising, carnal, and untenable theories, we give up the whole question as of the same nature with millenarianism' 841.

28. *Reformed Dogmatics*, 1966, 817.

29. The words are those of G. Eldon Ladd who further writes: 'This evil

Age is to last until His return. It will for ever be hostile to the Gospel and to God's people. Evil will prevail. . . . Wars will continue; there will be famines and earthquakes. Persecution and martyrdom will plague the Church.' *The Gospel of the Kingdom*, 1959, 124.

30. *The Whole Works of Thomas Boston of Ettrick*, edit. Samuel M'Millan, 1851, vol. 10, 420. John Owen also has a sermon on the text in his *Works*, vol. 9, 320.

31. *Biblical and Theological Studies*, 1951 reprint, 500, in an article 'The Prophecies of St. Paul'. A different view of Paul's eschatology is given in *The Pauline Eschatology*, Geerhardus Vos, 1961 reprint.

32. William Hendriksen, for instance, asserts that the gospel age 'will finally result in the complete destruction of the church as a mighty and influential organization for the spread of the Gospel'. *More than Conquerors*, 1947, 178. A text often appealed to as support for this contention is Luke 18.8, 'When the Son of man cometh, shall he find faith on the earth?' In view, however, of the context in which the question is found, at the end of a parable illustrating importunity in prayer there are grounds for believing that Christ is not referring to a disappearance of *saving faith* but to the danger of declension in that faith which it was the purpose of the parable to enforce, namely, 'faith which has endured in prayer without fainting' (Alford). John Owen takes the question in Luke 18.8 as an argument for Christians to seek a greater degree of holiness: 'It is not a godly conversation at an ordinary rate . . . which will suffice to meet Christ at his coming.' Owen also considers the text applicable to Christ's providential comings in history, for example in his judgment of the Jews in A.D. 70, though he says 'every such day is a lesser day of judgment – a forerunner, pledge, and evidence of that great day of the Lord which is to come' (*Works*, vol. 9, 140–1). Norval Geldenhuys writes on Luke 18.8, 'This question by no means implies that at Christ's coming the Christ church will no longer exist.' *Commentary on the Gospel of Luke*, 1950, 447.

33. *Epistle to the Romans*, 1568, 360.

v *The Hope and Puritan Piety*

1. *The Life and Work of C. H. Spurgeon*, G. H. Pike, vol. 3, 141.
2. *The Glorious Kingdom of Christ, Described and Clearly Vindicated*, 1691, 11. John Howe has an excellent discourse 'Concerning The Immoderate Desire Of Knowing Things To Come' as an appendix to his 'Of Thoughtfulness for the Morrow,' *Works*, 1837, 340.
3. *Common Places*, 1583, part 3, 386.
4. *Works of John Howe*, 566.
5. *Institutes*, translated by Henry Beveridge, vol. 1, 6.
6. *Commentaries on the Twelve Minor Prophets*, translated by John Owen (Calvin Translation Society), vol. 5, 510.
7. Ibid., vol. 3, 393.

8. *Commentary on a Harmony of the Evangelists* (C.T.S.), vol. 1, 320. See also *Institutes*, vol. 2, 189-90.
9. *An Exposition with Notes Unfolded and Applied on John 17* (Nichol's reprint, 1867), 380-1.
10. Sibbes, op. cit., vol. 5, 517.
11. *The First Two Stuarts and the Puritan Revolution*, 1876, 80-1.
12. *Life of John Eliot*, 7. (Lives of the Chief Fathers of New England, vol. 3.) The measure of Puritan concern for the overseas world has never been sufficiently appreciated. Ignorance of geography (of which a curious example can be seen in Christopher Love's *Heaven's Glory, Hell's Terror*, 1658, 191) and the language barrier, which was far greater in the seventeenth century than it was a hundred years later, were hindrances to further missionary expansion. The lives of Puritan leaders, as Joseph Alleine (who considered going to China) and Richard Baxter (who wrote 'No part of my Prayers are so deeply serious, as that for the Conversion of the Infidel and Ungodly World'), make it clear that the world's need was a subject often in view. See *Joseph Alleine*, Charles Stanford, 1861, 207, and, for Baxter, *The Theology of Missions in the Puritan Tradition*, Sidney H. Rooy, 1965.
13. *Magnalia Christi Americana*; or The Ecclesiastical History of New England, 1702. It was in this treasury of Puritan history that Mather gave Eliot's life. Quotation given is from the 1852 edition (reprinted 1967), vol. 1, 562.
14. Ibid., 564.
15. Ibid., 582.
16. *The Works of Thomas Shepard*, 1853, vol. 3, 449.
17. *Pioneers in Mission*, The Early Missionary Ordination Sermons, Charges, and Instructions, 1966, 26.
18. *Westminster Confession*, chapter 25, para. 3.
19. *The Works of Jonathan Edwards*, 1840, vol. 1, 609.
20. *Letters of Samuel Rutherford*, Bonar's edition, 88.
21. Ibid., 122-3.
22. Quoted from his 'Testimony to the Covenanted Work of Reformation from 1638 to 1649 in Britain and Ireland', to be found in the early editions of his *Letters*.
23. *The Whole Works of the Rev. Oliver Heywood*, 1827, vol. 1, 578. Philip Henry lists six things, 'the firm belief whereof will exceedingly promote our comfort in dying', the last of which is as follows: 'That God will certainly accomplish and fulfil, in due time, all the great things that he hath purposed and promised concerning his church and people in the latter days; as, that Babylon shall fall; the Jews and Gentiles be brought in; the gospel kingdom more and more advanced; divisions healed. Oh! how have some rejoiced, and even triumphed in a dying hour, in the firm belief of these things! As Abraham rejoiced to see Christ's day, now past, and died in the faith of it, so may we as to another day of his, which is yet to come, before and besides the last day.' *The Life of Philip Henry*, Matthew Henry, enlarged by J. B. Williams, 1825, 185-6.

24. *Exposition on 2 Timothy, 1 and 2,* 1632, 163. In this, one of a number of references Barlow makes to the Jews, he says, 'Pray we then for the conversion of the Jewes, and alter the order of the Patriarches petition, saying, *God persuade Shem to dwell in the tents of Japheth*; and either we or our posterity shall see it come to pass as we have requested'.

25. 'Pray for the calling of the Jewes, which shall bring so much good to the world: As the sisters sent to Christ in the behalf of their brother Lazarus; so let us Gentiles importune the Lord for our brethren the Jewes.' Parr, op. cit., 177.

26. *The Christian in Complete Armour,* 1964 reprint, vol. 2, 525.

27. *Works,* vol. 8, 266.

28. Quoted from *A Humble Acknowledgement of the Sins of the Ministry of Scotland,* undated.

29. *The Nonconformists Memorial: Being an Account of the Ministers, who were Ejected or Silenced after the Restoration,* 1775, vol. 2, 17.

30. Quoted in *The Theology of Missions in the Puritan Tradition,* by Sidney H. Rooy, 1965, 247.

31. *Oliver Heywood's Diaries,* edited by J. Horsfall Turner, 1882, vol. 1, 212.

32. *Richard Cameron,* John Herkless, 1896, 109. See also *Sermons Delivered in Times of Persecution in Scotland,* 426–33, where Howie's edited version of Cameron's sermon is given.

33. Given in *Six Saints of the Covenant,* Patrick Walker, 1901, vol. 2, 94.

34. *Lectures, Sermons, and Writings of the Rev. Lachlan Mackenzie,* 1928, 419.

35. *Works of Thomas Goodwin,* vol. 3, 365–6.

VI *The Eighteenth-Century Awakening: The Hope Revived*

1. *History of the Free Churches of England, 1688–1891,* H. S. Skeats and Charles S. Miall, 1891, 267.

2. Ibid., 101.

3. Ibid., 248.

4. *Works,* 1810, vol. 1, 253.

5. Skeats and Miall, op. cit., 250.

6. *The History of the Later Puritans,* J. B. Marsden, 1852, 473 and 470.

7. This well-known testimony and a number of others are given in Thomas Jackson's *Centenary of Methodism*. It is of course possible to exaggerate the darkness in the early eighteenth century and we are inclined to think this has sometimes been done. There were a number of earnest ministers who rejected the 'Easy-going God' generally believed in and whose work prepared the way for revival.

8. See *Memoir of the Life, Time and Writings of the Rev. Thomas Boston,* written by himself, with Introduction by the Rev. George H. Morrison, 1899.

9. *Memoirs of the Life of the Rev. Thomas Halyburton* (Free Church reprint), 261.

10. *Narratives of the Extraordinary Work of the Spirit of God*, James Robe and others, 1790, 43–4.

11. *The Complete Works of Matthew Henry*, 1859, vol. 1, 465.

12. *The Revivals of the Eighteenth Century, Particularly at Cambuslang*, D. MacFarlan (published about 1845), 31.

13. *The Whole Works of the Rev. Thomas Boston*, edited by Samuel M'Millan, 1848, vol. 3, 354–71.

14. John Gillies, *Historical Collections*, vol. 2, 23.

15. Ibid., 27.

16. *George Whitefield's Journals*, 1960, 88.

17. *The Life and Times of the Rev. John Wesley*, L. Tyerman, vol. 1, 206.

18. *The Works of the Rev. George Whitefield*, vol. 1, 54.

19. Ibid., 58.

20. The most reliable book in English on this thrilling period is *The Early Life of Howell Harris*, Richard Bennett, translated from the Welsh by Gomer M. Roberts, 1962.

21. Whitefield's *Works*, vol. 1, 179.

22. Ibid., 184, 188.

23. Ibid., 200.

24. Quoted by D. MacFarlan, op. cit., 18.

25. *The Practical Works of the Rev. John Willison*, 405.

26. Almost all the contemporary evidence on the revivals in the West of Scotland in 1742 comes from *Narratives of the Extraordinary Work of the Spirit of God at Cambuslang, Kilsyth, etc., Begun 1742*, by James Robe and others. These were reprinted together in 1790 and again in 1840. Dr. MacFarlan's book, mentioned above, gives a good deal of the original material.

27. Quoted by MacFarlan, op. cit., 225.

28. *Works*, vol. 1, 404.

29. Ibid., 409–10.

30. Letter given in Tyerman, *Life of George Whitefield*, vol. 2, 31. Unfortunately some of Whitefield's letters are not to be found in the three volumes of letters contained in his *Works*.

31. MacFarlan, op. cit., 237.

32. *The Signs of the Times*, 1742, 16. In this work Erskine, then aged twenty-one, advanced the view that the revival then commenced heralded the approaching 'glory of the latter days'.

33. Extracts from these case histories are given in MacFarlan. The originals are now in New College Library, Edinburgh. They were recently transcribed by S. M. Houghton of Oxford and a copy deposited at the Evangelical Library, London.

34. T. Prince, *Christian History*, Boston, vol. 2, 1745, 101. Quoted by Frank Baker, *William Grimshaw*, 1963.

35. *Memoir of the Rev. Robert Findlater*, William Findlater, 1840, 19.

36. *The Life of Thomas Charles of Bala*, D. E. Jenkins, 1910, 2, 90–1.

37. These figures are given in Tyerman's *Life of John Wesley*; he quotes the number of chapels from Myles' *Chronological History*.

38. Statistics given by R. Symons in his *John Wesley's Ministerial Itineraries in Cornwall*, 1879, 144.
39. Figure given by J. H. Whiteley, *Wesley's England, A Survey of 18th Century Social and Cultural Conditions*, 1938, 17.
40. *Life and Writings of William Grimshaw*, Wm. Myles, 1813, 67–8.
41. Tyerman, *Whitefield*, vol. 1, 556.
42. Tyerman, *Whitefield*, vol. 2, 259.
43. Ibid., 383.
44. Quoted by J. H. Whiteley, op. cit., 352.
45. *A Brief Memoir of the Life and Labours of Thomas Charles*, Edward Morgan, 1831 (second edition), 288.
46. *Memoir of John Elias*, Edward Morgan, 1844, 108.
47. *Welsh Calvinistic Methodism*, William Williams, 1884, 161.
48. *Some of the Great Preachers of Wales*, Owen Jones, 1885, 10.
49. *Memoir of Elias*, 168.
50. *A Brief Memoir of Thomas Charles*, Edward Morgan, chapter 8.
51. Ibid., 368.
52. *Sermons Preached in London at the Formation of the Missionary Society*, 1795 (September 22, 23, 24), 109.

VII *World Missions: The Hope Spreading*

1. The words are J. A. Bengel's, who was at Halle in 1713. Writing to his mother, he says: 'I can assure you that everything corresponds to the expectations I had formed of this seat of wisdom and piety. . . . What delights me above all is the harmony of these men among themselves, which they study to keep up by social prayer.' *Memoir of the Life and Writings of John Albert Bengel*, J. C. F. Burk, translated by R. F. Walker, 1837, 25–6.
2. *Memoir*, 316.
3. See his exposition of Romans 11 in his *Gnomon of the New Testament*, edited by M. E. Bengel and J. C. F. Steudel, translated by James Bryce, sixth edition 1866, vol. 3.
4. *Memoir*, 323.
5. *A History of Moravian Missions*, J. E. Hutton, 1922, 4.
6. See *A History of Wesleyan Missions*, W. Moister, 1871, 465, and *The Fathers and Founders of the London Missionary Society*, John Morrison, vol. 1, 188.
7. 'Memoirs of the Rev. Samuel Pearce' in *The Complete Works of Andrew Fuller*, 1841, 766.
8. *Works*, vol. 1, 396.
9. *Life of Wesley*, Tyerman, vol. 3, 478. The words are actually those of Dr. Coke. They were controverted by Charles Wesley 'with a very loud voice and in great anger', but, reports Pawson, 'Mr Mather got up and confirmed what Dr. Coke had said, which we all knew to be a truth'.

10. *The History of the Church Missionary Society*, Eugene Stock, 1899, vol. 1, 59.

11. *A Sermon Preached at Salter's-Hall, March 30th, 1792, Before the Correspondent Board in London of the Society in Scotland for Propagating Christian Knowledge*, 1793. This is a pamphlet which runs to 52 pages. It seems to have been the first of hundreds of great missionary sermons which were subsequently to be preached in London.

12. *William Carey*, S. Pearce Carey, 1923, 51.

13. See *Memoirs of the Life and Writings of Thomas Chalmers*, 1850, vol. 1, 337.

14. The popular story is repudiated by Ryland's son, John Ryland, Junior, who was Carey's close friend and a fellow member of the Northampton Association, being assistant minister at his father's church at the time when the incident was supposed to have happened. 'I never heard of it till I saw it in print, and cannot give credit to it at all.' Among the reasons he gives for rejecting its authenticity it is interesting to note that he says, 'No man prayed and preached about the *latter-day glory* more than my father'. *Life of Andrew Fuller*, John Ryland, 1816, 175.

15. S. Pearce Carey, op. cit., 154.

16. Ibid., 175.

17. Ibid., 198.

18. Ibid., 252.

19. Ibid., 193.

20. Quoted by C. H. Robinson, *History of Christian Missions*, 1915, 14.

21. S. Pearce Carey, op. cit., 326.

22. *A History of the Expansion of Christianity*, 1945, vol. 4, 65.

23. Ibid., 44.

24. Gillies, op. cit., 2, 153.

25. Ibid., 170.

26. *Works*, 4, 307 (Recommendatory Preface to Works of John Bunyan).

27. Ibid., 306.

28. Figures given by Le Roy E. Froom in *The Prophetic Faith of our Fathers*, 1954, vol. 4, 119. Froom adds, 'Henry's wide influence doubtless gave currency to the post-millennial view'.

29. Quoted in Tyerman, *Whitefield*, vol. 2, 27.

30. *The Life of the Rev. Thomas Scott*, John Scott, 9th edit., 1836, 114. Pearce Carey, in his standard life of William Carey, drops the reference to Dort in giving this quotation, which would not matter if he elsewhere gave some account of Carey's Calvinism, but unfortunately he does not.

31. The Form of Argument is reprinted as Appendix A in *William Carey, Especially the Missionary Principles*, A. H. Oussoren, 1945.

32. *Complete Works of Andrew Fuller*, xxv and lxvii. A 'moderate Calvinist', according to Fuller, was 'one that is a half Arminian'. A strict Calvinist, 'one that really holds the system of Calvin'. Of course, in Fuller's case, as with Sutcliff and Ryland, the change in beliefs was from a narrow 'high Calvinism' current among a number of eighteenth-century Strict Baptists which denied the universal obligation to faith and repentance which the gospel carries within its message. To move from this to the Puritan position was quite a radical change.

33. *Life of Andrew Fuller*, John Ryland, 545–6.
34. *The History of Dissenters During the Last Thirty Years*, James Bennett, 1839, 171.
35. S. Pearce Carey, op. cit., 267–8.
36. 'The Evangelical Revival and the Beginnings of the Modern Missionary Movement', The Congregational Quarterly, 1943, 223-236.
37. *Robert Morrison, The Pioneer of Chinese Missions*, W. J. Townsend, 52.
38. *The Fathers and Founders of the L.M.S.*, vol. 2, 61. These two volumes by Morrison contain a large amount of fascinating biographical material.
39. *Sermons Preached in London at the Formation of the Missionary Society*, 1795, 114.
40. *The Life and Letters of John Angell James*, edited by R. W. Dale, 1861, chapter 6, 'Student Life at Gosport'.
41. James was minister of Carr's Lane Church, Birmingham, from 1805 until his death in 1859. By his preaching and writing he exercised a wide influence, particularly among the Congregational churches.
42. *Works*, vol. 1, 379, 408, etc.
43. *Works*, vol. 4, 296.
44. See *Brief Memoir of Thomas Charles*, Edward Morgan, 348 and 355.
45. *Letters and Essays of John Elias*, Edward Morgan, 1847, 164. See also his denial of the pre-millennial view, 197.
46. *A Second Volume of Sermons*, Preached at the Celebration of the Lord's Supper 1750, xvi–xvii. Robe's entire preface makes frequent reference to prophecy.
47. See *Sermons Preached in London at the Formation of the Missionary Society*, 1795.
48. The sermon, entitled 'A Hope for the Heathen', was preached by John M. Mason on Isaiah 25.6, 7. See *Sermons, Lectures and Orations by John M. Mason*, 1860, 63. Also his sermon, *Messiah's Throne*, preached in London in 1802.
49. A sermon by John Love, 'The Glorious Prospects of the Church of Christ', in *Sermons Preached on Various Occasions*, John Love, 1846.
50. See a letter of Venn's dated October 28, 1786, in *Life of Henry Venn*, 6th edition, 1839, 417.
51. *Journals and Letters of the Rev. Henry Martyn*, edited by S. Wilberforce, 1839, 749–50.
52. Ibid., 740–1. See also p. 483.
53. *Works*, vol. 1, 607.
54. See S. Pearce Carey, op. cit., 409, and Martyn's *Journals*, 756.
55. *Complete Works*, 497–503.
56. *Charles Simeon*, H. C. G. Moule, 1892, 122.
57. W. T. Gidney, *The History of the London Society for Promoting Christianity Amongst the Jews*, 1908, 273. In E. Bickersteth's *The Restoration of the Jews to Their Own Land*, 1841, there is an interesting appendix giving Simeon's death-bed thoughts on the future conversion of the Jews.

VIII *The Hope and Scotland's Missionaries*

1. The most detailed report of this historic debate is in Heron's *Account of the Proceedings and Debate, in the General Assembly of the Church of Scotland,* May 21, 1796. In these pages I rely largely on Donald MacLean, 'Scottish Calvinism and Foreign Missions' in *Records of the Scottish Church History Society,* vol. 6, part 1, 1936. In the same *Records,* vol. 10, Hugh Watt has demonstrated the authenticity of the dramatic intervention of John Erskine in the debate.

2. For Calder and his family see John Kennedy, *The Days of the Fathers in Ross-shire.* Part of Calder's diaries was edited by William Taylor, *Diary of James Calder,* 1875, but a far larger part remains unpublished with Calder's descendants today.

3. *The Preachers of Scotland,* W. G. Blaikie, 1888, 226.

4. *The Missionary Ideal in the Scottish Churches,* D. MacKichan, 1927, 109.

5. *The Lives of Robert Haldane of Airthrey, and of his brother, James A. Haldane,* Alexander Haldane, 1856, 91. Though Haldane aimed to work in India, his greatest overseas influence was to be on the Continent. See Latourette, op. cit. 4, 133.

6. *Memoir of the Rev. Robert Findlater, to which are prefixed Memoirs of his Parents,* William Findlater, 1840, 78–9.

7. *Ibid.,* 41. *Three Sermons by Charles Calder* was published with a Preface by Malcolm MacGregor in 1877, the profit of sale to go to the Scheme of the Free Church for the Conversion of the Jews.

8. See the fine biography by John Kennedy.

9. Burns, father and son, are both well recorded, *The Pastor of Kilsyth, the Life and Times of W. H. Burns,* 1860, and *Memoir of Wm. C. Burns,* 1870, both by Islay Burns. One missionary, asked if he knew W. C. Burns, replied, 'All China knows him, he is the holiest man alive.'

10. *Memoirs of Alexander Stewart,* 1822, 143–4. This anonymous memoir gives the most accurate account of Simeon's visit and Stewart's conversion.

11. Quoted in an article 'Missions and Missionaries', *British and Foreign Evangelical Review,* vol. 29, 1880, 715.

12. *The Life of Alexander Duff,* George Smith, 1879, vol. 1, 8. Smith did outstanding work in the last century as the leading historian of missionary endeavour in India.

13. Quoted in *History of the Missions of the Free Church of Scotland in India and Africa,* Robert Hunter, 1873, 12.

14. Smith, op. cit., 25. See also the account in William Hanna, *Memoirs of the Life and Writings of Thomas Chalmers,* 1850, vol. 3, ch. 11.

15. Hunter, op. cit., 15.

16. Quoted from 'Two Modern Apostles', *The British and Foreign Evangelical Review,* vol. 30, 1881, 73.

17. S. Pearce Carey, op. cit., 375.

18. *British and Foreign,* vol. 30, 74.

19. *Duff,* George Smith, vol. 1, 300.

20. *Conquests of the Cross*, A Record of Missionary Work throughout the World, Edwin Hodder, 1890, vol. 3, 307.

21. Figure given by R. W. Weir, *A History of the Foreign Missions of the Church of Scotland*, 1900, 49.

22. Figures given by Hunter, op. cit., 26. I cannot account for the widely divergent and much higher figures given by Elizabeth G. K. Hewat in her recent survey of Scottish Mission work, *Vision and Achievement, 1796–1956*, 1960, 38. In 1866, Duff speaks of the aggregate annual revenue as £16,000, a sum with which he was far from satisfied.

23. The early convenors were Robert Gordon, James Buchanan and W. K. Tweedie.

24. Quoted from *Speech of the Rev. Dr. Duff on Foreign Missions and America*, 1854, 7–10. This speech runs to 45 pages!

25. *Foreign Missions: Being the substance of an Address Delivered Before the General Assembly of the Free Church of Scotland*, 1866, 23.

26. Hewat, op. cit., 47.

27. *Speech*, op. cit., 17.

28. *The Personal Life of David Livingstone*, W. G. Blaikie, 1880, 193. This fine life of Livingstone had gone through eleven impressions by 1906. Livingstone's own books had an immense circulation. His *Missionary Travels*, 12,000 copies, was published in November, 1857, but by the 10th of that month 13,800 copies had been ordered and a reprint begun!

29. Ibid., 123.

30. Ibid., 139.

31. Ibid., 434.

32. *The Life of John Macdonald*, Late Missionary Minister from the Free Church of Scotland at Calcutta, W. K. Tweedie, 1849, 482.

33. Blaikie, op. cit., 108.

34. *Evangelistic Theology*, An Inaugural Address Delivered in the Common Hall of the New College, Edinburgh, 1868, 47–8.

35. *A Narrative* of the mission was published in 1842, prepared by Andrew Bonar and R. M. M'Cheyne. Bonar was the only deputy of pre-millennial persuasion.

36. *Memoir and Remains of R. M. M'Cheyne*, Andrew Bonar, 1966 reprint, 489. M'Cheyne's manuscript notes, now in New College, Edinburgh, reveal that he had worked on the same subject earlier. A visit of M'Cheyne's to Ulster in 1840 to plead the interests of the Jews 'was blessed to awaken a deep interest'. The following year the Irish General Assembly unanimously resolved to establish work among the Jews, which they did in Syria in 1844 and Germany in 1845, believing that 'missionary enterprise is one of the means to bring about the restoration of Israel, in accordance with the Scriptures'. *Minutes of the General Assembly*, 1840–50, quoted in *Arnold Frank of Hamburg*, Robert Allen, 36.

37. See *Life of the late John Duncan*, David Brown, 334: 'Our hands now became so full of work that frequently we had not time so much as to eat bread; from early morning till late at night we were occupied in guiding, counselling and instructing those who were inquiring earnestly what they must do to be saved. . . . For a time the whole Jewish com-

munity was deeply moved, wondering whereunto these things would grow.'

38. *Rich Gleanings after the Vintage from 'Rabbi' Duncan*, edited by J. S. Sinclair, 1925, 384. This volume contains a number of Assembly addresses on the Jews given by Duncan.
39. *A Modern Apostle, Alexander N. Somerville*, George Smith, 1890, 348–50. The number of Jews was the estimate of Delitzsch at that date.
40. Ibid., 373.
41. *Missions, the Chief End of the Christian Church*, Alexander Duff, fourth edition 1840, 8.
42. *Sermons, Preached on Various Occasions*, John Love, 1846, 277–9.
43. Blaikie, op. cit., 123 and 150.
44. *John G. Paton, Missionary to the New Hebrides*, An Autobiography, 1965 reprint, 80.
45. *Report of Proceedings at the Conference on Foreign Missions, Held at Edinburgh*, 20th and 21st November 1861, 62.
46. *Indian Missions: Their Modes of Operation*, A Letter to the Rev. Dr. Tweedie, 1861, 22.
47. Quoted in *The British and Foreign Evangelical Review*, vol. 30, 73.
48. Blaikie, op. cit., 214.
49. Ibid., 181.
50. A letter to Tidman in 1855, quoted by Hewat, op. cit., 213.
51. Blaikie, op. cit., 142.
52. Ibid., 147–8.
53. Ibid., 143.
54. Ibid., 162.
55. Ibid., 478.

Note: It would have enlarged this chapter inordinately to have included any sketch of the overseas work of the branch of the Scottish Church which left the national Church in the eighteenth century. A full record of the earlier period is given by John M'Kerrow in his *History of the Foreign Missions of the Secession and United Presbyterian Church*, 1867.

IX *The Eclipse of the Hope*

1. *Discourses on the Millennium*, 1818, 17.
2. *The Life of Edward Irving*, Mrs. Oliphant, fourth edition, 96. This fascinating volume is the classic life of Irving.
3. Ibid., 104–5.
4. Further information on Lacunza is given in *The Prophetic Faith of our Fathers*, Le Roy E. Froom, 1946, vol. 3, 307. Lacunza's book was first published in Spanish in 1812. According to Froom there was a London edition before Irving's in 1826; it was Irving's two-volume edition, however, which did most to gain the attention of the public. Froom gives a mass of information but he is an unreliable guide to the history of Christian thought on prophecy.

5. *The Rev. Edward Irving's Preliminary Discourse to the Work of Ben Ezra entitled the Coming of Messiah in Glory and Majesty*, 1859 reprint, 7-8.

6. Irving reported the first conference in his *Preliminary Discourse*, op. cit., 197-202. Details of the later conferences are given in Irving's letters recorded by Mrs. Oliphant.

7. *Memoirs of the Life and Writings of Thomas Chalmers*, William Hanna, 1851, vol. 3, 221. In his Journal for Monday, May 26, Chalmers writes: 'For the first time heard Mr. Irving in the evening. I have no hesitation in saying that it is quite woful. There is power and richness, and gleams of exquisite beauty, but withal a mysticism and an extreme allegorization which I am sure must be pernicious to the general cause.' Ibid., 220.

8. Mrs. Oliphant, op. cit., 236.

9. Ibid., 255.

10. Ibid., 210. This was an accurate foreboding. 'The study of prophecy', writes W. G. Blaikie, 'came to give a special character to Irving's ordinary ministrations, which not only diminished his popularity, but prepared the way for opinions and practices that ultimately wrecked him'. *David Brown, A Memoir*, 1898, 37.

11. Mrs. Oliphant, op. cit., 275. For a good account of the alleged restoration of miraculous gifts in Irving's later ministry, see B. B. Warfield, *Miracles: Yesterday and Today*, reprinted 1965.

12. Froom, op. cit., vol. 3, 447.

13. *Memoir and Remains of Robert Murray M'Cheyne*, Andrew Bonar. For another assessment of Irving, see Alexander Haldane's biography of *Robert and James Haldane*, 1856, 528-9.

14. Andrew Bonar, *Sheaves After Harvest*, no date, 43. It is interesting to note that R. M. M'Cheyne did not share his close friend's change of view.

15. See *Scottish Theology*, John MacLeod, 1943, 278.

16. *John Ellerton, A Sketch of his Life and Works*, Henry Housman, 1896, 19.

17. *History of the Church Missionary Society*, Eugene Stock, 1899, vol. 1, 284. See also *Memoir of Edward Bickersteth*, T. R. Birks, 1851, vol. 2, 44 ff.

18. Ryle's volume *Coming Events and Present Duties*, 1867, is probably the rarest of his books today.

19. *Horae Apocalypticae: A Commentary on the Apocalypse*, 1851 (fourth edition), vol. 4, 522. See also Froom, op. cit., vol. 3, 716 ff.

20. Froom, op. cit., vol. 3, 706.

21. Ibid., vol. 4, 1193. G. R. Balleine, in his *History of the Evangelical Party in the Church of England*, first published in 1908, was of the opinion that the majority of the evangelical party did not adopt pre-millennial views 'and Waldegrave's Bampton Lectures against Millenarianism (1853) helped to confirm them in their decision'. 1911 edition, 137. The influence of the *Scofield Reference Bible*, however, was still to come when Balleine wrote.

22. F. Roy Coad, *A History of the Brethren Movement*, 1968, 106.

23. The personal contact between Moorhouse and Moody appears to date from 1867, see Froom, vol. 4, 1186, also *The Approaching Advent of*

Christ, Alexander Reese, 1937, 310–11. Darby also met Moody personally in America and could write, 'I know the man well'. *Letters of J.N.D.*, no date, vol. 2, 257.

24. Loraine Boettner gives this figure and comments on the influence of Scofield in his work, *The Millennium*, 1958, 369–73.

25. *Collected Writings of J. N. Darby*, edited by William Kelly, Prophetic, vol. 4, 514.

26. Ibid., 527.

27. Ibid., 531.

28. Ibid., 544.

29. Ibid., 410.

30. Ibid., 571.

31. Ibid., 547.

32. Two future leaders among the Brethren, Henry Craik and Anthony Norris Groves, were reading Irving in 1826, Coad, op. cit., 19.

33. Mrs. Oliphant, op. cit., 299.

34. See *Prophetic Developments with Particular Reference to the Early Brethren Movement* (A Christian Brethren Research Fellowship Occasional Paper). F. R. Coad, 1966, 24.

35. Support for belief in the rapture has been claimed from Victorinus, of the fourth century, and from Joseph Mede of the seventeenth. Whether this is so or not, it is clear that no group of Christians made it a matter of faith before the nineteenth century. According to S. P. Tregelles it was through a prophetic utterance by one of Irving's congregation claiming the gift of tongues that the notion of a rapture originated, but it appears that that view was expressed at Albury before the tongues' phenomena began in London (1831). B. W. Newton suggests that it was Irving who introduced it at one of the Albury Conferences; see Coad, *Prophetic Developments*, 22, and Froom, op. cit., vol. 4, 421–3. Tregelles, Newton and others of the early Brethren opposed Darby's insistence on the rapture and this became a major factor in subsequent divisions. Darby's position on prophecy came, however, to prevail throughout almost all sections of Brethren.

36. *Collected Writings*, Prophetic, vol. 4, 531–4. In Darby's *Letters*, vol. 1, a compact summary of his prophetic scheme will be found on pages 131–2. The link between Irving and Brethren prophetic beliefs seems to have been missed by most writers. Timothy C. F. Stunt covers some of the ground in an article, 'Irvingite Pentecostalism and the Early Brethren', *The Journal of The Christian Brethren Research Fellowship*, No. 10, December, 1965.

37. *Collected Writings*, Ecclesiastical, vol. 3, 417. Quoted by Clarence B. Bass in a good summary of Darby's position in *Backgrounds to Dispensationalism*, its Historical Genesis and Ecclesiastical Implications, 1960, 103. A good critical comment by A. N. Groves on Darby's theory that 'the Church is in ruins', is given in Coad, *History*, 122.

38. *Letters of J. N. Darby*, vol. 1, 7.

39. *Collected Writings*, Prophetical, vol. 1, 471 and 486.

40. *The Approaching Advent of Christ*, op. cit, 316.

41. *A History of the Plymouth Brethren*, 1901, 339. Coad's recent history does not replace Neatby's; the critical insights of the latter are particularly valuable.
42. Ibid., 228.
43. Ibid., 40 (quoted from *Phases of Faith*).
44. The words are those of Dr. Zahn, quoted by Reese, op. cit., 314.
45. *Aids to Prophetic Enquiry*, 1881, 2.
46. *Princetoniana*, Charles & A. A. Hodge, with Class and Table Talk of Hodge the younger, C. A. Salmond, 1888, 238–9.
47. *The Conflict of Christianity with Heathenism*, translated by E. C. Smyth and C. J. H. Ropes, 1879, 336.
48. Quoted by Alan Heimert, *Religion and the American Mind*, 1966, 60.

Note: The theme of this chapter is handled in detail by a recent writer, Ernest R. Sandeen, in his book, *The Roots of Fundamentalism*, British and American Millenarianism 1800–1930, University of Chicago Press, 1970.

x *Christ's Second Coming: the Best Hope*

1. Quoted by H. Berkhof, *Christ the Meaning of History*, 1966, 140.
2. *Works*, op. cit., 569.
3. Alfred Plummer, *The Pastoral Epistles* (The Expositor's Bible), 1891, 378.
4. *Letters and Essays of John Elias*, E. Morgan, 1847, 197.
5. *Sermons on Important Subjects*, by the Rev. George Whitefield, 1825, 608.
6. Quoted by David Brown, *Christ's Second Coming*, 29–30.
7. Quoted in *The Approaching Advent of Christ*, Alexander Reese, 304.
8. The phrase is Warfield's, *Biblical and Theological Studies*, 1952, 468. Isaac Ambrose, in his *Looking unto Jesus*, 1674, 611, says: 'All that ever the soul saw before in being with Christ in heaven till the Resurrection, shall be swallowed up with the sight of this glory of Christ at the Resurrection-day.'
9. Op. cit., 51.
10. *The Gospel of Forgiveness*, A Series of Discourses, 1878, Sermon XXIV.
11. *Memoir of the Life and Writings of J. A. Bengel*, C. F. Burk, 308.
12. *The Nonconformist's Memorial*, Samuel Palmer, vol. 3, 1803, 412.
13. *The Log College*, Archibald Alexander, 1968 reprint, 125.

xi *The Prospect in History: Christ our Hope*

1. *Exposition of 2 Timothy*, 1 and 2, 1632, 2, 99.
2. See *Religion and the American Mind*, From the Great Awakening to the Revolution, Alan Heimert, 1966, particularly Chapter 3.
3. *A History of the English-Speaking Peoples*, 1958, vol. 4, 53.
4. *Winston Churchill*, Lord Moran, 1966, 498.
5. Ibid., 636.
6. Ibid., 659.

7. Ibid., 659.
8. *William Carey*, op. cit., 336.
9. *Rich Gleanings after the Vintage from 'Rabbi' Duncan*, 386.
10. Dr. Warneck, quoted by C. H. Robinson in *History of Christian Missions*, 1915, 49.
11. *Speech of Dr. Duff on Foreign Missions and America*, 1854, 11.
12. *Foreign Missions, an Address before the General Assembly of the Free Church of Scotland*, 1886, 31.
13. *The New Theology in the Free Church*, a pamphlet by M. Macaskill, 1892, 14.
14. *Edinburgh 1910*, An Account and Interpretation of the World Missionary Conference, W. H. T. Gairdner, 1910, 21.
15. Ibid., 137–8.
16. Quoted by Ned B. Stonehouse in *J. Gresham Machen*, 1955, 473. Mrs. Buck's many words on the subject were all characteristically liberal, e.g. 'Above all, let the spread of the spirit of Christ be rather by mode of life than preaching'.
17. Ibid., 475.
18. Article, *Scottish Calvinism and Foreign Missions*, op. cit., 12.
19. *Life of Thomas Scott*, 1824, 384 (letter dated 18.11.1813).
20. *Address*, 1866, 26.
21. *Discourses on the Millennium*, 220–5.
22. Quoted by his son, A. A. Hodge, in *Evangelical Theology*, 1890. This question is discussed at some length by B. B. Warfield in an article 'Are They Few That Be Saved?' *Biblical and Theological Studies*, 1952. He writes: 'What saves the picture from being as dark as it is painted is that the contrast between the many and the few is not the only contrast which runs through our Lord's teaching and the teaching of His apostles. Side by side with it is the contrast between the present and the future. These small beginnings are to give way to great expansions. The grain of mustard seed when sowed in the field (which is the world) is not to remain less than all seeds: it is to become a tree in the branches of which the birds of heaven lodge. The speck of leaven is not to remain hidden in the mass of meal: it is to work through the meal until the *whole* of it is leavened' p. 348.
23. *The Year of Grace*, a History of the Ulster Revival of 1859, William Gibson, 1860, 89.
24. *Luther's Works*, vol. 24, 1961, 417.
25. *Metropolitan Tabernacle Pulpit*, vol. 20, 234.
26. Ibid., vol. 60, 198.

INDEX

INDEX TO SCRIPTURE REFERENCES